The school years

Since the first edition of *The School Years* was published in 1979, major social changes have occurred, many of them having a direct impact upon education and young people.

Poverty and unemployment, training of post 16 year-olds, the problems of sexual and emotional abuse, the phenomenon of AIDS, issues of gender, race and equal opportunities, increasing divorce rates – all these have affected the lives of children and adolescents. In addition, in the UK and many other countries, education reforms have altered the organization and ethos of the school setting, inevitably creating even greater challenges for the pupils themselves.

However, many of the themes addressed in the first edition remain central to our understanding of the socialization of young people today. The contributors to *The School Years* pay particular attention to these current questions and research dilemmas, and also provide a broad theoretical perspective on the subject.

They discuss the development of morality, the learning of gender roles, the role of the peer group, the origin of the concept of self, the causes of delinquency, and the relation between home and school. In doing so, *The School Years* explores key questions about human development in the context of the school setting.

John Coleman is Director of the Trust for the Study of Adolescence, Brighton and Editor of the *Journal of Adolescence*.

The school years

Current issues in the socialization of young people

Second edition

Edited by John C. Coleman

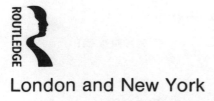

London and New York

First published in 1979 by Methuen & Co. Ltd.

This second edition published in 1992
by Routledge
11 New Fetter Lane, London EC4P 4EE

Simultaneously published in the USA and Canada
by Routledge
a division of Routledge, Chapman and Hall, Inc.
29 West 35th Street, New York, NY 10001

Typeset in Times by Witwell Ltd, Southport
Printed and bound in Great Britain by
Mackays of Chatham plc, Chatham, Kent

British Library Cataloguing in Publication Data

A catalogue record for this book is available from the
British Library.

Library of Congress Cataloging in Publication Data
The school years: current issues in the socialization of
   young people
   edited by John C. Coleman. – 2nd ed.
   p. cm. – (Adolescence and society)
   Includes bibliographical references and index.
   1. Adolescence. 2. Socialization. 3. Teenagers–Social
   conditions. 4. Teenagers–Great Britain–Social
   conditions.
   I. Coleman, John C., Ph. D. II. Series.
   HQ796.S4172 1992
   303.3′2–dc20   91–28498 CIP

ISBN 0-415-06169-5
     0-415-06170-9 (pbk)

Contents

Tables

Contributors

Dr Sally L. Archer is an Associate Professor of Psychology at Trenton State College. A developmental psychologist, she received her Master's degree from Tulane University in 1973 and her PhD from the University of Pennsylvania in 1980. Her research interests include adolescent development, identity and intimacy formation across the life-span, and gender-role socialization. She is a co-author of the forthcoming book *Ego Identity: A Handbook of Psychosocial Development* and editor of *Interventions for Adolescent Identity* to be published by Sage.

Professor Maurice Chazan is Emeritus Professor of Education at the University College of Swansea. He had experience as a teacher and an educational psychologist before moving to Swansea, where he was particularly involved in courses in educational psychology and special education. He has written extensively on early childhood education, educational disadvantage, and emotional and behavioural difficulties; and he has been co-director of a number of research projects.

Dr John Coleman is currently the Director of the Trust for the Study of Adolescence, a small independent research organisation and a registered charity based in Brighton. He trained as a clinical psychologist, and obtained his PhD from University College, London. He has published a number of books including *The Nature of Adolescence*, now in its second edition. For the last five years he has served as Editor of the *Journal of Adolescence*.

Dr David P. Farrington is Reader in Psychological Criminology at Cambridge University where he has been on the staff since 1969. His major research interest is in the longitudinal study of delinquency and crime, and he is Director of the Cambridge Study in Delinquent Development, a prospective longitudinal survey of over 400 London males from age 8 to age 32. He is also co-principal Investigator of the Pittsburgh Youth Survey, a prospective longitudinal study of over 1500 Pittsburgh males from age 7 to age 16. He is a Fellow of the British Psychological Society and of the American Society of Criminology. He received BA, MA, and PhD degrees in Psychology from Cambridge University, and the Sellin-Glueck Award of the American Society of Criminology (in 1984) for international contributions to criminology.

Dr Terry Honess is a Senior Lecturer in the School of Psychology at the University of Wales, Cardiff. His prime interests are with social policy issues such as youth unemployment and the impact of divorce on young people. In addition, he has a particular concern with qualitative research methods.

Dr Peter Kutnick is a Lecturer in Education (Social and Developmental Psychology) at the University of Sussex. His main interests centre on the effect of classroom processes/structure on the developing child. He has published a number of books including *Relationships in the Primary School Classroom* and *The Social Psychology of the Primary School*. Research and articles include aspects of cooperation skills, moral education and cognitive development. He is currently designing and implementing a classroom programme to enhance moral and social skills.

Dr Phillida Salmon worked for 11 years in the NHS as a clinical psychologist before moving into teaching. She has taught in a number of settings, most recently at London University Institute of Education. Her main concern as a pyschologist has been to establish the personal-social, rather than just the intellectual, character of learning and teaching. From 1989 to 1990 she was Chairperson of the British Psychological Society Psychotherapy Section. Publications include *Living in Time* (Dents 1985) and *Psychology for Teachers* (Hutchinson Education 1988). She is currently working on a book about the experience of doing a PhD.

Editor's introduction

The first edition of *The School Years* was published in 1979. Since that time major social changes have occurred, many of them having a direct impact upon education and young people. Poverty and unemployment, training of post-16-year-olds, the problems of sexual and emotional abuse, the phenomenon of AIDS, issues of gender, race and equal opportunities, and increasing divorce rates – all these have affected the lives of children and adolescents. In addition, in the UK and in many other countries, education reforms have altered the organization and ethos of the school setting, inevitably creating even greater challenges for the pupils themselves.

In spite of all this, however, many of the same topics which we addressed at the end of the 1970s remain central to our understanding of the socialization of young people today. The development of morality (Chapter 2), the learning of gender roles (Chapter 3), the origins and nature of the self concept (Chapter 4), the role of the peer group (Chapter 5), the causes of delinquency (Chapter 6), and the relationship between the home and the school (Chapter 7) are all areas of major concern to those wishing to make sense of the interaction between personality and environment. Key questions about human development in the context of the school setting remain. Where do the major influences upon children and young people lie? How can the adult world work best to engender pro-social behaviour among youth? What is the process whereby concepts of gender and gender roles become incorporated into adult behaviour? What is the nature of the self concept, and how is it shaped by experiences in school? What part does the peer group play in the genesis of anti-social behaviour?

These questions, among others, are addressed by the authors in this second edition of *The School Years*. I am grateful to them all, and to David Stonestreet, my editor at Routledge, for encouraging me to open the door again on such a worthwhile subject.

John C. Coleman

Chapter 1

Current views of the adolescent process

John C. Coleman

INTRODUCTION

Adolescence is a complex stage of human development, for the years 12 to 18 involve a wide range of major life changes. In fact it is unlikely that the individual undergoes greater changes at any other stage in the life cycle apart from infancy. During the teenage years the young person experiences puberty, which has an impact on physical, physiological and psychological systems. He or she undergoes a significant maturation of cognitive function. Major changes in the self concept are likely to occur, and there are radical alterations in all social relationships to be negotiated. How can we understand such fundamental transitions in human development, and make sense of the effects which they have upon the individual? Especially important in the context of the present book are the effects which these changes have upon the way the young person functions in the school setting, and it is primarily to this question that I shall address myself in what follows.

Broadly speaking there are two ways in which we can attempt to make sense of adolescent development. On the one hand we can look to theory. We can study theoretical notions of adolescence, and determine for ourselves the validity or logic of the different approaches. On the other hand we can turn to the research evidence. This will provide us with a factual base upon which to make an assessment of this period of the life cycle, but will inevitably leave a wide range of questions unanswered. It is my view that neither theory nor research can at present provide a complete answer. Both have limitations, and yet both have valuable insights to offer.

Clearly the scope of the present chapter must be limited. It seems important, however, to provide some form of introduction to the educational issues raised by adolescent development, and to offer a framework for those who wish to pursue further their study of adolescence, aided no doubt by the chapters that follow. I shall therefore review briefly two major theoretical views of adolescent development, and then turn to one or two of the issues which appear most pertinent to the school context. I have chosen to cover puberty, cognition and some aspects of social development, but have deliberately excluded the topic of the peer group, since this will be covered in a subsequent chapter.

TRADITIONAL THEORIES

There is general agreement by all who have written about adolescence that it makes sense to describe the stage as being one of transition. The transition, it is believed, results from the operation of a number of pressures. Some of these, in particular the physiological and emotional pressures, are internal; while other pressures, which originate from peers, parents, teachers, and society at large, are external to the young person. Sometimes these external pressures carry the individual towards maturity at a faster rate than he or she would prefer, while on other occasions they act as a brake, holding the adolescent back from the freedom and independence which he or she believes to be a legitimate right. It is the interplay of these forces which, in the final analysis, contributes more than anything to the success or failure of the transition from childhood to maturity.

So far two classical types of explanation concerning the transitional process have been advanced. The psychoanalytic approach concentrates on the psychosexual development of the individual, and looks particularly at the psychological factors which underlie the young person's movement away from childhood behaviour and emotional involvement. The second type of explanation, the sociological, represents a very different perspective. While it has never been as coherently expressed as the psychoanalytic view, it is none the less of equal importance. In brief, this explanation sees the causes of adolescent transition as lying primarily in the social setting of the individual and concentrates on the nature of roles and role conflict, the pressures of social expectations, and on the relative influence of different agents of socialization. Let us now look more closely at each of these explanations.

Psychoanalytic theory

The psychoanalytic view of adolescence takes as its starting point the upsurge of instincts which is said to occur as a result of puberty. This increase in instinctual life, it is suggested, upsets the psychic balance which has been achieved by the end of childhood, causing internal emotional upheaval and leading to a greatly increased vulnerability of the personality. This state of affairs is associated with two further factors. In the first place, the individual's awakening sexuality leads him or her to look outside the family setting for appropriate 'love objects', thus severing the emotional ties with the parents which have existed since infancy. This process is known as disengagement. Second, the vulnerability of the personality results in the employment of psychological defences to cope with the instincts and anxiety which are, to a greater or lesser extent, maladaptive. An excellent review of recent psychoanalytic thinking as it applies to adolescence may be found in Lerner (1987).

Regression, a manifestation of behaviour more appropriate to earlier stages of development, and ambivalence are both seen as further key elements of the adolescent process. According to the psychoanalytic view, ambivalence accounts for many of the phenomena often considered incomprehensible in adolescent behaviour. For example, the emotional instability of relationships, the contradictions in thought and feeling, and the apparently illogical shift from one reaction to another reflect the fluctuations between loving and hating, acceptance and rejection, involvement and non-involvement which underlie relationships in the early years, and which are reactivated once more in adolescence.

Such fluctuations in mood and behaviour are indicative also of the young person's attitudes to growing up. Thus, while freedom may at times appear the most exciting of goals, there are also moments when, in the harsh light of reality, independence and the necessity to fight one's own battles become a daunting prospect. At these times childlike dependence exercises a powerful attraction, manifested in periods of uncertainty and self-doubt, and in behaviour which is more likely to bring to mind a wilful child than a young adult.

A consideration of ambivalence leads us on to the more general theme of non-conformity and rebellion, believed by psychoanalysts to be an almost universal feature of adolescence. Behaviour of this sort has many causes. Some of it is a direct result of ambivalent modes of relating, the overt reflection of the conflict between loving and hating. In other circumstances, however, it may be interpreted as an aid to the disengagement process. In this context if the parents can be seen as old-fashioned and irrelevant then the task of breaking the emotional ties becomes easier. If everything that originates from home can safely be rejected then there is nothing to be lost by giving it all up.

Non-conformity thus facilitates the process of disengagement although, as many writers point out, there are a number of intermediate stages along the way. Baittle and Offer illustrate particularly well the importance of non-conformity and its close links with ambivalence:

> When the adolescent rebels, he often expresses his intentions in a manner resembling negation. He defines what he does in terms of what his parents do not want him to do. If his parents want him to turn off the radio and study this is the precise time he keeps the radio on and claims he cannot study. If they want him to buy new clothes, 'the old ones are good enough.' In periods like this it becomes obvious that the adolescent's decisions are in reality based on the negative of the parents' wishes, rather than on their own positive desires. What they do and the judgements they make are in fact dependent on the parents' opinions and suggestions but in a negative way. This may be termed the stage of 'negative dependence'. Thus, while the oppositional behaviour and protest against the parents are indeed a manifestation of rebellion and in the service of emancipation from the parents, at the same time they reveal that the passive dependent longings are still in force. The adolescent is in conflict over desires to emancipate, and the rebellious behaviour is a compromise formation which supports his efforts to give up the parental object and, at the same time, gratifies his dependence on them.
>
> (1971: 35)

To summarize, three particular ideas characterize the psycho-analytic position. In the first place adolescence is seen as being a period during which there is a marked vulnerability of personality, resulting primarily from the upsurge of instincts at puberty. Second, emphasis is laid on the likelihood of maladaptive behaviour, stemming from the inadequacy of the psychological defences to cope with inner conflicts and tensions. Examples of such behaviour include extreme fluctuations of mood, inconsistency in relationships, depression and non-conformity. Third, the process of disengagement is given special prominence. This is perceived as a necessity if mature emotional and sexual relationships are to be established outside the home.

Sociological theory

As has been indicated, the sociological view of adolescence encompasses a very different perspective from that of psycho-analytic theory. While there is no disagreement between the two approaches concerning the importance of the transitional process, it is on the subject of the causes of this process that the viewpoints diverge. Thus, while the one concentrates on internal factors, the other looks at society and to events outside the individual for a satisfactory explanation. For the sociologist, socialization and role are the two key concepts. By socialization is meant the process whereby individuals in a society absorb the values, standards, and beliefs current in that society. Some of these standards and values will refer to positions, or roles, in society, so that, for example, there will be expectations and prescriptions of behaviour appropriate to roles such as son, daughter, citizen, teenager, parent and so on. Everyone in a society learns through the agents of socialization, such as school, home, the mass media, etc. the expectations associated with the various roles, although these expectations may not necessarily be clear-cut. Furthermore, socialization may be more or less effective, depending on the nature of the agents to which the individual is exposed, the amount of conflict between the different agents, and so on. During childhood the individual, by and large, has his or her roles ascribed by others, but as he or she matures through adolescence greater opportunities are available, not only for a choice of roles, but also for a choice of how those roles should be interpreted. As will become apparent, it is implicit in the social-psychological viewpoint that both socialization and role assumption are more problematic during adolescence than at any other time.

Why should this be so? First, features of adolescence such as growing independence from authority figures, involvement with peer groups, and an unusual sensitivity to the evaluations of others all provoke role transitions and discontinuity, of varying intensities, as functions of both social and cultural context. Second, any inner change or uncertainty has the effect of increasing the individual's dependence on others, and this applies particularly to the need for reassurance and support for one's view of oneself. Third, the effects of major environmental changes are also relevant in this context. Different schools, the move from school to university or college, leaving home, taking a job all demand involvement in a new set of relationships which in turn lead to different and often greater expectations, a substantial reassessment of the self, and an acceleration of the process of socialization. Role change, it will be apparent, is thus seen as an integral feature of adolescent development.

While role change may be one source of difficulty for the adolescent, it is certainly not the only one. Inherent in role behaviour generally are a number of potential stresses such as role conflict. Here the individual occupies two roles, let us say son and boyfriend, which have expectations associated with them which are incompatible. The individual is thus caught in the middle between two people or sets of people, who expect different forms of behaviour. Thus in the case of son and boyfriend, the teenage boy's mother might put pressure on him to behave like a dutiful child, while his girlfriend will expect him to be independent of his parents and to care for her rather than for anyone else. Such a situation is one which few young people can avoid at some time or another.

Next there is role discontinuity. Here there is a lack of order in the transition from one role to another. Many years ago, Ruth Benedict (1938) drew attention to the fact that primitive cultures provided more continuity in training for responsibilities, sexual maturity and so on than western societies, and the situation has hardly improved today. Role discontinuity is said to occur when there is no bridge or ordered sequence from one stage to the next, or when behaviour in the second stage necessitates the unlearning of some or all of that which was learned earlier. One only has to think of the problem of transition for the young unemployed or the grossly inadequate preparation for parenthood in our society to appreciate the point. Third, there is role incongruence. Here the individual is placed in a position for which he or she is unfitted; in other words the role ascribed by others is not the one that the individual would have chosen. Good illustrations from adolescent experience would be parents who hold unrealistically high expectations of their teenage children, or who, alternatively, fight to maintain their adolescent sons and daughters in childlike roles. Implicit in these theoretical notions is the view that the individual's movement through adolescence will be very much affected by the consistent or inconsistent, adaptive or maladaptive expectations held by significant people in his or her immediate environment.

Up to this point our discussion has concentrated on the features of role behaviour which lead sociologists and social psychologists to view adolescence not only as a transitional period, but as one which contains many potentially stressful characteristics. However, the process of socialization is also seen by many as being problematic at this stage. In the first place the adolescent is exposed to a wide variety of competing socialization agencies, including the family, the school, the peer group, adult-directed youth organizations, the mass media, political organizations and so on, and is thus presented with a wide range of potential conflicts, values and ideals. Furthermore, it is commonly assumed by sociologists today that the socialization of young people is more dependent upon the generation than upon the family or other social institutions. Marsland goes so far as to call it 'auto-socialization' in his description of the process:

> The crucial social meaning of youth is withdrawal from adult control and influence compared with childhood. Peer groups are the milieu into which young people withdraw. In at least most societies, this withdrawal to the peer group is, within limits, legitimated by the adult world. Time and space are handed over to young people to work out for themselves in auto-socialization the developmental problems of self and identity which cannot be handled by the simple direct socialization appropriate to childhood. There is a moratorium on compliance and commitment and leeway allowed for a relatively unguided journey with peers towards autonomy and maturity.
>
> (Marsland 1987: 12)

Both the conflict between socialization agencies and the freedom from clearly defined guidelines are seen as making socialization more uncertain, and causing major difficulties for the young person in establishing a bridge towards the assumption of adult roles. Brake (1985), in his discussion of youth subcultures, makes similar points, and it is a common assumption among those writing from the sociological point of view that the social changes of the last twenty years or so have created ever-increasing stresses for young people.

In particular it should be noted that most writers see little of value in what they believe to be the decline of adult involvement and the increasing importance of the peer group. Among such writers the adolescent peer group is frequently described as being more likely to encourage anti-social behaviour than to act as a civilizing agent, and though it is accepted that the effects of peer involvement depend on the standards and activities of the peer group, there is undoubtedly a general feeling that when young people spend a considerable amount of time with individuals of their own age more harm than good is likely to come of it. While, on the one hand, there is clearly some logic in the view that the adolescent who is deprived of adult company is at a disadvantage in the transition towards maturity, on the other hand research does not bear out the myth of the all-powerful peer group, and it is still very much an open question as to what effect increasing age segregation has on the socialization process.

To summarize, the sociological or social-psychological approach to adolescence is marked by a concern with roles and role change, and with the processes of socialization. There can be little doubt that adolescence, from this point of view, is seen as being dominated by stresses and tensions, not so much because of inner emotional instability, but as a result of conflicting pressures from outside. Thus, by considering both this and the psychoanalytic approach, two mutually complementary but essentially different views of the adolescent transitional process have been reviewed.

PUBERTY

Puberty, and the physical growth that accompanies it, is important to those involved in education for a number of reasons. In the first place puberty has a range of physiological effects which are not always outwardly apparent to observers, but which can none the less have a considerable impact on the individual. Second, rates of maturation vary enormously, leading inevitably to questions of normality and comparability between young people. Furthermore, especially early or unusually late developers have particular difficulties to face, which again have marked implications for classroom performance and behaviour. Third, physical development cannot fail to have psychological consequences, often affecting self-concept and self-esteem, factors which themselves play a major part in motivation and learning. Thus it can be seen that an understanding of puberty is essential in making sense of adolescent development as a whole. I shall deal with each of these areas in turn.

Adults often fail to appreciate that puberty is accompanied by changes not only in the reproductive system and in the secondary sexual characteristics of the individual, but in the functioning of the heart and thus of the cardio-vascular system, in the lungs, which in turn affect the respiratory system, in the size and the strength of many of the muscles of the body, and so on. One of the many physical changes associated with puberty is the 'growth spurt'. This term is usually taken to refer to the accelerated rate of increase in height and weight that occurs during early adolescence. It is essential to bear in mind, however, that there are very considerable individual differences in the age of onset and duration of the growth spurt, even among perfectly normal children. This is a fact which parents and adolescents themselves frequently fail to appreciate, thus causing a great deal of unnecessary anxiety. In boys the growth spurt may begin as early as 10 years of age, or as late as 16, while in girls the same process can begin at 7 or 8, or not until 12, 13 or even 14. For the average boy, though, rapid growth begins at about 13, and reaches a peak somewhere during the fourteenth year. Comparable ages for girls are 11 for the onset of the growth spurt and 12 for the peak age of increase in height and weight. Other phenomena associated with the growth spurt are a rapid increase in the size and weight of the heart (the weight of the heart nearly doubles at puberty), accelerated growth of the lungs and a decline in basal metabolism. Noticeable to children themselves, especially boys, is a marked increase in physical strength and endurance (see Tanner 1978 for a full description).

Sexual maturation is closely linked with the physical changes described above. Again the sequence of events is approximately eighteen to twenty-four months later for boys than it is for girls. Since individuals mature at very different rates, one girl at the age of 14 may be small, have no bust and look very much as she did during childhood, while another of the same age may look like a fully developed adult woman, who could easily be taken for someone four or five years in advance of her actual chronological age. Such marked physical differences will have particular consequences for the individual's psychological adjustment.

The issue of especially early or late development is one to which considerable attention has been paid in the literature. Studies have shown that whether puberty occurs early or late bears little relation to abnormality in physical development. Thus, for example, slowness in beginning the growth spurt does not appear in any way to be indicative of later physical difficulty. However, there is good evidence from both Europe and North America to show that those who mature earlier physically score higher on most tests of mental ability and perform better in the classroom than their less mature peers. One implication of this is that in age-linked examinations physically fast maturers have an advantage over those who develop more slowly (Tanner 1978).

The age of onset of puberty is also associated with other psychological consequences. Results of work carried out at the University of California (for a review see Conger and Petersen 1984) have shown that where boys are concerned those who were among the slowest 20 per cent to develop physically were rated by adults as less attractive, less socially mature, and more restless, talkative and bossy. In addition they were seen by their peers as being less popular, and few of them were leaders. On a personality test the group revealed more feelings of inadequacy and negative self-perceptions. Many of these difficulties appear to persist over a period of time, for when they were followed up at the age of 33 the majority of the group still showed difficulties in personal adjustment.

Whereas for boys it is slow physical development which appears to be associated with poor psychological adjustment, the picture among girls is rather more complicated. Differences between early and late maturing girls are not as great, and furthermore the advantages and disadvantages of early versus late maturation may vary with time. At this age girls value more highly the personality traits associated with the pre-pubertal stage of development than those related to sexual maturity. However, by 14 or 15 the picture has changed, and traits associated with early maturation are, by this time, the more highly valued. Other studies have shown differences in interests between 13-year-olds who have reached puberty and those who have not. Thus there appears to be little doubt that the age of onset of puberty is associated with particular patterns of psychological adjustment. In general, apart from young adolescent girls, early maturation is related to general self-confidence and social maturity. This is hardly surprising given the advantages, both in terms of physique and self-image, which stem from early maturation. In view of this the most important task for adults in this sphere is undoubtedly to work to counteract the psychological disadvantages faced by the late maturer.

The changes discussed above inevitably exercise a profound effect upon the individual. The body alters radically in size and shape, and it is not surprising that many adolescents experience a period of clumsiness in an attempt to adapt to these changes. The body also alters in function, and new and sometimes worrying physical experiences, such as the girl's first period, have to be understood. Perhaps most important of all, however, is the effect that such physical changes have upon identity. As many writers have pointed out, the development of the individual's identity requires not only the notion of being separate and different from others, but also a sense of self-consistency, and a firm knowledge of how one appears to the rest of the world. Needless to say dramatic bodily changes seriously affect these aspects of identity, and represent a considerable challenge in adaptation for even the most well-adjusted young person. It is unfortunate that many adults, having successfully forgotten much of their own adolescent anxiety, retain only a vague awareness of the psychological impact of the physical changes associated with puberty.

Experimental evidence has clearly shown that the average adolescent is not only sensitive to, but often critical of, his or her changing physical self. Thus, probably as a result of the importance of films and television, teenagers tend to have idealized norms for physical attractiveness, and to feel inadequate if they do not match these unrealistic criteria. Studies have shown that adolescents who perceive themselves as deviating physically from cultural stereotypes are likely to have impaired self-concepts, and the important role that physical characteristics play in determining self-esteem, especially in the younger adolescent, has been underlined by many writers (see Brooks-Gunn and Petersen 1983). Other studies have been reported in which young people were asked what they did and did not like about themselves. Results showed that those in early adolescence used primarily physical characteristics to describe themselves, and it was these characteristics which were most often disliked. It was not until later adolescence that intellectual and social aspects of the personality were widely used in self-descriptions, but these characteristics were much more frequently liked than disliked (see Coleman and Hendry 1990).

It can be seen, therefore, that some understanding of puberty and its effects is essential in the school context. Research evidence has certainly underlined the wide-ranging implications of physical change in early adolescence but has not, in my view, provided much support for the psychoanalytic notion of psychological upheaval which is supposed to go hand-in-hand with puberty. It is clear that the self concept, particularly that aspect of it associated with physical characteristics, does undergo substantial change which may well result in some temporary instability.

None the less this hardly constitutes the sort of vulnerability of personality described in the theoretical literature; and while, on the one hand, it is obviously extremely important for adults to pay attention to the psychological effects of puberty, particularly for late developers, on the other hand, it seems essential not to exaggerate the extent of the effect of these aspects of maturation.

COGNITION

Those involved in education will no doubt be more aware than others of the significance of cognitive development during adolescence. In a short review such as this it is possible only to draw attention to the major themes, and to highlight one or two of the most significant areas of recent work in this field. For those wishing to read further, good general discussions of cognition in adolescence are to be found in Coleman and Hendry (1990), Serafica (1982) and Conger and Petersen (1984).

Changes in intellectual functioning during the teenage years have implications for a wide range of behaviours and attitudes. Such changes render possible the move towards independence of both thought and action; they enable the young person to develop a time perspective which includes the future; they facilitate progress towards maturity in relationships; and finally they underline the individual's ability to participate in society as worker, voter, responsible group member and so on. We cannot consider these changes without looking first at the work of Piaget, for it is he who has laid the foundation for almost all subsequent work on cognitive development. It will be worthwhile also to discuss briefly some work on adolescent reasoning and to review ideas on both moral and political thought in adolescence.

The work of Jean Piaget, the Swiss psychologist, is the most obvious starting place for a consideration of cognitive development during the teenage years. It was he who first pointed out that a qualitative change in the nature of mental ability, rather than any simple increase in cognitive skill, is to be expected at or around puberty, and he has argued that it is at this point in development that formal operational thought finally becomes possible (Inhelder and Piaget 1958). A full description of Piaget's stages of cognitive growth is not possible here. Most readers will be familiar with his assertion that in early adolescence the individual moves from a stage of concrete operations to one of formal operational thought. With the appearance of this stage a number of capabilities become available to the young person. Perhaps the most significant of these is the ability to construct 'contrary to fact' propositions. This change has been described as the shift of emphasis in adolescent thought from the 'real' to the 'possible', and it facilitates hypothetico-deductive logic. It also enables the individual to think about mental constructs as objects that can be manipulated, and to come to terms with notions of probability and belief.

This fundamental difference in approach between the young child and the adolescent has been neatly demonstrated in a study by Elkind (1966). He showed dramatic differences between 8- and 9-year-olds and 13- and 14-year-olds in their capacity to solve a concept-formation problem by setting up hypotheses and then testing them out in logical succession. However, it is clear that formal operational thought cannot be tested using a single problem task. Any investigator must use a range of tests in an attempt to construct some overall measure of the individual's ability to tackle problems of logical thought in a number of areas. In relation to this it is important to bear in mind that the development of formal thinking is certainly not an all-or-none-affair, with the individual moving overnight from one stage to another. The change occurs slowly, and there may even be some shifting back and forth before the new mode of thought is firmly established. Furthermore it is almost certain that the adolescent will adopt formal modes of thinking in one area before another. Thus, for example, someone interested in arts subjects may use formal operational thinking in the area of verbal reasoning well before he or she is able to utilize such skills in scientific problem solving.

In addition to these points recent research indicates that in all probability Piaget was a little too optimistic when he expressed the view that the majority of adolescents could be expected to develop formal operational thought by 12 or 13 years of age. While studies do not entirely agree on the exact proportions reaching various stages at different age levels, there is general consensus that up to the age of 16 only a minority reach the most advanced level of formal thought (Coleman and Hendry 1990).

Studies show that intelligence is likely to play a role in the development of formal operational thinking. Yet this variable is not sufficient to explain why formal operations appear in one child at 12, and in another at 16. Inhelder and Piaget (1958) paid remarkably little attention to this problem, contenting themselves simply with some speculation about the relation between intellectual and social development. They appear to suggest that as social pressures operate on the individual, encouraging him or her towards maturity and independence, so intellectual skills develop, enabling the young person to cope with the new demands of a more adult life. This is hardly a very satisfactory explanation, although it may indeed turn out that social and intellectual maturation are correlated.

Surprisingly there is little in the literature which sheds much light on such an important topic, as Niemark (1975) indicates. We may ask what other factors might be involved. Intelligence only contributes a small proportion of the total variance. Perhaps attention should be paid to the type of school and the attitudes of teachers. Studies have indicated that self-image might be important, but what about achievement motivation, or position in the peer group? Also, the impact of parental attitudes and the home environment should undoubtedly be examined. At this point, it must be accepted that there are no definite answers to the question of what it is which determines the appearance of formal operational thinking. It is already clear that many factors will be involved, and the solution is unlikely to be a simple one. However, one thing is certain; this is a question which needs to be answered as soon as possible if the psychology of Piaget is to remain relevant to the education of young people today.

To study adolescent reasoning is obviously another way of looking at cognitive development. David Elkind (1967) is a good example of someone seeking to extend Piaget's original notions in this way. He argues that while the attainment of formal operational thinking frees the individual in many respects from childhood egocentrism; at the same time, paradoxically, it entangles him or her in a new version of the same thing. This is because the achievement of formal operational thought allows the adolescent to think about not only his own thought, but also about the thought of other people. It is this incapacity to take account of other people's thinking, argues Elkind, which is the basis of adolescent egocentrism. Essentially the individual finds it extremely difficult to differentiate between what others are thinking about and his own preoccupations. He assumes that if he is obsessed by a thought or a problem then other people must also be obsessed by the same thing. One example given by Elkind is that of the adolescent's appearance. To a large extent teenagers are preoccupied with the way they look to others, and they make the assumption that others must be as involved as they are with the same subject. Elkind ties this type of egocentrism in with the concept of what he calls 'the imaginary audience'. Because of this egocentrism the adolescent is, either in actual or fantasy social situations, anticipating the reactions of others. However, these reactions are based on a premiss that others are as admiring or critical of him as he is of himself. Thus he is continually constructing and reacting to his 'imaginary audience', a fact which, according to Elkind, explains a lot of adolescent behaviour – the self-consciousness, the wish for privacy, and the long hours spent in front of the mirror. Recent work (reviewed in Conger and Petersen 1984) has provided strong corroboration for Elkind's views.

Another area of interest to researchers in the field of cognitive development is that of moral and political thought. How is this changed by formal operations? Do young people pass through different stages of thinking where morals and politics are concerned, and if so, what is the nature of such stages? As far as moral thinking is concerned it is once again Piaget's notions which have formed the springboard for later thinking on this subject, and although a number of different theories have been put forward to explain the development of concepts of morality in young people, the 'cognitive-developmental' approach of Piaget and Kohlberg has undoubtedly been the most influential. In his work on the moral judgement of the child, Piaget described two major stages of moral thinking. The first, which he called 'moral realism', refers to a period during which young children make judgements on an objective basis, for example by estimating the amount of damage which has been caused in an accident. Thus a child who breaks twelve cups is considered more blameworthy than one who only breaks one cup, regardless of the circumstances. The second stage, applying usually to those between the ages of 8 and 12, has been described as that of the 'morality of co-operation', or the 'morality of reciprocity'. During this stage, Piaget believed, decisions concerning morality were usually made on a subjective basis, and often depended on an estimate of intention rather than consequence.

Kohlberg (1969) has elaborated Piaget's scheme into one which has six different stages. His method has been to present hypothetical situations concerning moral dilemmas to young people of different ages, and to classify their responses according to a stage theory of moral development. Some of Kohlberg's most interesting work has involved the study of moral development in different cultures. He has shown that an almost identical sequence appears to occur in widely different cultures, the variation between cultures being found in the rate of development, and the fact that in more primitive societies later stages of thinking are rarely used.

As in the case of moral judgement the young person's political ideas are likely to be significantly influenced by his or her level of cognitive development. In recent years a number of writers have become interested in the shift which takes place during the adolescent years, from a lack of political thought to – in many cases – an intense involvement in this area of life. How does this occur and what are the processes involved? At what age do adolescents begin to show an increasing grasp of political concepts, and what stages do they go through before they achieve maturity of political judgement? One of the most important early studies was that undertaken by Adelson and O'Neill (1966). They approached the problem of the growth of political ideas in an imaginative way by posing for young people of different ages the following problem: 'Imagine that a thousand men and women, dissatisfied with the way things are going in their own country, decide to purchase and move to an island in the Pacific; once there they must devise laws and codes of government.' They then explored the adolescents' approach to a variety of relevant issues. They asked questions about how a government would be formed, what would its purpose be, would there be a need for laws and political parties, how would you protect minorities, and so on. The investigators proposed different laws, and explored typical problems of public policy.

The major results may be discussed under two headings – the changes in modes of thinking, and the decline of authoritarianism with age. As far as the first is concerned, there was a marked shift in thinking from the concrete to the abstract, a finding which ties in well with the work discussed above. The second major shift observed was the decline in authoritarian solutions to political questions. The typical young adolescent appeared unable to appreciate that problems can have more than one solution, and that individual behaviour or political acts are not necessarily absolutely right or wrong, good or bad. The concept of moral relativism was not yet available for the making of political judgements. In contrast, the 14- or 15-year-old is much more aware of the different sides of any argument, and is usually able to take a relativistic point of view. Thinking begins to be more tentative, more critical and more pragmatic.

Recent work in this area is well reviewed by Furnham and Stacey (1991). As they indicate, we now know a lot more about the ways in which thinking in the political arena develops. It is a topic of particular interest, not only because of its obvious implications for education and government, but also because of the manner in which intellectual change can be seen to interact with social behaviour. This is not to say that other areas of cognitive development are not of equal value and importance, and it is to be hoped that this section may have acted as a signpost, if nothing more, towards issues of general interest.

SOCIAL RELATIONSHIPS

I intend in this section to concentrate particularly on the role of adults, and on the nature and significance of relationships between young people and parents, teachers and important others. (Peer relationships will be dealt with in Chapter 5.) In selecting issues which will be of relevance to the educational context, I have chosen the development of independence, and adults as role models, since out of the many available these seemed to me to be two of the most obviously pertinent.

One of the central themes of adolescent development is the attainment of independence, often represented symbolically in art and literature by the moment of departure from home. However, for most young people today independence is not gained at one specific moment by the grand gesture of saying goodbye to one's parents and setting off to seek one's fortune in the wide world. Independence is much more likely to mean the freedom to make new relationships, and personal freedom to take responsibility for oneself in such things as education, work, political beliefs and future career choice.

There are many forces which interact in propelling an individual towards a state of maturity. Naturally both physical and intellectual maturation encourage the adolescent towards greater autonomy. In addition to these factors there are, undoubtedly, psychological forces within the individual as well as social forces within the environment which have the same goal. In the psychoanalytic view, mentioned earlier, the process of seeking independence represents the need to break off the infantile ties with the parents, thus making new mature sexual relationships possible. From the perspective of the sociologist, more emphasis is placed on the changes in role and status which lead to a redefinition of the individual's place in the social structure. Whatever the explanation, it is certainly true that the achievement of independence is an integral feature of adolescent development, and that the role of the adults involved is an especially important one.

In understanding this process it is necessary to appreciate that the young person's movement towards adulthood is far from straightforward. While independence at times appears to be a rewarding goal, there are moments when it is a worrying, even frightening, prospect. Childlike dependence can be safe and comforting at no matter what age, if, for example, one is facing problems or difficulties alone, and it is essential to realize that no individual achieves adult independence without a number of backward glances. It is this ambivalence which underlies the typically contradictory behaviour of adolescence, behaviour which is so often the despair of adults. Thus there is nothing more frustrating than having to deal with a teenager who is at one moment complaining about adults who are always interfering, and the next bitterly protesting that no one takes any interest. However, it is equally important to acknowledge that adults themselves usually hold conflicting attitudes towards young people. On the one hand they may wish them to be independent, to make their own decisions, and to cease making childish demands, while on the other they may be anxious about the consequences of independence, and sometimes jealous of the opportunities and idealism of youth. In addition it should not be forgotten that the adolescent years often coincide with the difficulties of middle age for parents in particular. Adjusting to unfulfilled hopes, the possibility of retirement, declining physical health, marital difficulties and so on may all increase family stress, and add further to the problems faced by young people in finding a satisfactory route to independence.

Research evidence has not provided much support for the notion that wide-ranging conflict between adults and young people is the order of the day. Noller and Callan (1991), in reviewing the data available, come to the conclusion that the general picture that emerges from experimental studies is that of relatively harmonious relationships with adults for the majority of young people. Of course adolescents do seek independence, of that there is no dispute, and so the question arises as to how common sense and research evidence can be fitted together. In the first place it is clear that some adolescents do, temporarily at least, come into conflict with or become critical of adults. In addition there is no doubt that some adults do become restrictive, attempting to slow down the pace of change. Research has shown that there are a number of factors which affect the extent of the conflict occurring between the generations. Cultural background, adult behaviour, age and social class all need to be taken into account.

Other aspects of the situation need also to be borne in mind. For example, there is undoubtedly a difference between attitudes towards close family members, and attitudes to more general social groupings, such as 'the younger generation'. Thus, for example, teenagers may very well approve of and look up to their own parents while expressing criticism of adults in general. Similarly, parents may deride 'drop-outs', 'skinheads', or 'soccer hooligans' while holding a favourable view of their own adolescent sons and daughters. Another fact that needs to be stressed is that there is a difference between feeling and behaviour. Adolescents may be irritated or angry with their parents as a result of day-to-day conflicts, but issues can be worked out in the home, and do not necessarily lead to outright rejection or rebellion. Furthermore, too little credit is given to the possibility that adults and young people, although disagreeing with each other about certain things, may still respect each other's views, and live or work together in relative harmony. Thus there seems to be little doubt that the extreme view of a generation gap, involving the notion of a war between the generations, or the ideas of a separate adolescent subculture, is dependent on a myth. It is the result of a stereotype which is useful to the mass media, and given currency by a small minority of disaffected young people and resentful adults. However, to deny any sort of conflict between teenagers and older members of society is equally false. Adolescents could not grow into adults unless they were able to test out the boundaries of authority, nor could they discover what they believed unless given the opportunity to push hard against the beliefs of others. The adolescent transition from dependence to independence is almost certain to involve some conflict, but its extent should not be exaggerated.

Adults fulfil many different functions for the developing adolescent, and one of these functions – one that is less visible than many others – is the provision of role models. Here the adult represents an example of the way such things as sex roles and work roles may be interpreted. The adult provides a model or an image, which the young person, in a partly conscious and partly unconscious manner, uses to develop his or her own role behaviour. It is of course true that children throughout their early lives depend on their parents and other adults for primary knowledge of such role behaviour, but obviously these models become crucial during adolescence, since it is at this time that the young person begins to make his or her own role choices. Thus, for example, while parents' attitudes to work will be pertinent all through childhood, these will become relevant in a somewhat more direct and more immediate way when the teenager is facing questions about what he or she is going to do after leaving school. As we have seen earlier, role change is likely to be a major feature of adolescent development, and it will be evident therefore that the role models available to the young person at this stage in life will be of great significance. It is important to be clear, however, that the likelihood of role decisions or role choices being influenced by adults will be determined not only by the nature of the role model, but also by the type of relationship between adult and young person. We cannot here enter into a discussion of identification, but we should note the obvious fact that role modelling is likely to be enhanced by a positive emotional quality in the relationship between the individuals concerned, as well as by the structure of the family, school or other institution, and the young person's involvement in decision-making processes.

It is unfortunate that almost all research on role modelling has concentrated on the family, since it is undoubtedly true that teachers, as well as other significant adults, have an important part to play in this sphere. To give one example of sex role modelling, research has indicated that boys whose fathers provide a moderately masculine role model, but who are also involved in the feminine, caring side of family life, adjust better as adults and experience fewer conflicts between their social values and their actual behaviour. Boys whose fathers provide role models which are at either extreme – excessively masculine, or predominantly feminine – appear to adjust less well (see Conger and Petersen 1984).

Where work role models are concerned, research has shown that close positive relationships are most likely to facilitate the use of the parents as a role model, although this does not necessarily mean taking the same type of job as the mother or father. Much more important here are the transmission of attitudes to work, and the general area of work interests. In one study women's attitudes to work were assessed as a function of their mothers' own attitudes and experiences. Results showed that women between the ages of 19 and 22 held attitudes towards work and everything associated with it which were directly related to (although not necessarily the same as) their mother's attitudes and experiences. In brief, where mothers had had positive experiences – in whatever work role they had chosen, including that of mother and housewife – then their daughters were likely also to be well adjusted in their attitudes to work and career. Where mothers had experienced conflict over work, or were dissatisfied with their own work experiences, it was likely that their daughters would have similar adjustment difficulties (Coleman and Hendry 1990).

Thus it can be seen that adults have a critical part to play in this sphere. Because the nature of the influence involved is usually indirect, the force of the impact that significant adults have in this respect is rarely fully acknowledged. What is certain is that more research is needed since, as all the reviews indicate, we are only just beginning to discover something of the process which occurs. Even in situations of unemployment role modelling is crucial. Here it has been shown that the attitudes that young people hold towards work, and the determination and persistence they apply to overcoming the enormous problems of being without work, are directly related to the behaviour of the role models they have available. Teachers and educationalists in particular should bear in mind that schools offer powerful, influential adult role models at just the time in the young person's life when role models are most needed. In my view it is part of the adult's responsibility, in his or her work with adolescents, to be aware of this aspect of the relationship that is created between them.

In brief then, two aspects of social relationships between adults and young people have been reviewed. Conclusions from both areas underline the critical part that parents, teachers and others have to play in facilitating the major transitions which occur during adolescence. Both theory and research provide support for this argument, and it is one which has a special relevance in the educational context. Here teenagers are in constant interaction with adults, and yet all too frequently this interaction is perceived, by both sides, as having a narrow and rather specific focus. As this chapter has tried to indicate, adults in the school setting are inevitably involved in far more than the conveying of information. It is to be hoped that the comments made here will encourage readers to consider the psychology of adolescence, and the lessons it has for all within education.

REFERENCES

Adelson, J. and O'Neill, R. (1966) 'The development of political thought in adolescence', *Journal of Personality and Social Psychology*, 4: 295–308.
Baittle, B. and Offer, D. (1971) 'On the nature of adolescent rebellion', in F. C. Feinstein, P. Giovacchini and A. Miller (eds) *Annals of Adolescent Psychiatry*, New York: Basic Books.
Benedict, R. (1938) 'Continuities and discontinuities in cultural conditioning', *Psychiatry* 1: 161–7.
Brake, M. (1985) *Comparative Youth Subcultures*, London: Routledge & Kegan Paul.
Brooks-Gunn, J. and Petersen, A. (eds) (1983) *Girls at Puberty*, New York: Plenum.
Coleman, J. C. and Hendry, L. (1990) *The Nature of Adolescence*, 2nd ed, London: Routledge.
Conger, J. and Petersen, A. (1984) *Adolescence and Youth*, 3rd ed, New York: Harper and Row.
Elkind, D. (1966) 'Conceptual orientation shifts in children and adolescents', *Child Development* 37: 493–8.
——(1967) 'Egocentrism in adolescence', *Child Development* 38: 1025–34.
Furnham, A. and Stacey, B. (1991) *Young People's Understanding of Society*, London: Routledge.
Inhelder, B. and Piaget, J. (1958) *The Growth of Logical Thinking*, London: Routledge & Kegan Paul.
Kohlberg, L. (1969) *Stages in the Development of Moral Thought and Action*, New York: Holt, Rinehart and Winston.
Lerner, R. M. (1987) 'Psychodynamic models', in V. B. Van Hasselt and M. Hersen (eds) *Handbook of Adolescent Psychology*, Oxford: Pergamon Press.
Marsland, D. (1987) *Education and Youth*, London: Falmer Press.
Niemark, E. D. (1975) 'Intellectual development during adolescence', in F. D. Horowitz (ed.) *Review of Child Development Research*, vol. 4, Chicago: University of Chicago Press.
Noller, P. and Callan, V. (1991) *The Adolescent in the Family*, London: Routledge.

Serafica, F. C. (ed.) (1982) *Social-cognitive Development in Context*, London: Methuen.
Tanner, J. M. (1978) *Foetus into Man*, London: Open Books.

Chapter 2

Moral development

Peter Kutnick

INTRODUCTION

Lines from a popular song of the 1960s, 'I was so much older then, I'm younger than that now . . .', aptly describe a moral development literature that was sure of itself in the 1970s but has more to learn in the 1990s. Educational psychology texts of the 1970s generally asserted that students should learn Kohlberg's (1969) theory, and this knowledge would substantially explain adolescent development and provide a sound basis for moral education in the classroom. Today, we still encounter moral problems such as: the adolescent who makes a nuisance of him/herself in class; the deputy head who (in prime ministerial fashion) asserts how much easier life would be if we all followed the 'rule of law'; clashes between 'cultures' such as fundamentalist assertion of moral convention and liberal abstraction of rules to underlying principles; and pupils who react with apathy when another person is in distress. We expect that moral education should help to overcome these problems.

Moral development theory often competes with a 'common sense' understanding that anyone (who cares to) can make statements or assertions about particular behaviour. In its defence, those who have studied moral development and its application in education have been forced to delineate clearly what they are studying and how their findings may affect aspects of moral character developed in schools. Damon (1988) has identified seven areas which are considered in the study of moral development:

1 Evaluation of 'good' and 'bad' behaviour.
2 Obligation to social and collective experience.
3 Concern for the welfare of others.
4 Responsibility for acting on one's concerns for others.

5 Concern for the rights of others.
6 Commitment to honesty.
7 Judgemental and emotional responses produced when rules or conventions are breached.

Moral development is not an individual process; it is generated and identified within individuals and groups. Studies show that children are not born moral; nor are they the amoral beasts described in William Golding's *Lord of the Flies*. Children are neither born into a state of sin (and must be made moral) nor are they born as an 'empty jug' (and must be taught to be good). From birth, children enter into and participate in social relations and are provided with many moral experiences; children are keen to enter into moral experiences to gain these understandings.

The importance of moral development research is its application to moral education (or personal, social and moral education). Outwardly one finds moral education curricula which are based on various theories of moral development. Also, the 'hidden curriculum' affects and constrains pupils' knowledge and understanding within school moral experience. Moreover, the school may be the only stable and long-lasting moral experience offered to many pupils; especially consider the breakdown of moralizing institutions such as the family (from extended to nuclear, from dual-parented to single-parented) and the loss of established religion and community life. Currently, though, schools are under legislative and political assault which limits their moral effectiveness to transmitting a traditional academic curriculum (in the form of a National Curriculum). To provide insights into how schools may more effectively plan for moral education this chapter will present a review of moral development literature, its substantiation and revisions; and a consideration of moral education in schools.

Before introducing the range of moral development theories that have been studied over the last few decades, a few qualifications should be made. Researchers whose theories are presented may appear to enhance, contradict and avoid each other. Weinreich-Haste (1987) explains this range of variation as a positive contribution to the literature and moral experience for the child. Researchers are bound to adopt a theoretical approach which specifies only a particular 'operational definition' of morality; this closely identifies what can be studied, appropriate methodology and distinction from other theories. The moral educator must weigh up different approaches and resolve the dilemma of indoctrination versus development of moral experience. Teachers are at the 'chalkface' of this dilemma; and are often held to account for the child's early and culturally established experience. But schools are only an aspect of the child's moral experience, which is also affected by parental histories, gender, social class, religion and other cultural affiliations.

TYPES OF THEORY

This review is limited in that it can only provide insights into moral development; there are numerous first hand writings and extended reviews available for the interested reader (see Lickona 1976; Kagan and Lamb 1987; Kurtines and Gewirtz 1987). Each of the theories covers a distinct approach to moral development. Several areas of overlap may appear between theories. The overlap will eventually lead to a call for the integration of approaches, especially with application to education. An initial distinction must be made between theories focusing on the 'normal' development of the child as opposed to deviations (abnormalities) from the normal.

Cognitive developmental theories

Cognitive developmental theories of moral development are cited most frequently in education. These theories identify a normal, sequential pattern of stage judgements known as moral reasoning and the relation of moral action to thought. All cognitive developmental theories consider the child as an active agent and collaborator in the construction of their understanding of morality. Cognitive developmental theories do not assume a 'virtues' approach to moral development, and therefore make little comment on singular issues such as cheating, resistance to temptation and specific acts of altruism. Lawrence Kohlberg (1969) identified the following assumptions for his (and other) cognitive developmental theories:

1 Moral development has a basic cognitive-structural or moral judgemental component.
2 Basic motivation for morality is a generalized motivation for

acceptance, competence, self-esteem or self-realization, rather than biological need or reduction of anxiety or fear.

3 Major aspects of moral development are culturally universal.

4 Basic moral norms and principles are structures arising through experiences of social interaction, rather than internalization of rules that exist as external structures.

5 Environmental influences in moral development are defined by the general quality and extent of cognitive and social stimulation throughout the child's development, rather than by specific experiences with parents or experiences of discipline, punishment and reward.

Cognitive developmental theories have a number of processes in common. Amongst them are the dominance of perception and action in the development of early thought and understanding; the fact that social interaction is necessary to break down egoistic 'centrations' in social and cognitive understanding; and that developmental movement may be characterized as embarking from here-and-now experiences towards abstract, principle-based behaviour. An example of the difference between here-and-now and principles is presented in the following confrontation between two children (aged 5 and 8) who discuss the agreement to share a toy:

8yr: Will you give it to me when you are finished?
5yr: Yes, when I'm done.
8yr: Do you swear to God and hope to die?
5yr: I don't think it's true.
8yr: Why?
5yr: Cause He's not down here.
8yr: That's not what it means. It means that you won't break a promise that you made.

Cognitive developmental, or stage, theories assume that the moral values embodied in higher stages are more complex and comprehensive than those of the lower stages. This assumption may undervalue the processes and thought of the less experienced child and limit insights which will help to advance the less developed child.

Piaget's (1932) research into moral development is the longest established but least drawn-upon of the cognitive developmental theories. His research integrated cognitive and social development, and showed how social experience relates to understanding. Piaget described moral stages from birth to adolescence, following from amoral to heteronomous to autonomous stages. Movement to the heteronomous stage is based on the realization of rules and authority; the creation of a 'morality of constraint' in which the child understands that rules exist and are to be followed. Generally, rules are handed down from loved ones, especially parents, who are more powerful than the child. Understanding of rules is 'sacred' and 'unchangeable'. Early understanding of rules is divorced from the intention behind the rules as shown in Piaget's comparative story of the boy who broke a cup while taking a forbidden biscuit and another boy who broke six cups while helping to put away the washing-up. Discussion about which boy was wrong and punishments for the breakage brought out a distinction between 'retributive' and 'distributive' justice; the younger child often states that the second boy was 'more wrong' because he 'broke more'.

Moving away from the domination of the home to the desire to maintain play requires that children change (parentally) established rules. Problems are confronted when children play with one another and different home-based rules clash. To maintain play children change rules, and reflection upon this process is the basis for the 'morality of co-operation'. The stage of autonomy may be entered into once the child has access to both constraint and co-operation. The child is neither constrained by adults or peers and is free to make judgements and take action. Key points from Piaget include:

1 The child does not advance without social interaction.
2 Main social interactors are, 'archetypically', parent (with superior power to the child) and peer (with the ability to share and create a mutual equality).
3 With advancement, the previous stage does not disappear, but can be drawn upon at a future date if the social circumstances demand.
4 The link between action and understanding is the 'law of conscious realization' through which the child's participation in relationships and rituals becomes reflected upon and understood.
5 Autonomy is the 'freedom' to make unconstrained decisions – these decisions cannot be described in advance.

The best known of the cognitive developmental theories of morality is presented by Kohlberg (1969; 1976). Kohlberg based his theory on Piaget's research, but soon took his own course and became known in both psychological and educational circles. Kohlberg's research began with adolescent boys in Chicago. In a longitudinal study he presented hypothetical problem stories and asked the boys to resolve dilemmas created by a clash of moral issues (such as authority versus justice, or the value of life versus property rights). A classic problem story is known as the 'Heinz dilemma', and is presented as:

> In Europe, a woman was near death from a rare form of cancer. There was one drug that the doctors thought might save her, a form of radium that a druggist in the same town had recently discovered. The druggist was charging $2000, ten times what the drug cost him to make. The sick woman's husband, Heinz, went to everyone he knew to borrow the money, but he could only get together about half of what the drug cost. He told the druggist that his wife was dying and asked him to sell it more cheaply or let him pay later. But the druggist said 'No'. So Heinz got desperate and broke into the man's store to steal the drug for his wife.

The story is followed up with a series of personal and general questions: 'Should the husband have done that? Why?', 'Does it matter if the wife is important or not?', and 'Is it better to save the life of one important person or a lot of unimportant people?' (see Kohlberg 1976 for more detail). Answers to the dilemmas led Kohlberg to identify three levels of moral reasoning, with two stages at each level (six stages in total). Stage sequence was based on development of rational understanding, and Kohlberg drew on the work of several philosophers to validate his assertion that justice was the main issue underlying morality. The three broad levels are described as:

1 Pre-conventional – in which the individual 'has not yet come to really understand and uphold conventional or societal rules and expectations'.
2 Conventional – 'conforming to and upholding the rules and expectations and conventions of society or authority just because they are society's rules, expectations, or conventions'.
3 Post-conventional – the individual 'understands and basically accepts society's rules, but acceptance of society's rules is based on formulating and accepting the general moral principles that underlie these rules. These principles in some cases come into

conflict with society's rules, in which case the post-conventional individual judges by principle rather than by convention', and may break the law in order to change the law for more rightful purposes (1976: 33).

Within each level, there is a narrow and person-dominated stage and a more advanced and general-oriented stage (see Table 2.1 for a full depiction of the stages). The three levels have been equated to emotivism, positive law and natural law (Shweder and Much 1987). Kohlberg noted that, with development, moral relativism will evolve to positive action (in philosophical terms he has committed the 'naturalistic fallacy'); hence, with the development of moral judgement one is more able and better prepared to take moral action (a monotonic relationship).

Extensions and developments of Kohlberg's research have led to a 'bootstrapping' of new findings and gradual evolution and application of the theory. An important bootstrapped aspect is the 'necessary but not sufficient' structure of moral development, which integrates the child's socio-perspective-taking ability (see Selman 1980) and logical-mathematical development (especially the necessity of formal operational thought to reach Stage 4). Several further studies have been undertaken which show that moral progress follows the stage sequence (Blatt and Kohlberg 1975); that the identified progression is found in countries other than the United States (Weinreich 1974); and that educational applications could be written into a moral curriculum (Fenton 1976).

Kohlberg's theory is not without critics and qualifiers. The qualifications show earlier development in children than 'theoretically' expected; the importance of friendships and social relationships (in preference to rational judgement); differentiation between moral and conventional reasoning; and gender differences in approach to judgement problems. On the first point, Damon (1977; 1988) has consistently shown that children are capable of moral decisions and actions at earlier ages than one would expect after reading Kohlberg. Damon asserts that chidren learn justice through sharing experiences, especially in play. From late infancy through adolescence children become more skilled and sensitive at incorporating other children into their activities; they develop from an object orientation (desire to play with the same toy), to an empathic awareness of playmates, to a reasoned obligation of sharing (in order to maintain play). Adults may easily overlook this ability as

Table 2.1 Kohlberg's six moral stages

	Content of stage		
Level and stage	What is right	Reasons for doing right	Social perspective of stage
LEVEL I–PRE-CONVENTIONAL Stage 1– Heteronomous morality	To avoid breaking rules backed by punishment, obedience for its own sake, and avoiding physical damage to persons and property.	Avoidance of punishment, and the superior power of authorities.	*Egocentric point of view.* Doesn't consider the interests of others or recognize that they differ from the actor's; doesn't relate two points of view. Actions are considered physically rather than in terms of psychological interests of others. Confusion of authority's perspective with one's own.
Stage 2– Individualism, instrumental purpose, and exchange	Following rules only when it is to someone's immediate interest; acting to meet one's own interests and needs and letting others do the same. Right is also what's fair, what's an equal exchange, a deal, an agreement.	To serve one's own needs or interests in a world where you have to recognize that other people have their interests, too.	*Concrete individualistic perspective.* Aware that everybody has his own interests to pursue and these conflict, so that right is relative (in the concrete individualistic sense).
LEVEL II– CONVENTIONAL Stage 3–Mutual interpersonal expectations, relationships, and interpersonal conformity	Living up to what is expected by people close to you or what people generally expect of people in your role as son, brother, friend, etc. 'Being good' is important and means having good motives, showing concern	The need to be a good person in your own eyes and those of others. Your caring for others. Belief in the Golden Rule. Desire to maintain rules and authority which support stereotypical good behaviour.	*Perspective of the individual in relationships with other individuals.* Aware of shared feelings, agreements, and expectations which take primacy over individual interests. Relates points of view

Level and stage	What is right	Reasons for doing right	Social perspective of stage
	about others. It also means keeping mutual relationships, such as trust, loyalty, respect and gratitude.		through the concrete Golden Rule, putting yourself in the other guy's shoes. Does not yet consider generalized system perspective.
Stage 4–Social system and conscience	Fulfilling the actual duties to which you have agreed. Laws are to be upheld except in extreme cases where they conflict with other fixed social duties. Right is also contributing to society, the group, or institution.	To keep the institution going as a whole, to avoid the breakdown in the system 'if everyone did it', or the imperative of conscience to meet one's defined obligations. (Easily confused with Stage 3 belief in rules and authority.)	*Differentiates societal point of view from interpersonal agreement or motives.* Takes the point of view of the system that defines roles and rules. Considers individual relations in terms of place in the system.
LEVEL III–POST-CONVENTIONAL, or PRINCIPLED Stage 5–Social contract or utility and individual rights	Being aware that people hold a variety of values and opinions, that most values and rules are relative to your group. These relative rules should usually be upheld, however, in the interest of impartiality and because they are the social contract. Some nonrelative values and rights like *life* and *liberty*, however, must be upheld in any society and regardless of majority opinion.	A sense of obligation to law because of one's social contract to make and abide by laws for the welfare of all and for the protection of all people's rights. A feeling of contractual commitment, freely entered upon, to family, friendship, trust, and work obligations. Concern that laws and duties be based on rational calculation of overall utility, 'the greatest good for the greatest number'.	*Prior-to-society perspective.* Perspective of a rational individual aware of values and rights prior to social attachments and contracts. Integrates perspectives by formal mechanisms of agreement, contract, objective impartiality, and due process. Considers moral and legal points of view; recognizes that they sometimes conflict and finds it difficult to integrate them.

Level and stage	What is right	Reasons for doing right	Social perspective of stage
Stage 6–Universal ethical principles	Following self-chosen ethical principles. Particular laws or social agreements are usually valid because they rest on such principles. When laws violate these principles, one acts in accordance with the principle. Principles are universal principles of justice: the quality of human rights and respect for the dignity of human beings as individual persons.	The belief as a rational person in the validity of universal moral principles, and a sense of personal commitment to them.	Perspective of a moral point of view from which social arrangements derive. Perspective is that of any rational individual recognizing the nature of morality or the fact that persons are ends in themselves and must be treated as such.

Source: Kohlberg 1976

children 'work-out' their problems among themselves without adult intervention. A method of exposing children's sharing skills is to provide a small group (of four children) with six chocolate bars, ask them to divide the bars among themselves, and observe the ensuing discussion. The perception that children cannot 'get along' among themselves without adult guidance is contradicted and development of friendship illuminated.

On the second, Youniss' (1980) comparison of adult and peer relations found peers essential for 'interpersonal sensitivity' and the acknowledgement of the perspective of others. It is in the development of close and intimate friendships during adolescence that mutuality and trust among social equals are engendered. This study describes the generation of altruism, closeness and co-operation through interpersonal activities.

On the third, drawing upon 'real' dilemmas (as opposed to Kohlberg's hypotheical situations), Turiel (1983) explored children's understanding of the obligations and regularities characteristic of the conventional social system in which they lived. Conventional understanding followed a progression from an awareness of the behaviours that people present, to acknowledging that characteristic behaviours are maintained by specific types of people (positional responsibilities as parents, teachers, prime ministers, etc.), to an understanding that rules are co-ordinated between types of people in a social system. Conventions are followed to maintain the system and understanding of the system is qualified by the child's logical thinking abilities. Conventional understanding is distinct from moral judgement.

On the fourth point, when Carol Gilligan (1982) sought to replicate Kohlberg's research using real life dilemmas (such as women's decisions concerning an abortion), she found a dimension of 'care' that had not been uncovered. Girls generally responded differently to these dilemmas from boys; they showed 'connectedness and attachment' versus 'individualism and separation', respectively. Gilligan identified three levels of caring: for self in order to survive; responsibility for another's welfare (a caring and responsible orientation); and an interconnection between self and other (where care enhances both self and other). Care (female) versus justice (male) orientation in moral development may be a cultural example of 'macho' American society where the studies were undertaken. Thus, Damon (1988: 103) noted 'gender can influence a child's moral orientation if and only if gender makes a difference to the child's social context', and movement to different social circumstances (for example, a woman entering the legal profession, a male taking full houseperson responsibilities) may cause a dramatic change in orientation.

Social learning theories

Social learning theories of moral development were much in evidence through the 1970s. Social learning is based on behaviourist principles in which overt behaviours are reinforced and shaped, and assume a characterological orientation in which specific 'virtues' are identified for positive reinforcement, while other behaviours may be discouraged by non-reinforcement or punishment. From birth, children find themselves in day-to-day situations where they may observe 'moral' behaviour and accept appropriate external reinforcement until they are able to reinforce themselves ('internalization') in similar situations. Social learning theories can explain processes through which emotional reactions and learnt responses are utilized in the acquisition of specific virtues, although the theories are at a loss to explain systematic moral development without the recognition of 'cognitive mediation' to tie thought and behaviour together. In such a description, moral development becomes equivalent to socialization. The outcome of this moral development is conformity to rules and norms of society. Children must learn how to control their impulses and learn social rules. Kohlberg (1969) characterized social learning theories thus:

1 Moral development is growth of behavioural and affective conforming to moral rules.
2 Basic motivation for morality is rooted in biological needs or the pursuit of social rewards and avoidance of social punishment.
3 Moral developoment is culturally relative.
4 Basic moral norms are the internalization of external cultural rules.
5 Environmental influences on moral development are defined by quantitative variations in strength of reward, punishment, prohibitions, and modelling of conforming behaviour by parents and other socializing agents.

Insights arising from these theories (Gewirtz 1969; Aronfreed 1976; and others) include the child's realization of and relationship to 'significant others' (who may serve as models for the child); an indication that early development is important for altruism and empathy through somatic conditioning (see Hoffman 1976); and the recognition that moral socialization will vary between cultures which reinforce different values.

Cultural variation was the topic for one of the most insightful and holistic moral socialization theories. Bronfenbrenner (Garbarino and Bronfenbrenner 1976) undertook extensive comparisons of dilemmas in a variety of (pre-1989) communist and western countries. Using a dilemma such as:

You and your friends accidentally find a sheet of paper which the teacher must have lost. On this sheet are the questions and answers to a quiz that you are going to have tomorrow. Some of the kids suggest that you not say anything to the teacher about it, so that all of you can get better marks. What would you really do?

Answers to this and other dilemmas were conceptualized into five types of moral judgement and behaviour:

1 Self-oriented: the individual is motivated by impulses of self-gratification.

2 Authority-oriented: the individual accepts parental strictures and values as immutable, and generalizes the orientation to include other adults and authority figures.

3 Peer-oriented: the individual is a conformist who goes along with the peer group.

4 Collective-oriented: the individual is committed to a set of group goals which take precedence over individual desires.

5 Objectively-oriented: the individual's values are functionally autonomous, and the individual responds to situations on the basis of principles.

The orientations do not follow a developmental sequence. Moreover, adolescents in different societies tend to group their responses around a singular orientation. Children in western societies use authority-oriented answers, while those in communist societies use collective-oriented answers. Differences between the cultural orientations are due to the models and reinforcement contingencies characteristic of these distinct societies.

Anti-social behaviour (delinquency) within society was explained by Eysenck (1976) as a function of incorrect models displayed or the wrong behaviours reinforced. A social learning approach to moral education would recommend that teachers decide on which virtues are to be reinforced; what is the most appropriate contingency of reinforcement; and how to maintain themselves as significant others in the pupil's life. (In the light of the breakdown of family structure and disuse of religious and other moral institutions, the moralizing qualities of the school become very important.) The social learning approach may be difficult to maintain in that it is easier to identify incorrect behaviour and threaten punishment (which is not as effective as positive reinforcement), than to plan and pursue a programme of positive character virtues. Where social learning programmes are effective, one would expect conformity to moral conventions; but conformity does not provide a background for change and adaptation of rules.

Psychoanalytic theories

Psychoanalytic theories have evolved from early Freudian conceptions to focus on the attachment relationship between child and parents and the general effect of living within a family. The theory describes moral development by citing those who 'fit in' or conform to society, and the role of empathy/emotionalism as a root of altruism. A simplified account of Freudian moral development describes the libidinous desires of the oedipal (5- to 7-year-old) child for the parent of the opposite sex (see Edme *et al.* 1987 for a fuller explanation). This 'desire' leads to an identification with the actions and authority of the same-sex parent to achieve 'love' of the opposite-sex parent (for example, father's actions become a model for the son). Behaviour of the same-sex parent becomes an 'ideal' to follow, which is internalized and described as 'superego' or conscience. The superego enables the child to overcome the conflict between the gratification of immediate egoistic desires and conventions of the adult world by comparing the desire to the internalized 'ego ideal'. With internalization, moral development is no longer dependent on the presence of parents and the child's self-esteem will be enhanced when the child reflects upon her/himself as 'acting like an adult'; deviations from the ego ideal will cause socially induced shame or internal feelings of guilt. As the oedipal stage roughly equates to the start of schooling, the teacher may also be included within the ego ideal. Increases in frequency of children's amoral behaviour in the current cultural climate may be explained by the demise of the two-parent family and materialism leading to exaggerated parental egoism; this situation places undue reliance on the school as an 'ideal' purveyor of norms.

The original Freudian formulations have been untestable, although a number of points identified in psychoanalytic theory add to our insight. Judith Dunn (1987) discussed moral development as a process drawing upon the emotional relationships which tie child to parent and become the basis for empathy and altruism. This 'attachment' (described in greater detail by Ainsworth *et al.* 1974) between parent and child is enhanced by parental sensitivity, responsiveness and desire to communicate. Children who have a strong attachment tend to become more self-assured and curious. Upon starting school, well-attached children are more competent at forming new learning and social relationships (Waters and Srouf 1983) than other children. Zahn-Waxler *et al.* (1979) found emotional arousal of parents related to the child's understanding of emotions, and Hoffman (1976) described the conditioning of empathy in children leading to sympathy and altruism.

Dunn expanded beyond Freudian conceptualization to show that family relationships promoting moral growth also include siblings and birth order placement. The presence or lack of siblings provides experience of sharing and responsibility, dependent on the role that children are allotted in the family. In this vein, Damon (1988) cited research undertaken in China in which only children were less likely to share and co-operate than children brought up with brothers and sisters; a problematic future may be in store for this collective society given their one-child-per-family policy.

Psychoanalytic theory, then, describes the family as a small social system where ties of emotion and identity between children and parents form the basis for internalizing moral conventions. Emotion generated between loved ones and the child initiates moral traits of empathy, sympathy and altruism; without the emotional or close tie, children's relations with others will be seriously limited.

Relational theory

Relational theory of moral development draws upon aspects of previous theories and qualifies moral outcome by the type of relationship and the persons with whom the child enters into relationships. As in cognitive development, experience provides for conceptual understanding and participation in moral life.

The earliest relationships with caregivers are seen to set rules and regularities in an atmosphere of love and affection. The emotional tie (as attachment) opens the social world for the child while introducing authority and power relations. A 'reciprocity of complement' (Youniss 1980) lays the experiential groundwork for empathy and obligation. Not all parental relationships are the same and the quality of the parental relationship will affect the child's moral presence in social situations. Baumrind's (1971) comparison of parental authority conceptualized three main types: authoritarian, authoritative and permissive. The authoritative parent established, explained and negotiated home rules; and his or her children were able to control egoistic impulses and establish competent social and learning relationships in schools. The relationship with parents is one of 'close' affection and is different from mere social or acquaintance relationships. Closeness is the basis for empathy which allows the child to 'feel for' others.

Peers present two different relationships for the child. Moral socialization among peers may be similar to parents, especially in mixed age groups; where older children induct younger children into dominance hierarchies and pass on traditional conventions in

Table 2.2 Development of social relationships, with logical-mathematical, moral and social perspective (developmental) parallels

Social relationships	Logical-mathematical	Moral	Social perspective
0 Reflex behaviour/neonatal capacities	Sensori-motor	Autistic	
1 Sensori-motor-affective schemes			
2 Development of dependent relationship	Pre-operational	Heteronomous	Egocentric
3 Early rule/authority application, reflective egocentric understanding			
4 Concrete and rational rule/authority application; self-reflective questioning	Concrete operational	Co-operative	
5 Involvement with peers, reflective mutual social development			Socio-centric
6 Reflective ability to balance and apply constraining and/or co-operative principles	Formal operational	Autonomous	

Source: Kutnick 1988b

play, games and gender. Alternatively, a 'mutual reciprocity' (Youniss 1980) can develop between peers who perceive themselves as equals. As equals, the will to overcome common problems can lead to co-operation, intimacy and security among a small number of close friends. Co-operation is not necessarily the norm of many peer groupings; a misconception found in many schools and embodied in the child-centred ideals of the Plowden Report (1967).

Relational theory identifies the distinct qualities possible in various relationships and emphasizes that moral relationships maintain a closeness and affectional tie amongst individuals if they are to promote moral growth. The development of relationships is described in Table 2.2. Relationships with logical, social and moral parallels present a similar approach to that of Piaget.

Cultural theory

Cultural theory (see Shweder and Much 1987) is anthropological in origin, and describes the conventional systems that characterize societies and countries. Cultural theory stresses that the moral individual conforms to societal expectations, that each society sanctions its own moral conventions, and that there is a clear distinction between developing and western cultures. As moral development is societal, morals are relative between cultures and there are no universal moral principles (in distinction to Kohlberg's theory). Sanction systems (a social learning perspective) of any given society will place greater or lesser significance on the role of parents, siblings and peers and the range of conventions that each group may 'transmit'. Developing and agrarian societies emphasize collective behaviours among groups and the moral virtues of harmony, communalism and respect for elders (as described in pre-colonial Nigeria by Iheoma 1985). Whiting and Whiting (1975) found children in western and materialistic (i.e. individualized and parentally dominated) societies to be assigned less societal responsibilities, and their behaviour was more egoistic and less altruistic than children in less developed countries. The dislocation of western societies from agrarian and communal roots enforces differentiation between moral and conventional life. Cultural theory, as with social learning, emphasizes conformity to dominant social groups and internalization of transmitted conventions as its explanation of moral development.

SUBSTANTIATION AND REVISION OF THEORIES

With the passage of the 1970s, there were no noticeable expansions in theories of moral development. Many studies and applications were undertaken, but they qualified and tested discrete aspects of the theories. Most of the continuing research was undertaken from a cognitive developmental perspective, with the main focus on Kohlberg. These studies have led to substantive revisions and a trend to integrate the approaches.

Cognitive developmental theories

Cognitive developmental theories, especially as espoused by Kohlberg, were tested and revised substantially. Studies showed and supported the developmental stage sequence (see Turiel 1969; Rest 1975) but now argued that children must be exposed to reasoned argument at a level only slightly more advanced than their current stage; access to reasoning at too advanced a level was shown to be ineffective at promoting moral growth. McNamee (1977) found a direct correlation between stage of (Kohlbergian) moral reasoning and willingness to help a 'stooge' feigning a bad drug problem during an interview session. Kohlberg's revised identification of stages substantiated a positive relationship between moral stage and participation in real events, such as Berkeley Free Speech sit-ins and non-obedience in Milgram's studies of authority (see Kohlberg and Chandee 1984). To explain the 'monotonic' relationship, Kohlberg expanded the theory to assert that the individual must make a moral judgement *and* feel responsible for taking the appropriate action. Responsibility required an understanding as to why one may feel responsible for others and training to take on the responsibilities for others; the type and quality of relationships between people has been added to the theory. Moral reasoning was also found to be correlated to role-taking and social perspective skills (Kurdek 1978).

Reviews of Kohlberg's work (especially see Blasi 1980) found that relatively few individuals achieved the highest Kohlbergian stages (thus, a complete testing of deontic action could not be made and provided Shweder and Much (1987) with the argument that the general masses are found at the conventional level – challenging both the universality of morals and the need to 'go beyond the law'); and correlations between lower levels of moral reasoning and delinquent or conformist actions were found, a reminder that each stage of moral reasoning has here-and-now actions to support that line of reasoning. Kohlberg's applied research into moral education evolved with the realization that moral discussion does not overcome problems of responsibility, care and the moral atmosphere of schools.

Social learning theory

Social learning theory moved away from a simplistic 'learning' of morals. Reformulations of social learning expanded the theory to include an awareness of social environment, social relationships, and the child's ability to conceptualize. Kurtines (1987) found that qualities of specific relationships effect the ability to interact and reflect upon socio-moral actions. As the individual lives in a socially defined system of rules and roles, integration or internalization of that system takes place through the reinforcements (undertaken by communication) between individuals and their role placements. Interaction provides the opportunity to learn of conventional standards and mutual obiligations between adults and peers. Levels of communicative competence closely parallel the development of social relationships described in Table 2.2. Similarly, Eisenberg (1987) explored attributions that children made when explaining their own and others' behaviour. She found that children used 'authority and punishment-oriented' reasons to explain compliance with adults. Peer-instigated compliance was used with reference to pro-social behaviour that met 'others' needs and one's relationship with or liking for another person'. A critical overview of developments within learning theory (Weinreich-Haste 1987) suggests that the concept of morality has become pluralistic and has taken on a developmental rather than characterological orientation.

Psychoanalytic theory

Psychoanalytic theory has moved away from the Freudian, oedipal explanation of morality. Current research has shown: pre-oedipal conflict with parents lying at the root of the internalization of conventional and authoritative behaviours; early child–parent relationship bringing together aspects of social, emotional and cognitive developments (as in attachment); and various types of parental power assertions as being correlated with behaviours expressed by children. An example of a bridge between parental and child moral behaviour is empathy: the stage when the child comes to realize that his/her emotional states are similar to those of his/her parents (as describe by Hoffman 1984) is seen as the root of empathy; and empathy has been found to be a natural constraint on later aggressive behaviour (Edme et al. 1987). Edme also stated that moral emotions develop through constant checking of communication with a loved one, reinforcing appropriate behaviour by positive affect and deviations with negative. Parents, or loved ones, can be said to 'scaffold' or provide the boundaries and opportunities for moral behaviour, according to Edwards (1987).

A deviation from classic psychoanalytic theory introduces effects of peers and the mutual/sharing attributes that they encourage. Desire for peer interaction has been found at an earlier age than one would expect from developmental sequences identified in Table 2.2. If children are allowed the opportunity for interaction, as Vandell and Mueller (1980) found, they will look at one another in preference to adults, from the age of 2 months; and by 2 years they will show complex patterns of behaviour to maintain 'friendship' and reciprocated affection. The closeness of child–parent relationships can also be found amongst children at an early age if they are allowed the opportunity and continuity of interaction. Examples of peer attachment have also been found (Freud and Dann 1951) if children have a communal upbringing. Psychoanalytic concepts such as socially induced shame and internalized guilt have been found to develop interpersonally and are dependent on experiences scaffolded by parents.

Relational theory

Relational theory appears to be the main beneficiary of further research and revisions in moral development. The deconstruction of Kohlberg's approach has coincided with a re-evaluation of Piaget, which emphasizes the role of peers as a relational development of equal significance to parents (Damon 1988; Kohlberg and Higgins 1987). Child–adult relationships have long been associated with the identification and enforcement of social regulations and conventions. Sharing and intimacy among peers appears in social situations where common interests, symmetrical turn-taking, empathic responses and the desire to stay in the good graces of playmates has high priority. Mere exposure to other children is not enough for peer relations to take on these dynamic qualities. Their relationship must develop a closeness or dependence which will affirm an affectional tie. Relational theory integrates a dynamic approach which explains how and why particular relationships may be more effective at providing the experience and conceptualizing of moral development; especially the differentiation between adult-inspired conventions and peer-inspired mutality.

Relational theory cannot provide a universal explanation for all moral conventions, especially as they relate to various cultures throughout the world. A cultural/relational hypothesis may be advanced to explain the existence of 'individualist' as opposed to 'collectivist' cultures: the difference is based on the amount, legitimacy and closeness of exposure to peers in each culture. As an example, it has been found that Israeli children brought up in collectivist kibbutzim were more likely to co-operate (as opposed to compete) on games (Shapira and Madsen 1969) and score at higher stages on Kohlbergian dilemmas (Power and Reimer 1978) than their peers brought up in Israeli cities.

In summary of the above revisions, Damon (1988) presents the following as secure bases for moral development:

1 Through participation in essential social relationships, children will encounter classic moral issues.
2 Moral awareness is shaped and supported by natural emotional reactions to observations and events, especially in the family.
3 Relations with parents, teachers and other close adults introduce the child to important standards, rules and conventions.
4 Relations with peers introduce norms of direct reciprocity and standards of sharing, co-operation and fairness.
5 Because children's morality is shaped (or scaffolded) through social influence, there will be a wide variation between the experiences offered to all children.
6 Moral growth characteristic of the school setting is governed by the same developmental processes that apply to moral growth everywhere.

EDUCATIONAL APPLICATIONS

Moral education – the use of schools to promote the moral development of children – is found in all countries. Education acts and plans broadly define developmental outcomes that are seen as moral and socializational as well as academic. Programmes of moral education have been designed to include a knowledge of moral issues, sensitivity towards others and self, an ability to reason about moral issues (especially conventions, justice, and fairness) which enables action to be taken in relation to that moral concern, with an awareness that moral experience is generated within the social context of the school. Programmes for moral development are often confused with indoctrination of societal values at the expense of autonomy, freedom and creativity (McPhail 1982).

While schools may be charged with moralization responsiblities, it is the teachers who are held accountable for both moral and academic education. In relation to moral education, Lickona (1990) stated that teachers have the responsibility to promote pupils' self-respect, pro-social behaviour, and moral reasoning and achievement. The responsibility is found in curricula presentation as well as the example set by teachers. With this responsibility it is odd that teacher education rarely includes training for moral education (in the UK and elsewhere, for example, see Plas 1985; Devuyst 1983; and others). The current movement to promote core (3Rs) subjects through the introduction of a National Curriculum also limits the importance of moral education, as academic subjects take precedence over social education. Yet schools will be blamed if their pupils do not show (as Pring 1987 lists) concern for other people, ability to articulate feelings, achievement of self-esteem and self-worth, engagement in principled thinking, reflection upon their experience, and a critical acceptance of values and attitudes (especially of the school).

Perhaps too much emphasis is placed on the moralization that can take place in schools. One sociological approach to the study of education stated that schools can only replicate the relationships and norms characteristic of society (Bowles and Gintes 1976); schools can only enhance moral behaviour characteristic of that society. Weinreich-Haste (1987) reminds us that the groundwork for guilt, anxiety, and basic peer relationships has already been laid before entering school at the age of 5 years. Damon (1988) stated that the child enters school with decision-making competence and a working knowledge of justice and fairness. It is easy to structure an argument that schools are not necessary for moral development.

On the other hand, the experience of attending school has been found to expand interpersonal and cognitive skills (especially through cognitive conflict) and to assert institutional norms consistently amongst the mass of children that attend. Behaviour and understanding of children fostered by a particular school 'ethos' (see Rutter et al. 1979) affects both academic achievement and the upholding or breaking of norms (of truancy and delinquency). Thus, in the attempt to plan for the moral development of pupils, schools must acknowledge what is meant by moral education and the limitations of its assertion within the school. From the previous review of theory, schools should be aware that:

1 Schools are responsible for the assertion of cultural values, although they may also prepare the child to challenge conventional values if necessary.
2 Moral development covers multiple experiences including logical-mathematical, social-perspective-taking and emotional aspects.
3 Relationships are essential for moral development. The most

effective moral relationships are 'close' and meaningful for the child. These relationships involve the child with both adults and peers.

4 Children learn effectively through an action orientation, better known as the 'Law of Conscious Realization'.

5 Virtues of good character, habit in conventions, and mutuality are diverse but essential aspects of moral development.

6 Teachers are in the best place to scaffold moral experiences for pupils in school.

What can school achieve?

Any social analysis of schools (for example, Cohen and Manion 1981) finds that a range of norms (conventional and moral) are imposed upon the pupil population. Norm assertion appears to be handled in a contradictory way in schools; some schools and teachers may approach the normative role through overt planned experience as opposed to *laissez-faire* 'just letting it happen'. Teachers' attitudes to their role in schooling may range from purely academic to a combination of academic with pastoral/moral responsibility. Teachers whose attitude is purely academic assert the importance of the overt curriculum and play down the importance of the 'hidden curriculum' (Meighan 1981), although the hidden curriculum has been found to be of major importance in moral development strategies for schooling.

Initial approaches to moral education have been based upon the overt curriculum, and planned according to the (unrevised) assertion of moral development theories. First, character education adopts a social learning approach which identifies a set of 'virtues' (of good character) and didactically teaches towards those virtues. One programme, which has isolated a range of virtues, has been constructed by Wilson (Wilson *et al.* 1967) and states that children should be trained in rational skills to: identify with other people; identify and describe feelings; relate knowledge of consequences to actions; identify and acknowledge rules and principles; and relate these rules to one's own interests.

Second, North American approaches to moral education have been dominated by models of cognitive discussion (described as a liberal rationalist ideology by Vine 1983). Discussion approaches include values clarification and Kohlberg's use of the Socratic method. Values clarification asks pupils to consider and discuss contemporary issues. Teachers are to remain 'value-neutral' so as not to dominate or indoctrinate the moralizing. Pupils are encouraged to choose among values brought into discussion, to affirm their choice of values, and take action on these values in their everyday life. (Values clarification is similar to Stenhouse's Humanities Curriculum Project (1970) in the UK.) The cognitive developmental, or Socratic, approach formulated by Kohlberg noted that it was difficult for teachers to be in a position where they are not a model of values. Within the hierarchy of moral reasoning, pupils should be encouraged to move from 'less mature' to more advanced forms of reasoning. And teachers should use discussion of conflicting moral issues (as with the Heinz dilemma) to expose pupils to slightly higher levels of reasoning (a strategy which has proved effective in school trials, Blatt and Kohlberg 1975).

Third, relational approaches (as in McPhail's (1982) Startline and Lifeline packages for primary schools) draw upon the child's capacity for interpersonal relationships and their developing understanding of others. Social and significant situation are created in expressive activities, role play, drama, simulation and discussion. Through the situations children actively participate in the formation and questioning of their own and others' views; they are asked to draw upon common emotions and feelings, communication and conceptualization. This action/reflection places the teacher in an influential role where barriers between subjects are not rigidly defined, learning is a balance between individual and co-operative activity, and emotional ties between individuals are used to bring them together.

The relational approach at the secondary school level is found in the Developmental Group Work Curriculum designed by Button (1974). Button identified the need for self-discovery and experience as the root for moral and personal development. His curriculum looks upon the school as an interacting organization which must be supported if it is to develop. Support is developed in pupil groups, which participate in exercises (sensitivity, trust, sociodrama and others) to promote communication skills and explore relationships engendered. Developmental Group Work is designed to be used by individual teachers as a timetabled school activity; thus whole school involvement is required if planned social, emotional, moral and cognitive developments are to be effective.

Finally, no overt psychoanalytic programmes have been identified except for the use of school 'counsellors' and pastoral 'care', although this is a comparatively ineffective approach, according to Topping (1983).

Classroom realities and empirical comparisons

Classroom realities and empirical comparisons challenge and clarify the possibilities of moral education in schools. The assertion that traditional values of character education (social learning) have been more effective than other approaches (see Wynne 1986) draws upon memories of better behaviour and conventional values found in Victorian times; and neglects the fact that most western cultures are now more pluralistic and there are more models competing for the child's interests (through media, etc.). Character education is criticized in that values are being 'transmitted' as an abstraction without fostering of the 'capacity to make autonomous judgements' (see Damon 1988). But teachers generally use the character education approach in preference to other curricular approaches in both western and developing countries (see Kutnick 1988a; Kutnick 1990; Iheoma 1985). When asked about their understanding and use of moral education, teachers provided lists of character virtues that they wished to see in their pupils. Without careful planning much of their time was taken up with disciplining pupils who contravened norms, although negative reinforcements are notoriously ineffective in producing pro-social behaviour and leave the child dependent on the teacher for positive examples and reinforcement (see Beihler and Snowman 1982).

Empirical comparisons between approaches show the cognitive developmental approach to be the most effective. Bredemeier *et al.*'s (1980) comparison of social learning and cognitive developmental approaches found children able to produce a reasoned understanding for their behaviour in a cognitive programme only. Comparisons betwen value clarification and cognitive developmental approaches (Lockwood 1978; Leming 1980) found the cognitive developmental approach most effective; although Damon (1988) adds that the cognitive approach should include peer discussion, empathy training and role-taking in addition to teacher leading moral discussions.

Teachers and classroom activity are central to effective moral education, but the reality of classrooms often finds ritualized roles of power assertion and subservience for teacher and pupil respectively. Children, from a very young age, are found to be dependent on the teacher for direction and support (Bennett *et al.* 1984), and even primary school classrooms that appear as child-centred are taught didactically (Galton *et al.* 1980). With such dependence on the teacher it is neither easy nor possible for the teacher to judge children's developing moral capacities and provide the appropriately advanced argument (Damon 1988) nor is it possible for pupils to act 'autonomously'. The expectation that children will co-operate among themselves (required in many approaches) when asked to work in groups is not supported in classroom studies (Galton 1990), and teachers may have to adopt particular schemes to promote co-operation (see Slavin 1990). The realization that the moral atmosphere of schools enforces didactic and hierarchical commitments on children has caused a fundamental rethink by Kohlberg, and his cognitive developmental approach has now taken on a holistic 'just community' approach (Kohlberg and Higgins 1987) within classroom and school. The just community affirms the use of relationships, decision-making, and sharing of responsibilties as well as moral discussion.

CONCLUSIONS

Moral education, like moral development, disguises a multiplicity of approaches. Each approach has something to contribute to the development of the child; this includes learning of specific conventions, awareness and use of relationships with others, reasoning ability and linkage with action, and close ties with others. Approaches to promote moral development must be supported in the school generally and practised in the classroom if they are to be effective. Development must be accounted for. Teachers must scaffold experiences of the classroom and cannot take a *laissez-faire* attitude to their moral responsibilities. Social and relational requirements of effective moral education contradict movement towards an academic National Curriculum where the moral curriculum is a low priority. Curiously, the reverse approach (i.e. dominated by the moral curriculum, co-operation, communication, etc.) has been found to promote academic and cognitive achievement (see Slavin 1983; Rogers and Kutnick 1990). The chalkface of the classroom need not be bound by existing didactic practices which constrain autonomous thinking and action. To achieve benefits of moral education four principles have been identified in the literature, each of equal importance:

1 Responsibility for actions of self and others must be promoted among children, even if it is as simple as cleaning up after themselves and others.
2 Development is promoted through the positive, active, engagement of the child – real situations (through models, role play, directed discussion, etc.) are most effective.
3 Active engagement informs development through 'conscious realization', the ritualized patterns of interaction between children, peers and teachers being the experience that they come to know and expect.
4 The relationship and closeness of co-operation is necessary to draw the child out of egocentric and constraining perspectives, and is the most likely route to allow the development of autonomy.

Have there been any programmes that promote all the above principles? Thomas Lickona (in press) has been working on a process model of moral education over a number of years. The model suggests that the child and teacher work as partners. The teacher is responsible for orchestrating the following: the building of a moral community and self-esteem through sensitivity, supportive and affirmatory contacts; co-operative learning, enabling individual pupils to share knowledge, extend and compare viewpoints, co-ordinate actions with others and share in the success of group members; moral reflection, tying cognition with affect through discussion of classroom events and the joint resolve of difficult dilemmas; and participatory decision-making about rules, plans and problems of the classroom.

The 'class circle' is one particular example which integrates the above aspects for classrooms of all age groups. Lickona describes the circles as a meeting for whole class interactive discussion, where leadership is shared (there is no classroom hierarchy, as everyone sits on a chair in a circle), lasting only a limited amount of time (10 to 40 minutes) but meeting regularly (not just of necessity), and for particular (decision-making) purposes. The operation of the class circle fulfils all aspects of the process described above. Other programmes such as Developmental Group Work, Startline and Lifeline also fulfil the above principles. The programmes make simultaneous use of the overt and hidden curricula.

Critical change and revision of moral development theory with educational applications over the last three decades have expanded our awareness of the range, complexity and need for integration of this work. We can no longer simply identify one theoretical approach to development, operationally define morality solely within the scope of that theory, and formulate an 'effective' programme for moral education. Significant aspects of each of the major theories and integrated models appear as the effective way forward for application in schools. There is no easy transfer from theory to practice. Two certain conclusions can be made from this review: any programme of moral education will be constrained by traditional and institutional practice, and there will be many more interesting developments to come in the future.

REFERENCES

Ainsworth, M., Bell, S. and Stayton, D. (1974) 'Infant–mother attachment and social development: "socialization" as a product of reciprocal responses to signals', in M. P. Richards (ed.) *The Integration of a Child into a Social World*, London: Cambridge University Press.

Aronfreed, J. (1976) 'Moral development from the standpoint of a general psychological theory', in T. Lickona (ed.) *Moral Development and Behavior*, New York: Holt, Rinehart & Winston.

Baumrind, D. (1971) 'Current patterns of parental authority', *Developmental Psychology Monograph* 4: 1–103.

Beihler, R. F. and Snowman, J. (1982) *Psychology Applied to Teaching*, Boston: Houghton Mifflin.

Bennett, N., Desforges, C., Cockburn, A. and Wilkinson, B. (1984) *The Quality of Pupil Learning Experiences*, London: Lawrence Erlbaum Associates.

Blasi, A. (1980) 'Bridging moral cognition and moral action: a critical review of the literature', *Psychological Bulletin* 88: 1–45.

Blatt, M. M. and Kohlberg, L. (1975) 'The effects of classroom discussion on children's level of moral judgement', *Journal of Moral Education* 4: 129–61.

Bowles, S. and Gintes, H. (1976) *Schooling in Capitalist America*, New York: Basic Books.

Bredemeier, B. J., Weiss, M. R., Shields, D. L. and Shewchuk, R. M. (1980) 'Promoting moral growth in a summer sport camp: the implementation of theoretically grounded instruction strategies', *Journal of Moral Education* 15: 212–20.

Button, L. (1974) *Developmental Group Work with Adolescents*, London: Hodder & Stoughton.

Cohen, L. and Manion, L. (1981) *Perspectives on Classrooms and Schools*, Eastbourne: Holt, Rinehart & Winston.

Damon, W. (1977) *The Social World of the Child*, San Fransisco: Jossey-Bass.

——(1988) *The Moral Child: Nurturing Children's Moral Growth*, New York: The Free Press.

Devuyst, L. (1983) 'Moral education in Belgium', *Journal of Moral Education* 12: 51–5.

Dunn, J. (1987) 'The beginnings of moral understanding: development in the second year', in J. Kagan and S. Lamb (eds) *The Emergence of Morality in Young Children*, Chicago: University of Chicago Press.

Edme, R., Johnson, W. F. and Easterbrooks, M. A. (1987) 'The do's and don'ts of early moral development: psychoanalytic tradition and current research', in J. Kagan and S. Lamb (eds) *The Emergence of Morality in Young Children*, Chicago: University of Chicago Press.

Edwards, C. P. (1987) 'Culture and the construction of moral values: a comparative ethnography of moral encounters in two cultural settings', in J. Kagan and S. Lamb (eds) *The Emergence of Morality in Young Children*, Chicago: University of Chicago Press.

Eisenberg, N. (1987) 'Self-attributions, social interaction and moral development', in W. Kurtines and J. Gewirtz (eds) *Moral Development Through Social Interaction*, New York: Wiley.

Eysenck, H. J. (1976) 'The biology of morality', in T. Lickona (ed.) *Moral Development and Behavior*, New York: Holt, Rinehart & Winston.

Fenton, E. (1976) 'Cognitive-developmental approach to moral education', *Social Education* 4: 186–222.

Freud, A. and Dann, S. (1951) 'An experiment in group upbringing', *Psychoanalytic Study of the Child* 6: 127–68.

Galton, M. (1990) 'Grouping and group work', in C. Rogers and P. Kutnick (eds) *The Social Psychology of the Primary School*, London: Routledge.

Galton, M., Simon, B. and Croll, P. (1980) *Inside the Primary Classroom*, London: Routledge and Kegan Paul.

Garbarino, J. and Bronfenbrenner, U. (1976) 'The socialization of moral judgement and behavior in cross-cultural perspective', in T. Lickona (ed.) *Moral Development and Behavior*, New York: Holt, Rinehard & Winston.

Gewirtz, J. (1969) 'Mechanisms of social learning: some roles of stimulation and behavior in early human development', in D. Goslin (ed.) *Handbook of Socialization, Theory and Research*, Chicago: Rand MacNally.

Gilligan, C. (1982) *In a Different Voice*, Cambridge, MA: Harvard University Press.

Hoffman, M. L. (1976) 'Empathy, role-taking, guilt, and development of altruistic motives', in T. Lickona (ed.) *Moral Development and Behavior*, New York: Holt, Rinehart & Winston.

——(1984) 'Empathy, its limitations and its role in a comprehensive moral theory', in W. Kurtines and J. Gewirtz (eds) *Morality, Moral Behavior and Moral Development*, New York: Wiley.

Iheoma, E. O. (1985) 'Moral education in Nigeria: problems and prospects', *Journal of Moral Education* 14: 183–93.

Kagan, J. and Lamb, S. (eds) (1987) *The Emergence of Morality in Young Children*, Chicago: University of Chicago Press.

Kohlberg, L. (1969) 'Stage and sequence: the cognitive-developmental approach to socialization', in D. Goslin (ed.) *Handbook of Theories of Socialization, Theory and Research*, Chicago: Rand McNally.

——(1976) 'Moral stages and moralization: the cognitive developmental approach', in T. Lickona (ed.) *Moral Development and Behavior*, New York: Holt, Rinehart & Winston.

Kohlberg, L. and Chandee, D. (1984) 'The relation of moral judgement to moral action', in W. Kurtines and J. Gewirtz (eds) *Morality, Moral Behavior and Moral Development*, New York: Wiley.

Kohlberg, L. and Higgins, A. (1987) 'School democracy and social interaction', in W. Kurtines and J. Gewirtz (eds) *Moral Development Through Social Interaction*, New York: Wiley.

Kurdek, L. (1978) 'Perspective-taking as a cognitive basis of children's moral development: a review of the literature', *Merrill-Palmer Quarterly* 24: 3-28.

Kurtines, W. (1987) 'Sociomoral behavior and development from a rule-governed perspective: psychosocial theory as a nomotic science', in W. Kurtines and J. Gewirtz (eds) *Moral Development Through Social Interaction*, New York: Wiley.

Kurtines, W. and Gewirtz, J. (eds) (1987) *Moral Development Through Social Interaction*, New York: Wiley.

Kutnick, P. (1988a) *Relationships in the Primary School Classroom*, London: Chapman.

——(1988b) 'I'll teach you! Primary school teachers' attitudes to and use of moral education in the curriculum', *Journal of Moral Education* 17: 40-51.

——(1990) 'A survey of primary school teachers' understanding and implementation of moral education in Trinidad and Tobago', *Journal of Moral Education* 19: 48-57.

Leming, J. S. (1980) 'Curricular effectiveness in moral/values education: a review of research', *Journal of Moral Education* 10: 147-64.

Lickona, T. (1990) 'Moral development in the elementary school classroom', in W. Kurtines and J. Gewirtz (eds) *Moral Behavior and Development*, New York: Erlbaum Associates.

Lickona, T. (in press) *Teaching Respect and Responsibility: The Fourth and Fifth Rs*, New York: Bantam Books.

Lickona, T. (ed.) (1976) *Moral Development and Behavior*, New York: Holt, Rinehart & Winston.

Lockwood, A. L. (1978) 'Effects of values clarification and moral development curricula on school age subjects: a critical review of recent research', *Review of Educational Research* 48:325-64.

McNamee, S. (1977) 'Moral behavior, moral development and motivation', *Journal of Moral Education* 7: 27-31.

McPhail, P. (1982) *Social and Moral Education*, Oxford: Blackwell.

Meighan, R. (1981) *A Sociology of Educating*, Eastbourne: Holt, Rinehart & Winston.

Piaget, J. (1932) *The Moral Judgement of the Child*, New York: Free Press.

Plas, P. L. van der (1985) 'Moral education in Holland', *Journal of Moral Education* 14: 111-19.

Plowden Report (1967) *Children and Their Primary Schools*, London: HMSO.

Power, C. and Reimer, J. (1978) 'Moral atmosphere: an educational bridge between moral judgement and action', in W. Damon (ed.) *New Directions for Child Development*, San Francisco: Jossey-Bass.

Pring, R. (1987) 'Implications of the changing values and ethical standards of society', in J. Thacker, R. Pring and D. Evans (eds) *Personal, Social and Moral Education in a Changing World*, Windsor: NFER-Nelson.

Rest, J. (1975) 'Longitudinal study of the defining issues test', *Developmental Psychology* 11: 738–48.

Rogers, C. and Kutnick, P. (1990) *The Social Psychology of the Primary School*, London: Routledge.

Rutter, M., Maughan, B., Mortimore, P. and Ouston, J. (1979) *Fifteen Thousand Hours: Secondary Schools and their Effects on Children*, Harmondsworth: Penguin.

Selman, R. (1980) *The Growth of Interpersonal Understanding*, New York: Academic Press.

Shapira, A. and Madsen, W. (1969) 'Cooperative and competitive behavior of kibbutz and urban children in Israel', *Child Development* 40: 609–17.

Shweder, R. A. and Much, N. C. (1987) 'Determinations of meaning: discourse and moral socialization', in W. Kurtines and J. Gewirtz (eds) *Moral Development Through Social Interaction*, New York: Wiley.

Slavin, R. (1983) *Cooperative Learning*, New York: Longman.

——(1990) 'Co-operative learning', in C. Rogers and P. Kutnick (eds) *The Social Psychology of the Primary School*, London: Routledge.

Stenhouse, L. (1970) *Humanities Curriculum Project*, London: Heinemann.

Topping, K. (1983) *Educational Systems for Disruptive Adolescents*, London: Croom Helm.

Turiel, E. (1969) 'Developmental processes in the child's moral thinking', in P. Mussen, L. Langer and M. Covington (eds) *Trends and Issues in Developmental Psychology*, New York: Holt, Rinehart & Winston.

——(1983) *The Development of Social Knowledge: Morality and Convention*, Cambridge, MA: Cambridge University Press.

Vandell, D. L. and Mueller, E. C. (1980) 'Peer play and friendship during the first two years', in H. C. Foot, A. J. Chapman and J. R. Smith (eds) *Friendship and Social Relations in Childhood*, Chichester: Wiley.

Vine, I. (1983) 'The nature of moral commitments', in H. Weinreich-Haste and D. Locke (eds) *Morality in the Making*, Chichester: Wiley.

Waters, E. and Srouf, F. (1983) 'Social competence as a developmental construct', *Developmental Review* 3: 79–97.

Weinreich, H. (1974) 'The structure of moral reason', *Journal of Youth and Adolescence* 3: 135–45.

Weinreich-Haste, H. (1987) 'Is moral education possible? A discussion of the relationship between the curricula and psychological theory', in J. Tacker, R. Pring and D. Evans (eds) *Personal, Social and Moral Education in a Changing World*, Windsor: NFER-Nelson.

Whiting, B. and Whiting, J. M. W. (1975) *Children of Six Cultures*, Cambridge, MA: Harvard University Press.

Wilson, J., Williams, N. and Sugarman, B. (1967) *Introduction to Moral Education*, Harmondsworth: Penguin.
Wynne, E. A. (1986) 'The great tradition in education: transmitting moral values', *Educational Leadership* 43: 4–9.
Youniss, J. (1980) *Parents and Peers in Social Development*, Chicago: University of Chicago Press.
Zahn-Waxler, C., Radke-Yarrow, M. and King, R. A. (1979) 'Childrearing and children's pro-social initiation toward victims of distress', *Child Development* 50: 319–30.

Chapter 3

Gender role learning

Sally L. Archer

INTRODUCTION

'It's a boy!' or 'It's a girl!' This is a brief statement uttered at the birth of each child. The societal ramifications of the designation of this biological distinction will be profound. From culture to culture, being labelled male or female places an immediate structure on what is deemed optional as opposed to expectation or requirement in such spheres as physical appearance, personality attributes, family roles, work, ethnic/ideological ritual, and recreation. The attitudes expressed by significant members of one's society will strongly influence the form and manner of teaching one's youth what it means to be a male or female. Thus, it is important that we understand the language of sex and gender. It is essential that we document which distinctions are biologically determined and which are societally constructed. It is important to know where and how cultural expectations develop. It is crucial, as well, to determine the manner in which our cultural perceptions may limit our knowledgeability about the roles of sex and gender in our development and daily living.

The primary purpose of this chapter is to examine gender role learning as a complex and pervasive developmental process formed in a strong, societal context. The primary goals are to increase the reader's gender role knowledgeability in order to understand these processes better and to sensitize the reader to opportunities for choices regarding one's gender expectations for self as well as for others. This chapter has four foci. Addressed first is the issue of the language of sex and gender with an introduction to the multiple factors that contribute to the construction of gender. These sections are entitled 'Definitions' and 'The content of gender roles and stereotypes'. The second focus is on explanations as to why and how a gender role is learned as described in numerous, sometimes contrasting, sometimes complementary, theories. This section is entitled 'Socialization processes and consequences'. Addressed third is the impact of socialization agents, such as parents, teachers, and media, on the developing child and adolescent; this section is entitled 'Learning gender roles: the interfacing of socializing agents and children'. The final focus is on recommendations for changes to the learning environment. Encouraged is the consideration of flexible options for healthy, personally expressive growth for boys and girls, unhindered by artificially constructed stereotypes. These proposals for change are found in the section on 'Learning to make choices'.

DEFINITIONS

There are a number of labels that have been generated pertaining to our selves as males and females, such as sex and gender. Two categories, one based on our biology and the other on social construction, focus our attention on the determinants of the perceived differences between males and females. It is important that we recognize the reasons for the distinctions as well as the meanings of the sex and gender labels so that communication and understanding are maximized, and misconceptions and confusion minimized.

Biological determinants

The most basic label is that of defining individuals in terms of their *sex*. One is labelled male or female due to one's sex chromosomes and/or anatomical sex structures, equating males with the presence of, for example, xy sex chromosomes and a penis, while females are usually defined by xx sex chromosomes and the presence of a vagina. As Unger (1979) has noted, hormones and other physical characteristics based on biological origins have also been used to distinguish the sexes. Height and percentage of body fat and muscle are typical examples. However, given the work of John Money and others (e.g. Baker and Ehrhardt 1978; Money and Wiedeking 1980), we have become increasingly aware of the fact that it may be inappropriate to categorize individuals as strictly male or female. Rather, levels of hormones and physical appearance exist along a continuum with extreme maleness anchoring one end and extreme femaleness anchoring the other end. There are males with rounded hips and breasts as well as females who are very flat-chested. Some individuals, usually genetic females, may experience *androgenital syndrome* whereby they receive an overabundance of the masculinizing androgen and, unless treated early with cortisol, will appear male-like in their external genital structures and be raised as boys, perhaps requiring surgical procedures at adolescence. Some genetic males may be insensitive to the masculinizing effects of androgen – *androgen insensitivity syndrome* – and develop external female-like genitals and be raised as girls. Other individuals who carry the sex chromosomes of one sex, and who are born with ambiguous genitalia, undergo surgery in the first years of life with their genitalia corrected for consistency with the sex opposite to that designated by their sex chromosomes (in line with the likelihood of surgical success given the genital structure with which the child is born), and are reared as this opposite sex. There are also intersex children who have been reared as one sex, undergone substantial physical change at puberty, and have been redefined in terms of their sex at adolescence (Imperato-McGinley *et al.* 1974; Lott 1987). Still others are born with sex chromosomal abnormalities, such as *Turner's syndrome, Klinefelter's syndrome* or the *double-y syndrome* that impact on physical appearance, the ability to reproduce and/or psychological profiles that may include impaired intellectual functioning, impulsivity/excitability, etc. For the most part, however, the members of differing societies would concur as to the assigned sex of most individuals as male or female based on their biological constitution.

Although sex has been described in terms of biological determinants, psychological comfort with one's sex is a basic and essential factor to be understood. With regard to individuals themselves, establishing one's *sex identity*[1] would refer to the construction of a personal definition of their subjective experience and comfort with their biological self as male or female. Between the ages of 2 and 4, children begin to know the connection between the label boy/girl, and body and body image. By the age of 5 or 6 they understand that having a penis and being a boy go together, as having a vagina and 'probably' making babies go with being a girl. Understanding that one is of a single sex and will remain so throughout life also emerges at about this time and is referred to as *sex constancy*. Adolescence appears to be an age when discomfort with one's biological sex is likely to surface as questions pertaining to pubertal change and reproductive capacities emerge. It is also at this time that developmental sex identity concerns may become apparent for homosexuals, bisexuals, and heterosexuals that convey the complexity of this task (e.g. Anderson 1990). Developmental sex identity concerns become complicated by their interaction with gender role demands.

Social construction determinants

While one's sex label is determined by one's biological features, one's ascribed gender is determined by the socio-cultural dictates of one's environment. *Gender* refers to the social, cultural, and psychological aspects of those clusters of characteristics, traits, and behaviours that have been associated with being male or female but 'should be thought of as independent of a person's biological sex' (Doyle and Paludi 1991: 5). Because this is a societally constructed differentiation, it is useful to examine the components of gender separately and in relationship to one another. These include gender roles, gender norms, gender stereotypes, gender identity, gender typing, and gender constancy.

Gender role refers to the functions of sets of behaviours, beliefs, and attitudes socially defined as appropriate for one's sex. *Gender norms* should refer to the 'normative' or 'typical' expression of these behaviours, beliefs, and attitudes found in a given population. It should serve a descriptive function of documenting actual behaviour. Unfortunately, gender norms have historically and sociologically been defined as the societal prescriptions of what the 'shoulds' and 'should nots' are for each sex, equating 'norms' with external dictates. With this historical and sociological usage, 'gender norms are the prescriptive guidelines that form the gender roles' (Doyle 1985: 88). *Gender stereotypes* are oversimplified 'socially shared beliefs that certain qualities can be assigned to individuals, based on their membership in the female or male half of the human race' (Lips 1988: 2). Thus males share one cluster of traits, to include as examples aggression and objectivity, while females share another, to include emotionality and passivity, etc. Gender stereotypes are a rigid and simplified version of gender roles that provide little or no flexibility for individual difference.

Gender identity[2] has been described in terms of process as well as product. The process refers to decision-making as to whether and to what degree these externally defined gender roles are appropriate to one's self-definition (Archer 1985). One begins to formulate a gender identity in childhood. At that time the individual primarily accumulates, and clusters into schemas by 'boy versus girl', the messages provided by significant others in one's society. The evaluative component of gender definition largely emerges during adolescence, and becomes increasingly refined throughout the adult years. It requires sophisticated cognitive capacities and ego strength to examine the range of roles; assess their appropriateness to one's uniqueness in the face of societal expectations; and accept, select from among, and/or discard gender roles in terms of their 'goodness of fit' for the individual in the existing societal context.

The product refers to the actual content of one's gender identity that one deems appropriate. *Gender typing* refers to the degree to which an individual acquires a traditional masculine or feminine gender identity role. *Gender constancy* refers to the degree to which an individual consistently maintains gender characteristics, behaviours, and beliefs throughout life.

THE CONTENT OF GENDER ROLES AND STEREOTYPES

When male and female are thought of in terms of their biological distinctions, there is a tendency to envision just the two units: male and female. When male and female are thought of in terms of their socially constructed gender, complications emerge because many physical characteristics, traits, occupations, and roles are assumed to 'belong' appropriately to one sex as opposed to the other. Thus, based on biology, males and females are perceived in a unitary fashion; but based on social constructions, one is forced to a multi-faceted perception of their distinctiveness. A basic assumption appears to have been that certain clusters of characteristics, behaviours, and goals are in fact necessary to each sex. As will be noted, one's biological constitution makes less demands for correlates in the social environment than social stereotypes would suggest is necessary or appropriate. Lack of gender role consistency between cultures (e.g. Lii and Wong 1982), changes in gender roles over historical points in time (e.g. Feingold 1988), changes with chronological age (e.g. Cazenave 1984), and clarifications of perceptions (e.g. Deaux and Lewis 1984; Eagly and Steffen 1984) with improved research questions, designs and measures all point to the artificial construction of many of the expected correlates.

Perhaps one of the strongest conveyors of the social dichotomy between male and female has been the research focused on the usage of the personal qualities associated with the terms masculinity and femininity. In the 1930s and 1940s the assumption that males were masculine and females feminine encouraged a perception of an opposition of behaviours and traits as characterizing the biological male and female (e.g. Hathaway and McKinley 1943; Terman and Miles 1936); for example, males engage in aggressive acts, females are emotional. In the 1960s and 1970s masculinity and femininity were recognized as independent constructs; both expressible in males and females. With Bem's Sex Role Inventory (1974) it was proposed that *individuals* might be 1) high on masculinity, low on femininity, labelled masculine; 2) high on femininity, low on masculinity, labelled feminine; 3) high on both, labelled androgynous; or 4) low on both, labelled undifferentiated with regard to gender role. Paralleling this advance was that of Spence, Helmreich and Stapp (1974) who developed the Personal Attributes Questionnaire. So, for example, males and females who are masculine in gender role orientation are probably agentic; males and females who are feminine in gender role orientation are probably nurturant.

What were the personal qualities that were being associated with male and female, masculine and feminine? A number of studies were designed with the purpose of examining lists of personality traits to determine which are typically associated with males and females. As noted by Lips (1988), Williams and Bennett (1975) found that 75 per cent of students at an American university agreed that of 300 adjectives, thirty typically described women and thirty-three described men. Women were characterized by such adjectives as appreciative, charming, dependent, fickle, gentle, nagging, and submissive. Men were characterized by such adjectives as adventurous, assertive, boastful, dominant, loud, severe, and stable. There appeared to be considerable cross-cultural agreement on many, although not all, of the distinctions.

Williams and Best (1982) engaged in a thirty-country cross-cultural set of studies focused on sex trait stereotypes, 'those psychological characteristics or behavioural traits that are believed to characterize men with much greater (or lesser) frequency than they characterize women (1982: 16). Working with university men and women in twenty-five different countries, using a 300-adjective checklist, they found agreement across all countries on three single items for females – sentimental, submissive and superstitious – and six items for males – adventurous, dominant, forceful, independent, masculine and strong. Dropping one country from the assessment, four additional adjectives would be included for females – affectionate, dreamy, feminine and sensitive; and six additional items for males – aggressive, autocratic, daring, enterprising, robust and stern. At least 67 per cent of the respondents from a country had to agree that the given adjective was more appropriate for one sex than the other in order for it to be deemed a sex role stereotype. For approximately one-half of the countries, the male stereotype was rated as somewhat more favourable (e.g. especially in Japan, South Africa, Nigeria and Malaysia), whereas in approximately another half of the countries, the female stereotype was rated as somewhat more favourable (e.g. especially in Italy, Peru and Australia). 'On this basis one would conclude that there was no cross-cultural tendency to evaluate one stereotype more favourable than the other' (1982: 90). Several phenomena appeared to be pervasive across the studied cultures. Male-associated traits had connotations of strength and far greater activity, whereas female-associated traits had connotations of weakness and low activity. In additional cross-cultural studies (Williams and Best 1982) conducted with children of the ages of 5 and 8 years in twenty different countries, it was found that differentiating stereotypes increased between the 5- and 8-year-old groups, male stereotypes were better understood than female stereotypes at each age, and in those countries demonstrating highly differentiated sex trait stereotypes among the university males and females, a comparable high differentiation was found among the 8-year-olds.

In many of these gender studies questions are focused on ideals, expectations about unknown others, and what is 'generally associated' with each gender. With these questions one is primarily tapping stereotypes as opposed to actual characteristics and behaviours. Several further studies typically identified with early assessment of stereotypes by gender have been those of Broverman and her colleagues (*et al.* 1972) and Rosenkrantz and his (*et al.* 1968). Here, too, lists were generated as more 'typical' of one gender than the other. From these studies, characteristics were clustered; males being associated with competency and females with warmth and expressiveness, not unlike the distinctions of agency and communion made by Bakan (1966), and instrumentality and expressiveness made by Parsons and Bales (1955). However, as Lips (1988: 5) reminds us, in each of these instances 'such findings describe the extent to which people in various parts of the world *know* the male and female stereotypes, not necessarily the extent to which they actually believe them to be true.' Nor does it address the descriptive norms of actual behaviours, characteristics and choice patterns as people actually experience and live them.

During the 1980s the work of people like Kay Deaux (Deaux and Lewis 1984), Alice Eagly (Eagly and Steffen 1984) and Jay Orlofsky (1981) led us to a more sophisticated appreciation of the complexity of gender construction. Orlofsky (1981) teased apart gender role interests/behaviours (those that were ideal, typical, or self-rated) from attitudes and personality traits (as measured by the Attitudes Toward Women Scale and Personal Attributes Questionnaire), finding a general independence of these components of gender. The complexity of perceptions of the gender construct was particularly revealed by findings that a number of behaviours and interests typically identified as stereotypically male or female were deemed, in practice, acceptable for both sexes although others were rigidly maintained to be sex-specific. Providing examples, Orlofsky noted that sex-specific stereotypes particularly adhered to in sporting activity areas for males were physical competition and aggression (e.g. hunting, boxing, football) while sex-specific stereotypes adhered to for females in the areas of socio-emotionally-oriented vocations and familial behaviours included greater self-subordination or domesticity (e.g. kindergarten teacher, nurse, mending clothes, infant care).

As an additional example of gender role complexity, Eagly and Steffen (1984) conducted a sequence of experiments in which they manipulated several variables, to include gender, status of employment role by its title and setting, employment versus homemaker, employment versus marriage and parenting, and employment by choice versus necessity. *Individuals*, male and female, who were engaged in the role of homemaker were perceived as high in communion and low in agency, whereas employed *individuals* of both genders were perceived as agentic. Employed women were perceived as even more agentic than were the employed men. It was thought that this might be due to the perception that employed women are in this role by choice. Thus, these gender-stereotypic beliefs appear to be associated with particular roles, rather than with the biological male or female. Being a homemaker requires one to engage in communion. Because homemakers are typically female, females engage in communion. If males are the homemakers, then they, too, engage in communion. Being employed requires agency; being employed out of choice suggests extensive agency. Because men are employed out of necessity, rarely out of choice, employed women are perceived as comparatively more agentic – which counters another gender stereotype. Thus, suggest Eagly and Steffen (1984) gender stereotypes stem from the distribution of women and men into social roles, such as homemaker and employee.

How do our children and adolescents learn these societal expectations of the appropriateness of specific roles for each gender? Let us examine the possible socialization processes as proposed by various theorists, as well as the documented behaviour of children and adolescents.

THE SOCIALIZATION PROCESSES AND CONSEQUENCES

Psychoanalytic theories of identification

The oldest perspective on gender role learning is that of the *psychoanalytic theory of identification*, first formulated by Sigmund Freud (1927). This theory was heavily influenced by the societal context of its time, focused on anatomy, male dominance, and hence father–child relationships. Freud proposed that young children make their first identification with their primary caretaker, typically mother. But at about the age of 3, children develop a sexual attraction for the opposite-sex parent. The male phallus plays a primary role in this process. Boys, having identified closely with their mother since infancy, intensify their relationship with her in a sexual manner. But this places them in the position of having to rival their father for their mother's affections. Fearing retribution from their father, in the form of castration, they relinquish or repress this attraction at about the age of 5 or 6 and rigidly identify with him.

Girls have great difficulty continuing their initial identification with their mother. This is because they discover that they must have 'lost' their penis, a calamity blamed on mother who also lost her penis. Father, who has a penis, is to be envied and coveted. Girls ultimately resign themselves to their female identification, but attempt to maintain some masculine identification as well. For boys and girls, the identification process results in gender role learning, expressed through the internalization of the same-sex parent's characteristics, behaviours, and beliefs deemed appropriate to one's maleness or femaleness. Behaviour consistent with this gender role learning would be demonstrated by the early school years.

In a more recent societal context, female psychoanalytic theorists (e.g. Chodorow 1978; Horney 1978) have proposed a different perspective on the identification process, making the mother–child relationship the focal point. Summing up across their individual orientations, the all-powerful 'mother image' is given as a primary reason for the male's rigid masculine identification and the female's difficulty in establishing a same-sex gender identification. They argue that, in order to maintain male dominance in our societies, it becomes necessary for the male to overcome his awe and envy of female womb and breasts as well as the power of mother over infant; thus, he rejects his attachment to mother and relates to father. In contrast, the female has difficulty establishing her same-sex identification for two reasons: the 'myth' of the all-powerful 'mother image' generates an expectation of a demanding role to incorporate as one's own, and the status and privilege provided exclusively to males are envied and desired. It should be noted that neither theory of *identification* has undergone rigorous research investigation to support its position. Both perspectives focused on explaining *why* identifications would take place and are good examples of the impact of the societal context on theory development.

Social learning theory

By contrast, the *social learning theory* has undergone extensive empirical investigation that has resulted in an increase in our awareness of the complexity of processes that impact on the development and maintenance of one's gender role throughout the life span. Initially proposed by Bandura and Walters (1963) and Mischel (1970), the basic mechanisms of this behaviourally-oriented model include reinforcement, observation of models, and imitation. In infancy and throughout the pre-school years, the basic principles of reinforcement are already at work. Significant others – such as parents, media heroes, and peers – provide positive reinforcement for engaging in behaviour deemed appropriate for one's sex. Positive consequences following one's behaviour increase the likelihood that the particular behaviour will be repeated.

Positive reinforcements include such things as praise, smiles, physical contact, desired foods and toys. For example, females tend to be exposed to doll-like toys with faces more extensively than are boys. If the girl interacts with a doll, she is likely to be encouraged with smiles, strokes, and expressions of 'Ah, isn't it a nice baby! Hug the baby.' In consequence, her contact with doll-like toys should increase. Negative consequences following one's behaviour should lead to the avoidance of or decrease in the likelihood of repeating that behaviour. Typical negative consequences or punishment might include sharp negative exclamations, frowns, and/or the denial or removal of favoured foods or toys. For example, young male children interacting with the same doll-like toy may well receive adult frowns, wrinkled nose, and/or comments of 'You don't want to play with that. That's for girls. Here, play with this.' The child is then given a small-scale football or action figure (in the USA dolls 'for boys' are not called dolls but rather action figures, e.g. GI Joe) with which to interact. As a consequence, the boy decreases interactions with what others have chosen to label girl-type toys and increases contact with what have been identified as boy-type toys, evidenced by the approval of significant others.

The second form of learning that influences what behaviours are to be enacted comes from observing models and choosing to imitate those models that provide or show evidence of that which is deemed positive. Children observe how others perform specific behaviours and tasks, but the choice to imitate that behaviour rests on many possible factors about the model (e.g. Fagot 1985; Perry and Bussey 1979). Research findings have revealed that young children observe whether the models are themselves rewarded or punished for the behaviour in which they engage. If the model is punished for their actions, children typically do not imitate that behaviour. If the model is reinforced, the likelihood is heightened that the child will also engage in that behaviour. In addition, some models are more likely to be imitated than other models. Perceived similarity between the child and the model is an extremely important factor. The similarity may include being of the same sex, liking comparable gender-labelled activities, sharing certain physical characteristics, personality traits, or having the same name, etc. In addition, models who exude warmth, maintain power over the child's reinforcements, and are available, are all factors into whether someone will be imitated or not. Children are more likely to imitate same-sex models who engage in gender-typed behaviours than same-sex models engaged in cross-typed behaviours. They tend not to imitate opposite-sex models, although this decision can be complicated by other variables, such as the ones previously mentioned to include warmth, power, or availability. Children begin to engage in gender-stereotyped ways during the pre-school years. Because this occurs before they have developed a sense of gender constancy, it poses a problem for cognitive developmental theory.

Cognitive developmental theory

The basic premiss of the *cognitive developmental theory* is that children are provided at an early age with labels denoting one's sex. The child actively seeks cognitive consistency and understanding as to the meaning of the label with its concomitant behaviours. Focusing on cognitive capacities from a developmental orientation, the learning of gender roles is placed in a stage sequence as described by Kohlberg and others (Kohlberg and Ullian 1974). It is assumed that 'children cannot understand generalized concepts such as their own sex and its accompanying gender-role expectations until their cognitive abilities are sufficiently developed to a stage or level at which they can understand the constancy' of their sex (Jacklin 1989: 130).

In the first stage children's concepts of gender and gender role are relatively 'amorphous and confused' (Douvan 1979: 83). Around 2 years of age, children begin to learn that there are two sexes, labelled 'boy' and 'girl' and that certain genital structures (or their absence) as well as certain characteristics and behaviours seem to go with that label. Sex identity and stereotypic gender-role behaviour begin to emerge. For example, a child may hesitantly state that they are a boy because they have a penis and 'She's a girl because she doesn't have one.' One is further informed that girls have long hair and boys have short hair, girls wear dresses and boys don't. This is particularly fascinating when said by a child whose father has long hair, whose mother rarely wears dresses, and whose older sister has very short hair. The categorizing by early gender assumptions can be discrepant with individual experience, yet at this age does not appear to cause dissonance. During the intermediate phase, beginning at about the age of 5 to 7, gender rules become understood and 'are applied rigidly and defensively' (Douvan 1979: 83). Sex constancy has been learned and gender role behaviour is brought sharply into line, especially for boys. Thus, based on cognitive developmental theory, sex (gender) identity is learned first, followed by a high valuation being placed on consonant behaviours and characteristics as well as same-sex models. Imitation and emotional attachment to the same-sex parent thus follow sex (gender) identity. And therefore, beginning with the traditional school years, the child has a cognitive set for learning the complex structure of gender role expectations that will now be reinforced, especially by same-sex significant others. It is thought that there is a final stage 'in which understanding combines with flexibility and appreciation for individual differences' (Douvan 1979: 83). Unfortunately the extensiveness with which gender stereotypes are reinforced in many cultures would suggest that much like principled moral reasoning, this stage may be attained by few. With regard to the first two stages, 'it has been shown that children know much about their own sex-appropriate [gender] behaviour and attitudes well before [this] stage theory would predict that they should have this knowledge' (Jacklin 1989: 130). However, it is also likely that children easily parrot others without cognitively understanding the ramifications of this classification system.

Gender schemata theory

A recent theoretical orientation that combines aspects of the cognitive-developmental theory and social learning theory (Bem 1983; Liben and Signorella 1987; Martin and Halverson 1983) is that of the *gender schemata theory*. As described by Jacklin (1989), schemas are sets of ideas that help individuals organize information. Gender schemas refer to all the diverse information that an individual acquires regarding modes of behaviour, properties of objects, attitudes, and even feeling-states that are categorized in line with one's present understanding of gender and one's need to understand the category better. Gender schemata are useful for several reasons: 1) to document what knowledge an individual has about the genders, and 2) to assess the importance of gender schema to the individual by noting the degree to which it is used as a guide for processing information and determining one's behaviour. A primary focus is thus on the individual as opposed to the identification figures or models or agents of reinforcement. The child, for example, is described in terms of its activity of constructing gender categories and its responsiveness to environmental cues.

This also affords an opportunity to examine how the socio-cultural value placed on gender influences the individual's acquisition of gender roles.

Research findings to date suggest that gender role knowledge increases with increase in age and that children focus on their own sex's gender role. However, the male role tends to be learned earlier (Stangor and Ruble 1987). This is not surprising because male gender behaviour tends to be more rigidly stereotyped and thus more obvious.

Through the research efforts of Signorella and Liben (as reported in Liben and Signorella 1987), it has been found that children are highly knowledgeable about activity stereotypes (e.g. doll play, cooking, truck-driving) by kindergarten (5–6 years of age), and about trait stereotypes (e.g. passivity versus aggression) by second grade (7–8 years of age), thus leaving little room for variation by middle childhood. In addition, among kindergarten to fourth-grade children (9–10-year-olds), high-stereotype children have difficulty remembering pictures of men and women in non-traditional gender roles. However, low-stereotype children remember equal numbers of traditional and non-traditional pictures. In some instances low-stereotype children have been found to recall more non-traditional pictures than traditional pictures. Even more interesting may be the fact that high-stereotype children were more likely to reconstruct their remembrances in light of converting non-traditional pictures to traditional ones (e.g. recalling female doctors as male doctors), an activity that would reinforce gender rigidity. Children who accept non-traditional preferences for themselves and for others were found to process traditional and non-traditional information equally well.

These findings suggest that as early as the elementary school years, gender information that is perceived as relevant and fits a schema is attended to and processed, while information that does not relate to an existing schema may be distorted or ignored. 'Thus, a person with a strong gender schema [might] spontaneously sort people, characteristics, and behaviours into masculine and feminine categories, regardless of their differences on other dimensions unrelated to gender' (Lips 1988: 48). One of the strengths of gender schemata is as a measure of the primacy the gender concept has for individuals in a given culture over other possible organizing concepts (Bem 1983; Jacklin 1989) as a basis for norms, taboos, group memberships, and institutional arrangements.

Other relevant theories

Several other theories pertaining to gender role learning have recently emerged, hold promise, each focused differently, each providing additional direction to our understanding of this complex process, each requiring empirical investigation. Constantinople's (1979) *sex-role-as-rule-model* expands our appreciation of a gender-schemata-type theory. Within her proposed cognitive orientation, she also provided a social learning emphasis, to include, for example, the behavioural processes of generalization and discrimination. As the child experiences new situations associated with gender, the child shifts the information to other similar situations and experiences, thus transferring the information to broader contexts, to include different environmental settings and activities. Increasingly complex schema can then combine with direct teachings and observational learning from significant others, constantly resulting in attention being drawn to gender-relevant stimuli and refined discriminations within and between the classification system for the sexes. The significant models can provide reinforcement that adds a positive or negative emotional component to gender-related behaviours. These behavioural processes (e.g. generalization, discrimination, reinforcement) are important for the development of data-driven categories (e.g. Aaron and Jeremy play with trucks; Rae and Leigh play with dolls), emerging first during early childhood. Conceptually-driven information-processing follows (e.g. boys must be strong and therefore cannot cry) and is motivationally directed by the need to fulfil expectations. When predictions lead to error (Daddy is crying), accommodation and thus change in schema content should result (e.g. either Daddy is not strong, or boys can cry). Constantinople anticipates that a major consolidation of gender role categories occurs at the time of gender identity stability (Lips 1988).

With Pleck's theory of *sex role strain* (Pleck 1984) which is focused on male gender role development, it is hypothesized that gender-related behaviours and consequently gender roles develop mainly out of a person's need for social approval or as a consequence of situational adaptation (see Doyle 1985: 77-8). Typically, a society operationally prescribes gender roles that are based on overly rigid, inflexible, inconsistent and conforming gender stereotypes and norms. yet to be perceived as psychologically mature and healthy, one is expected to abide by these prescriptions. These demands place a personal strain on many individuals in their work and family lives because the roles are, at least in part, incompatible with their personal values, interests and goals. A refusal to abide by the conformity expectations typically results in social condemnation. A fear of penalty can also result in overconformity and psychologically dysfunctional behaviour. Conformity can also result in denial of one's individuality and pursuit of personal goals, leaving one with a lack of personal fulfilment.

Althought Pleck's theory can be applied to both genders, his focus is on the difficulties inherent in the social system for males in particular. John Hill's *gender intensification hypothesis theory* (Hill and Lynch 1983) also directs our attention to social pressure to behave in gender-appropriate ways, but he proposed that the demand intensifies during adolescence, especially for girls. Thus differences between girls and boys at the time of puberty may not be due so much to biological differences as to an acceleration in their socialization to act in stereotypically masculine or feminine ways. In line with Pleck's theory, lack of conformity to stereotypes probably results in loss of popularity and acceptance. Hill and Lynch noted that adolescent girls become more self-conscious and experience more disruptions in self-image than boys, and achievement becomes more gender-stereotyped, with girls beginning to excel in verbal skills and boys in spatial skills. Interestingly, Keyes and Coleman (1983) working with 15- to 17-year-old British pupils did not find sex differences for measures of personal adjustment, although 'females appeared to experience more conflict over sex role issues' (Coleman and Hendry 1990: 52). One might also have anticipated greater stress in females with high academic ambition since this is contrary to gender role stereotypes for women but instead they found that high ambition did not equate with less adequate adjustment for females than for males. Rather, individuals of both sexes who experienced highest sex role conflict (perceived self-deficiency in instrumental 'masculine' attributes revealed as well by contrast with perceived social expectations) experienced more personal adjustment problems, to include low self-esteem, high psychological malaise and low academic ambition than did individuals experiencing lesser sex role conflict.

In a final theory Archer (1984) proposed a separate *gender roles developmental pathways* approach to the process of acquiring gender roles. He proposes four related dimensions of gender role acquisition that may fundamentally differ over the life span:

1) rigidity or flexibility with regard to crossing gender-typed behaviour; 2) simplicity or complexity of the content of the gender role; 3) internal consistency or inconsistency of the role requirements; and 4) the degree of continuity or discontinuity in role development over time. He exemplifies the developmental use of the dimensions by noting (Archer 1984; Lips 1988) that in childhood societal demands for boys' stereotypes are more rigid, complex, and inconsistent but that at adolescence, girls become more rigid, inflexible, and narrowly defined. As adults, females become more consistent and same-sex-typed as they take on spousal and parenting responsibilities while males are perceived as becoming more flexible and cross-gender-typed if they, as adults, take on parenting roles.

LEARNING GENDER ROLES: THE INTERFACING OF SOCIALIZING AGENTS AND CHILDREN

Culling research findings[3] as discussed in Doyle (1985), Doyle and Paludi (1991), Lips (1988), and Lott (1987), it would appear that flexible or rigid gender-role development will depend in large part on the messages provided by significant others as well as the individual's ability to accommodate to new information, adjust the content of gender schemas, or assimilate by distorting reality to fit rigid perspectives. During early childhood, US culture bombards boys and girls with stereotyped gender-role messages. Even parents, consciously in support of gender-aschematic environments, reinforce and model some traditional values, beliefs, and goals as evidenced by the colour schemes, choice of dress, toys, and range of physical activity provided at home. Typically, boys are given significantly more opportunities to explore while girls are restrained in close proximity to parents. Boys are provided with a plethora of exploratory, active, and manipulative toys while girls are given passive or domesticating toys. Media (books as well as commercialized television programmes) typically glorify adventurous male behaviour, while placing females in family helper positions. These factors and more provide clear messages as to the delineation and valuation of roles for males and females before the traditional school years even begin. Although initially boys and girls may cognitively find these social roles 'amorphous and confusing', rewards, punishments, and models at every turn provide public statements regarding the content of the gender schema

categories for boys versus girls. Indeed as noted earlier, by kindergarten children are able to distinguish activities appropriate for
boys versus girls. And thus it is not surprising that even by the age
of 4, many children will react strongly and selectively to different
toys because of their packaging alone. Typically there are boys *or*
girls on the cover conveying a very clear message that this is (or is
not) for you based on your biological sex. Ergo, as boys creatively
manipulate tinker toys (and other types of construction sets), girls
wash their babies.

Once in school, teachers tend to perpetuate the gender distinction
by attending to boys more, to include scolding as well as instruction, with messages that poor performance for boys implies lack of
effort, whereas for girls it suggests incompetency. Children harshly
penalize each other, especially boys, if they deviate from the rigid
and inflexible rules of gender roles. Boys, in particular, use tactics
of labelling non-conforming boys as 'sissy' and publicly demean
'girl things'. In contrast, girls are permitted greater flexibility;
'tomboy' is not necessarily greeted as an offensive label (during
childhood, at least in the USA). However, although girls may not
be severely penalized for inconsistent gender-role behaviours, it is
impossible to avoid the environmentally rigid messages of 'appropriate grown-up feminine behaviours and goals'. In school for
many hours of the day, children see female nursery and elementary
school teachers, male principals and superintendents. Females
teach home economics and English, males teach science and maths.
Textbooks in fields such as history and the sciences continue to be
androcentric, exhorting the accomplishments of males and ignoring
or giving minimal note to the efforts brought to fruition by females.
Even magazines for teenagers that could focus on egalitarian
concepts expend enormous time and money on themes of glamour,
make-up and fashions for the popular and successful girl who must
snare her man, marry and have babies, versus themes of adventure,
determination, and struggle for the young man who strives for
success in a tough, competitive world out there. And it is just this
image of the female versus male that permeates the adolescent
years. Puberty culminates in a focus on physical appearance and
physical attractiveness, as secondary sex characteristics, reproductive capacity and athletic prowess emerge. Sex and gender identity
strongly converge and result in a demand for rigid adherence to
gender stereotypes if one is to be popular and receive the stamp of
approval from peers as well as adults.

For males, there appears to be a substantial continuity between childhood and adolescence with regard to the form of the gender role expectations. Having been required to walk the more rigid and consistent pathway from early childhood, their more difficult task may be the attempt to match the intensity of the ideal 'macho' image of the male provided by the public and expected by their female peers. As one twelfth-grade male (17–18 years of age) said in response to a request to describe his expectations of his male role in society, 'You have to be strong, tough, able to withstand pain; carry most of the responsibilities in a marriage' (Archer 1985).

For females, there is a disruption of the flexibility previously 'permitted'. Thus, they experience not only the discontinuity of physical appearance from child to adult form, but also have conferred on them a set of rigid social expectations that sharply contrast with the social approval previously received for academic accomplishments and competition with boys. Popularity becomes the coveted achievement. The public message from all sides is that the adult male is to be valued and the successful female must ensnare the best possible catch. 'He' then will determine her identity and her future life course. Music videos primarily focused on sexual exploitation with female victimization, soap operas in which even professional women succumb to their men, books of popular gothic romance in which pretty women, after great suffering, are finally chosen by their Prince Charming, all enhance the expectation of a traditional role for females. As well, significant family members are inclined to provide messages that boys will not like you if you 'show them up'. Under such circumstances it is not surprising that females demonstrate lowered self-esteem and increased self-consciousness as well as lack of clarity with regard to life plans. Indeed a sobering, consistent research finding has been that females are not inclined to value their own qualities until or unless approved by significant others. As a consequence, it would appear that adolescent girls do not use their own abilities, talents and skills as the aspiration for their personal life directives. Rather, while boys examine the future in light of their *abilities*, females appear to do so in light of their *opportunities* given the anticipated expectations of future marital partner and children who will define their options for them.

LEARNING TO MAKE CHOICES

This constant and consistently rigid bombardment makes it difficult to counter traditional gender schemas successfully. As noted by gender schema researchers, children with traditional stereotyped perceptions assimilate external stimuli in line with their already established learning, even going so far as to distort new knowledge about egalitarian and/or gender-aschematic orientations to fit their traditional perspectives on the gender role world. Children with non-traditional or low-stereotype cognitions are significantly more likely to retain information of flexible content accurately.

If our children and youth are to develop aspirations for life plans that are consistent with their abilities, talents and skills, if they are to have the opportunity to engage in personally expressive and self-fulfilling activities, they need to have choices. There are several ways in which the learning environment could be modified to enhance this likelihood. One requires the adults to make choices; another requires teaching our children to make choices.

Adults must consciously decide whether life choices are to be made on the basis of socially constructed *gender* expectations or *individual* ability and interest. If one places individual ability above socially constructed dictates, then it behoves the adults in the society to work towards an increasingly gender-aschematic environment. Clothing, books (beginning with nursery rhymes), movies, songs, toys, etc. should be designed and packaged about and for children, not boys versus girls. Career options should be introduced in the context of those *individuals*, male and female, who have the ability, talent, and interest to pursue them. Marriage and parenting options should be introduced in the context of those *individuals* who seek this form of interpersonal connection and have the ability and desire to care for others and be cared for by these others in this capacity. Schematic categories should be learned and shared in terms of appropriate and real requirements and limitations; for example, if height or physical strength of the *individual* is a necessary characteristic for a given career or task then that information should be factually presented.

The capacity to bear children is a real biological difference between males and females. We must learn to distinguish these biological realities from generalized, extended social role expectations that are constructed as if they are biologically determined or part of a biological package. For example, the capacity to bear babies is biologically determined, changing diapers is not. Individuals in all capacities in our societies, parents, teachers, policy makers, corporate leaders, etc. must become cognizant of their values framework and be held accountable for the modelling and rewarding of rigid stereotypes and the punishing of exploration for individual personal expression. Increasingly, theorists are focusing on the psychological maladjustments that may accompany gender role strain. Research findings are emerging that document this correlation. The adults of our various cultures must become sensitized to the negative impact of rigidly held gender role expectations and should learn how to make choices available to our children and youth, who, in turn, must develop their capacity to explore options, a process to be encouraged by significant others. Indeed in one study in which adolescents were asked about the interrelationship of their gender roles, career expectations, and family plans (Archer 1985), few of the boys but a large minority of the females sensed a collision course over which they had little control and for which society would provide them with little support. As one twelfth-grade female said, 'If I work, I'll be a journalist. I'll have deadlines to meet. I'll have to make a choice. I don't know what I'll do.' Not only does she not know what to do, she has not been taught how to assess these roles from multiple perspectives. Our youth are just learning how to engage in formal operational thought and social reasoning. They have not honed the skills needed to appreciate the complex interrelationship between social gender constructions, individual abilities, talents, and ambitions, approval for self by self versus others, or the potentially interlocking dynamics of the various components of life choices, such as religious ideology, family, and career.

Theorists, researchers and practitioners have spent much of our time documenting stereotypes and how well they are learned and enforced. An important goal of the school years should be to disrupt gender stereotypes and to encourage the cognitive skills of schematizing in line with the generation of gender-free possibilities from selection of toys to selection of life goals. Envision the possibilties if all children were encouraged equally to play spatial, verbal, nurturing, and computer games. What options would our children have if their choices were based on their abilities, talents, skills, and interests? What differences in opportunities would we see if the limitations imposed by socially constructed, artificial gender stereotypes were removed. To theorists, researchers, and practitioners alike long-term studies will be needed to determine whether low gender-role stereotype children are able to maintain their flexiblity into adulthood, given the tremendous societal pressures to abide by prescribed gender norms. As well, we should be asking what strategies can be developed to instil flexibility into high gender-role stereotype children and the adult models who structure their environment.

NOTES

1 In line with the thinking of James Doyle, C. W. Sherif and Rhoda Unger, this author has attempted to further separate variables associated with the biological sex of the individual from that of the socially constructed gender. Thus, the terms sex, sex identity, and sex constancy are offered as separate from and in contrast to gender, gender identity, and gender constancy.
2 The product of gender identity refers to what has traditionally been labelled gender identity content. The process refers to the use of exploration and commitment to arrive at a self-chosen set of values, beliefs and goals. This process of choosing one's gender role, described as one of numerous domains in the ego identity literature (Archer 1985; Marcia 1980), has not typically been integrated into the gender literature.
3 Individual references for this section can be found in the cited reviews of Doyle (1985), Doyle and Paludi (1991), Lips (1988) or Lott (1987).

REFERENCES

Anderson, D. (1990) 'Homosexuality in adolescence', in M. Sugar (ed.) *Atypical Adolescence and Sexuality*, New York: W. W. Norton & Company.

Archer, J. (1984) 'Gender roles as developmental pathways', *British Journal of Social Psychology* 23: 245–56.

Archer, S. L. (1985) 'Identity and the choice of social roles', in A. S. Waterman (ed.) *Identity in Adolescence: Processes and Contents*, San Francisco: Jossey-Bass.

Bakan, D. (1966) *The Duality of Human Experience*, Chicago: Rand McNally.

Baker, S. and Ehrhardt, A. (1978) 'Prenatal androgen, intelligence, and cognitive sex differences', in R. Friedman (ed.) *Sex Differences in Behavior*, Huntington, NY: Krieger Publishing.

Bandura, A. and Walters, R. (1963) *Social Learning and Personality Development*, New York: Holt, Rinehart & Winston.

Bem, S. L. (1974) 'The measurement of psychological androgyny', *Journal of Consulting and Clinical Psychology* 42: 155–62.

——(1983) 'Gender schema theory and its implications for child development: raising gender-aschematic children in a gender-schematic society', *Signs: Journal of Women in Culture and Society* 8: 598-616.

Broverman, I. K., Vogel, S. R., Broverman, D. M., Clarkson, F. E. and Rosenkrantz, P. S. (1972) 'Sex-role stereotypes: a current appraisal', *Journal of Social Issues* 28: 59-78.

Cazenave, N. A. (1984) 'Race, socioeconomic status, and age: the social context of American masculinity', *Sex Roles* 11: 639-56.

Chodorow, N. (1978) *The Reproduction of Mothering*, Berkeley, CA: University of California Press.

Coleman, J. C. and Hendry, L. (1990) *The Nature of Adolescence*, 2nd edn, London: Routledge.

Constantinople, A. (1979) 'Sex-role acquisition: in search of the elephant', *Sex Roles* 5: 121-33.

Deaux, K. and Lewis, L. L. (1984) 'Structure of gender stereotypes: interrelationships among components and gender labels', *Journal of Personality and Social Psychology* 46: 991-1004.

Douvan, E. (1979) 'Sex role learning', in J. C. Coleman (ed.) *The School Years*, London: Methuen.

Doyle, J. A. (1985) *Sex and Gender*, Dubuque, IA: Wm C. Brown.

Doyle, J. A. and Paludi, M. A. (1991) *Sex and Gender*, Dubuque, IA: Wm C. Brown.

Eagly, A. H. and Steffen, V. J. (1984) 'Gender stereotypes stem from the distribution of women and men into social roles', *Journal of Personality and Social Psychology* 46: 735-54.

Fagot, B. I. (1985) 'Beyond the reinforcement principle: another step toward understanding sex role development', *Developmental Psychology* 21: 1097-1104.

Feingold, A. (1988) 'Cognitive gender differences are disappearing', *American Psychologist* 43: 95-103.

Freud, S. (1927) 'Some psychical consequences of the anatomical distinction between the sexes', *International Journal of Psycho-Analysis* 8: 133-42.

Hathaway, S. and McKinley, J. (1943) *The Minnesota Multiphasic Inventory*, New York: Psychological Corporation.

Hill, J. and Lynch, M. (1983) 'The intensification of gender-related role expectations during early adolescence', in J. Brooks-Gunn and A. Petersen (eds) *Female Puberty*, New York: Plenum Press.

Horney, K. (1978) 'The problem of feminine masochism', in J. Miller (ed.) *Psychoanalysis and Women*, New York: Penguin.

Imperato-McGinley, J., Guerrero, L., Gautier, T. and Peterson, R. E. (1974) 'Steroid 5-reductase deficiency in man: an inherited form of male pseudohermaphroditism', *Science* 186: 1212-15.

Jacklin, C. N. (1989) 'Female and male: issues of gender', *American Psychologist* 44: 127-33.

Keyes, S. and Coleman, J. (1983) 'Sex-role conflicts and personal adjustment: a study of British adolescents', *Journal of Youth and Adolescence* 12: 443-57.

Kohlberg, L. A. and Ullian, D. Z. (1974) 'Stages in the development of psychosexual concepts and attitudes', in R. C. Friedman, R. M. Richart and R. L. Van de Wiele (eds), *Sex Differences in Behaviour*, New York: Wiley.

Liben, L. S. and Signorella, M. L. (eds) (1987) *Children's Gender Schemata*, London: Jossey-Bass.

Lii, S. and Wong, S. (1982) 'A cross-cultural study in sex-role stereotypes and social desirability', *Sex Roles* 8: 481-91.

Lips, H. M. (1988) *Sex & gender: an Introduction*, Mountain View, CA: Mayfield Publishing Company.

Lott, B. (1987) *Women's Lives*, Monterey, CA: Brooks/Cole Publishing Company.

Marcia, J. E. (1980) 'Identity in adolescence', in J. Adelson (ed.) *Handbook of Adolescent Psychology*, New York: Wiley.

Martin, C. L. and Halverson, C. F., Jr (1983) 'Gender constancy: a methodological and theoretical analysis', *Sex Roles* 9: 755-90.

Mischel, W. (1970) 'Sex-typing and socialization', in P. Mussen (ed.) *Carmichael's Manual of Child Psychology*, 3rd edn, New York: Wiley.

Money, J. and Wiedeking, C. (1980) 'Gender identify/role: normal differentiation and its transpositions', in B. Wolman and J. Money (eds) *Handbook of Human Sexuality*, Englewood Cliffs, NJ: Prentice-Hall.

Orlofsky, J. L. (1981) 'Relationship between sex role attitudes and personality traits and the Sex Role Behavior Scale-1: a new measure of masculine and feminine role behaviors and interests', *Journal of Personality and Social Psychology* 40: 927-40.

Parsons, T. and Bales, R. (1955) *Family, Socialization and Interaction Process*, New York: Free Press.

Perry, D. G. and Bussey, K. (1979) 'The social learning theory of sex differences: imitation is alive and well', *Journal of Personality and Social Psychology* 37: 1699-1712.

Pleck, J. (1984) 'The theory of male sex role identity: its rise and fall, 1936 to the present', in M. Lewin (ed.), *In the Shadow of the Past: Psychology Portrays the Sexes*, New York: Columbia University Press.

Rosenkrantz, P. S., Vogel, S. R., Bee, H., Broverman, I. K. and Broverman, D. M. (1968) 'Sex-role stereotypes and self-concepts in college students', *Journal of Consulting and Clinical Psychology* 32: 287-95.

Sherif, C. W. (1982) 'Needed concepts in the study of gender identity', *Psychology of Women Quarterly* 6: 375-98.

Spence, J., Helmreich, R. and Stapp, J. (1974) 'The personal attributes questionnaire', *JSAS Catalog of Selected Documents in Psychology* 4: 127.

Stangor, C. and Ruble, D. N. (1987) 'Development of gender role knowledge and gender constancy', in L. S. Liben and M. L. Signorella (eds) *Children's Gender Schemata*, San Francisco: Jossey-Bass.

Terman, L. and Miles, C. (1936) *Sex and Personality*, New York: McGraw-Hill.

Unger, R. K. (1979) 'Toward a redefinition of sex and gender', *American Psychologist* 34: 1085-94.

Williams, J. E. and Bennett, S. M. (1975) 'The definition of sex stereotypes via the adjective checklist', *Sex Roles* 1: 327-37.
Williams, J. E. and Best, D. L. (1982) *Measuring Sex Stereotypes: A Thirty Nation Study*, Beverly Hills, CA: Sage.

Chapter 4

The development of self

Terry Honess

DEVELOPMENT: WHAT IS TO BE ACHIEVED?

The concept of 'development' must be distinguished from change. It is not sufficient to provide an account of either what happens to an individual, or an account of what happens to most people. The concept of development involves *prescription* as well as description, and therefore the idea of improvement towards some desired or ideal state. Two kinds of question follow for the practitioner: 'What is to be achieved?' and 'How is it to be achieved?' Such questions invariably involve values as to what are the most appropriate ways of living in our particular society. This argument is developed with particular reference to three classic authorities on the nature of development, all of whom employ the concept of 'self'. These authors are Havighurst, Erikson and Allport.

The focus for the discussion of these three authors will be their exposition of what constitutes a relatively 'healthy' or 'desired' outcome for young people at the end of their school years. This is necessary if we are to understand the development of self through the school years.

Havighurst (1953; 1956; 1972) acknowledges the shaping role of physical maturation, societal expectations, and self-aspirations in determining 'developmental tasks'. Havighurst identified these tasks through empirical means: observation of children and adults at different ages, and asking them about their principal concerns and aspirations. These data, in conjunction with a review of extant literature, led Havighurst to specify nine tasks for 'middle childhood', and eight for 'adolescence'. The full list for adolescence is given in Table 4.1.

The concept of 'task' is important because it emphasizes the need for successful coping and adaptation. A number of researchers have

Table 4.1 The developmental tasks of adolescence: the views of Havighurst

Achieving an appropriate masculine or feminine role
Accepting one's physique and using the body effectively
Achieving more mature relations with both sexes
Achieving emotional independence from parents and other adults
Preparing for marriage and family life
Achieving assurance of economic independence
Developing a set of values and an ethical system that guide
　behaviour
Desiring and achieving socially responsible behaviour

Source: adapted from Havighurst 1953

successfully exploited this link: see Bosma and Jackson's (eds 1990) review of empirical studies that relate coping to self-concept in the school years. For example, Siffge-Krenke (1990) investigated coping behaviours used by teenagers in dealing with everyday problems, and Offer, Ostrov and Howard (1981) talk of the 'coping self' in their extensive studies of the adolescent self-concept.

The central assumptions of Havighurst are clearly echoed in the writings of Erikson (1950; 1968). Erikson also argues that to understand an individual's actions or feelings requires taking account of three factors: somatic process, social context, and ego process or identity. The last is the way in which a person resolves conflicts and makes sense of him or herself. In his account, Erikson charts the human life cycle in terms of eight different phases of ego development. However, it is important to stress that although each phase is prototypical for a particular age, each phase can be revisited or anticipated at any stage. This is particularly so during adolescence (see Table 4.2).

Erikson is one of the most influential figures in research and writing on 'the development of self'. However, direct *empirical* examination of his theory is relatively sparse. An important exception is the work of Marcia (1966; 1980). He has sought to develop standardized interviews in order to make operational the concepts of 'diffusion', 'foreclosure', 'moratorium' and 'achievement' in respect of different identity statuses. Marcia's methods have been taken up by a number of other researchers: for example, Grotevant *et al.* (1982) have extended the identity status interview into the interpersonal domain, and Josselson (1987) discusses sex differences in an important reworking of the Marcia

Table 4.2 The developmental tasks of adolescence: the views of Erikson

Eight phases or ages of ego development	Successful outcome represented in adolescence
Basic trust vs. mistrust	Realistic time orientation
Autonomy vs. shame and doubt	Self-certainty
Initiative vs. guilt	Role experimentation
Industry vs. inferiority	Apprenticeship
Identity vs. identity confusion	Coherent identity
Intimacy vs. isolation	Responsible heterosexuality
Generativity vs. stagnation	Leadership and being guided
Ego integrity vs. despair	Ideological commitment

Source: adapted from Erikson 1968

Table 4.3 Features of the mature personality: the views of Allport

Extension of the sense of self
Intimacy and compassion
Emotional security
Realistic perceptions and skills
Self-reflection
Unifying philosophy of life

Source: adapted from Allport 1955

framework. Nevertheless, Erikson's primary contribution has been, and still is, in respect of his ideas. In his own words, the theory is 'a tool to think with', not 'a prescription to abide by' (1950: 243).

Finally, in this section, we shall outline the work of Allport (1955; 1964). Six features of the mature personality are identified by Allport which characterize the desired ways of operating in the world (see Table 4.3).

1 *Extension of the sense of self*: involves activity in arenas such as work, family or politics which result in an extension of self-investment and meaning.
2 *Intimacy and compassion*: intimacy involves a sharing with, acceptance of, and trust in, particular others; compassion is this quality applied to others in general.
3 *Emotional security*: self-acceptance is necessary, which is manifest in a recognition of one's strengths and weaknesses, and the

concern to realize one's potential. Other characteristics include 'frustration tolerance' and the capacity to express one's own views.

4 *Realistic perceptions and skills*: involves accurate perception of objective tasks, and the possession of appropriate problem-solving skills.

5 *Self-reflection*: relates closely to emotional security and realistic perceptions – a mature personality has insight, not affectation.

6 *Unifying philosophy of life*: maturity involves 'a clear perception of life's purpose in terms of an intelligible theory'. (Allport 1964: 294)

Taken together, the developmental goals specified by Havighurst, Erikson and Allport are strikingly similar. Two key processes appear to underwrite the achievement of these goals: a challenging but secure self-reflection, and finding a recognition within society, i.e. a social identity.

Gender identity and self-esteem are among the most researched areas concerned with children's developing self-perceptions, and since both address the 'key processes' identified above, these areas are reviewed here. First, *the development of gender identity*. Both Havighurst and Erikson emphasize the importance of achieving an appropriate masculine or feminine role; and achieving more mature relations with both sexes. Gender identity at least partly constitutes the individual's social as well as personal sense of self. Second, *the development of a secure sense of self*. All three authors stress the importance of self-acceptance and a coherent identity. Psychologists have primarily focused on the course and correlates of measures of 'self-esteem'.

RESEARCH ON THE DEVELOPMENT OF GENDER IDENTITY

It is well documented that by the age of 2 to 3, children are able to assign 'appropriate' (i.e. stereotyped) male and female talk to male and female dolls (e.g. Kuhn *et al.* 1978). Gender identity involves more: an unambiguous self-referral as either male or female. The usual procedure for determining such constancy is that developed by Slaby and Frey (1975) and consists of a series of questions such as 'if you put on girl's [boy's] clothing, would you become a girl [boy]?'; 'If you wanted to be, could you be a Mummy [Daddy] when you grow up?' Researchers suggest that gender constancy determined by such questions is established by 4 to 6 years of age (e.g. Ruble *et al.* 1981). This is before the establishment of ethnic or personality self-constancy (e.g. Aboud 1984; Semaj 1980).

Gender constancy is important because it is assumed (e.g. Kohlberg 1966; and more recently Bem 1981 on gender schema) that there are motivational and behavioural consequences of such constancy. Ruble and Stangor (1986) provide a review of relevant empirical studies. However, a relatively early acquisition of gender constancy does not imply more stereotyped behaviour: Aboud and Ruble (1987) suggest that constancy acquisition is a necessary condition for *influencing* a child's individual feelings of what constitutes sex-appropriate behaviour for him or herself.

Other authors (e.g. Hollway 1989) go further and argue that gender identity is not simply a cognitive 'achievement'. Rather it is an all-pervasive feature of social life, and that it is necessary to speak of 'gendered subjectivity'.

RESEARCH ON THE 'SELF-CONCEPT'

Researchers have sidestepped the issue of 'What is the self?' by seeking to measure the 'self-concept' or the 'academic self-concept', i.e. school children's reports of their own sense of self or self-worth. Following her widely quoted reviews of the self-concept literature (e.g. 1979), Wylie concludes (1987): 'in view of the disproportionate attention to overall self-esteem, it is quite provocative that many of the theoretically predicted relationships have turned out to be weak or null'. Problems with measuring the self-concept are discussed later in this chapter; here we confine ourselves to a review of important research studies.

Simmons (1987) is able to address some of the Wylie criticisms by demonstrating the value of relating overall self-esteem to social, biological and behavioural phenomena, rather than to other psychological constructs. In her review, Simmons is able to demonstrate that simple questionnaire measures do show significant relations with non-questionnaire indicators that are important in the lives of adolescents. For example, she provides good empirical support, using self-esteem measures, for the proposition that changes such as entry into high school, onset of dating, puberty, independent decision-making and so on can be managed if such changes are met sequentially rather than simultaneously.

Other authors have sought to redress the imbalance identified by Wylie through focusing on children's 'open-ended' self-descriptions. The most thorough programme of this kind is that carried out by McGuire and his colleagues (1979 *et seq.*) who have asked children of different ages: 'Tell me about yourself', and, more recently, 'Tell me what you are not'. A significant feature of this work is the demonstration that children's spontaneous descriptions are directly influenced by the salience or distinctiveness of particular aspects of their social circumstances.

TALKING ABOUT THE SELF

In discussing goals for development it is clear that appropriate ways of living in our particular society have been paramount in the writings of Havighurst, Erikson and Allport. One further quotation will suffice here: Havighurst describes developmental tasks 'as those things that constitute healthy and satisfactory growth in our society'. This 'assumes an active learner interacting with an active social environment' (1972: 2). It has also been argued above that there are two processes central to this active accommodation between the individual and his or her social environment. These processes are the development of a challenging but secure self-reflection, and finding a recognition within society, i.e. a social identity.

Turning now to methodology, it is also clear that what children and young people write about or talk about has been the principal source of data for researchers. In the remainder of this chapter, we shall therefore adopt the position that 'self' is to be found not inside people, but in their talk. This will make us particularly sensitive to how questions are asked – how interviews progress, and how analysis should proceed. It means that interviews are not simply a matter of finding the right question to *reveal* the respondent's 'self', but that interviews set a context for *constructing*, as well as making manifest, the individual's sense of self. It will be seen that this approach allows a considerably more significant role for the educationalist than an approach that merely suggests 'measures' of the 'self-concept'. The format for the development of this argument is based around six questions:

1 *Where is the self?*: Extracts from interviews with a 16-year-old boy – 'John' – and a 16-year-old girl – 'Julia' – are provided to

allow the discussion to develop from an empirical base. Older chidren are chosen to help articulate what it is that constitutes a *relatively* advanced progression in respect of the 'development of self'.

2   *What is 'maturity'?*: Both scripts are used to identify key features of development, which are then compared against the tasks identified by Havighurst and Erikson, as well as the features of the mature personality identified by Allport. One further concern in this section will be a discussion of 'gender differences'.

3   *What is the 'self'?*: The proposition that selves are, to a significant degree, socially constructed is developed. The features identified above – a developing capacity for 'self-reflection' and an emerging 'social identity' – are brought together in this account.

4   *How is the 'self' developed?*: Constructionist views are integrated with psychoanalytic and cognitive accounts of the development of self. This is summarized in a model which stresses the school child's active accommodation to his or her family and school environment.

5   *How is the 'self' to be measured?*: Questionnaires and interviews are discussed, and the problems of analysis are introduced with illustrations from John and Julia's scripts.

6   *Does it make any difference to the practitioner?*: In answering 'Yes' to this question the particular examples of completing pupils' Records of Achievement and careers counselling are discussed. The conclusion emphasizes the need to help school children to construct rather than simply find their 'selves'.

The following are brief extracts from interviews with 16-year-old John and 16-year-old Julia, eight months after they had finished in the fifth form, and were expecting to leave school. It was one of a series of case study interviews with young people, which are part of a research programme concerned with identity development and the school-leaving transition (see Honess and Edwards 1987; 1990; Honess 1989a; 1989b; 1989c).

1a   Where is the self?: John's talk

John's talk about his work

I ('I' refers to the 'Interviewer'): And you started work in June and it sounds like it was a yeah . . . a pretty dreary time in a way . . . sort of sweeping up and things . . .

John: No . . . it didn't because umm . . . you know all . . . everyone starts at the bottom and work your way up like and uhh . . . I knew it was one part of my duties like, to do sweeping up. Oh . . . there was a lot of blokes like they teach me you know . . . they say 'Come and have a look at this a minute' or 'Leave the sweeping up and . . .' . . . very helpful. A great bunch of lads there anyway. I like them a lot . . . [but] sometimes they tell me 'Don't be so enthusiastic'.

John: On the weekend we do [get homework] from college. It's . . . don't get me wrong, it's not like school, they treat you like adults in college right, they treat you as young adults right, like they don't treat you as children right . . . you can get into arguments over it . . . a lot of them swear in the class, and it's not a classroom, it's a lecture room.

John's talk about his activities, friends and girlfriend

John: Well, you know, you change as you get older, so a . . . it's you know . . . you meets someone at work, and he says 'Are you coming out tonight?' . . . 'Yeah, all right then, all right, I'll come out like.' And you go out and you think, 'Oh this is it, this is great like!' You know, 'Must do this more often'.

John: She [John's girlfriend] fitted in so well along the line. 'Cause when I . . . when I started going out right, and I met no mates at all right . . . she used to live for me, and I used to live for her! But nowadays it's a . . . different! I've had such a good time with my mates up there [living away from home for his apprenticeship], so I may as well come back home here and have a good time with my mates home here. It's as I told her, I won't . . . when I come back, I won't be seeing so much of her, say about three days a week. Three nights out!

I: Was she quite happy about that?

John: Umm . . . [pauses] . . . no, I don't think she is.

I: I mean, how strong . . . I mean, you said just now, that you vowed you're not going to throw your life away on some stupid girl.

John: See . . . it's a decision that my father's put into my head really. If my father wants the very best for me and I want to prove to him that a . . . I can get the very best!

John's talk about his parents

John: Umm . . . do the dishes after tea, when you [the interviewer] just picked me up just now, I was doing the washing for her [John's mother], she was still in bed – put my washing in the washing machine . . . when she gets up then she'll take it out and she'll peg it out . . . You know, if I have a day . . . if I have a day, you know, if I don't help in any way, I'll always make up for it.

I: So have you always been this responsible, always doing your own . . . ?

John: No . . . since I started paying my mother housekeeping I've been sort of responsible, you know.

I: You obviously get on well with your mum, has that relationship changed in any way.?

John: Gained more than anything . . . I find it far better to get on with my mum nowadays . . . she don't push me into doing anything. If I don't want to do it, I'll tell her I don't want to do it.

I: Why do you think you're getting on better?

John: umm . . . [long pause] . . . well, it's . . . it's something . . . it's a trivial thing, you know, it's umm . . . when I first got the job, she was over the moon like, she didn't think I would honestly get it . . . she thought . . . I'm glad like in a way I've made her happy. In a way. I've got a job and if she goes to her friend she could probably say, 'My son's got a job!' That's what a . . . that's what makes me chuffed, you know, not being big-headed or nothing.

I: Do you think you're getting on better with your dad than you were?

John: Yeah! Much better. He comes to watch me on Saturday afternoons in football . . . It's like one of the boys says, if you gets whacked in the face, like your old man will run on and hit him, and I said, 'No, I want to get on with it'.

I: But you are finding that you can talk to him better, or not?

John: Working and football.

John's 'talk about himself' in response to explicit questions about self

The interviewer is referring back to the pre-leaving interview, when John was still at school (see Honess and Edwards 1990 for the questions used):

I: Do you still feel confident about yourself, do you feel . . . ?

John: Umm . . . yeah in a way, you know, I'm not a defeatist, I won't let anyone beat me, you know, if they beat me then you know, a . . . well, they must have worked awful hard to beat me.

I: You said, you were asked if you were worried about not having any job, and you said, 'Yes, I'm a great worrier'. Are you still a great worrier?

John: It's like if a job don't turn out right, that worried . . . that worries me like. If you do something wrong, you think, 'Oh you're putting your job in jeopardy'.

I: Do you worry about losing the job?

John: Yeah! A lot.

I: Why?

John: Umm . . . I don't know really. Have you ever had the feeling that umm . . . [pauses] . . . that every move you make, people are watching you? Umm . . . this is how I feel, you know. I don't know whether it's just me, I don't know . . . but a . . . it's like glare . . . eyes are glaring at you like when you're in work, you're doing a job . . . and a . . . if it don't turn out like, that a . . . if you don't get something right, that you should get right, but a . . . you think, 'Oh I'm putting my job in jeopardy like' . . .

John: [talking about unemployment and government policy] As long as I'm happy, you know, I don't particularly care . . . what happens to the rest of the country, what ever happens around me, yeah, of course . . . but umm . . . [long pause] . . . but that's as far as it goes.

John is now describing himself in the third person:

John: Everything, well I think, everything revolves around work. His life revolves around work . . . Well, when he was in school he was classed as umm . . . you know, 'lower' than what we was, because I was in a lower class, but he's got a better job than most of us now . . . Work gave him an environment which . . . with elder people, with older men, it's umm . . . it's brought him down . . . more down to earth. [long pause] Umm . . . he's a better 'all-round' person. He's umm . . . you can discuss things – personal things with him, more that what you could in school, otherwise he'd laugh at you. But . . . umm . . . that's about it.

1b Where is the self?: Julia's talk

Julia's talk about her unforeseen return to school because of her failure to pass any exams

Julia: I started crying when I got my results, so did my mother . . .
It was terrible! [pause] My mother said just go back to school and
try again . . . She knows I don't really like it in school now, just
before Christmas I wanted to leave, and I still can't find a job.
   I: So right, what got you fed up with school then?
   Julia: You can't really read in here 'cause you've got all the boys
in the common room, making too much noise . . . and playing
football. When . . . when I came back here . . . I mean the boys they
were really awful. So you had to be mouthy to them, because they
just run . . . run you over! They're terrible! But now . . . I'm getting
on easier with them now, they treat me . . . treat me like one of the
boys, and the one I really . . . I really used to hate, but now I get on
really well with him. You've just got to give them a 'taste of their
own medicine'.
   Julia: Doing the same work, over and over again . . . started just
about December. I didn't come in a lot, but it's been picking up
because for two weeks I've been in every day and the boys that have
been there all the time, since I've been away, and they're getting
poorer marks than I am.

Julia's talk about friends and her boyfriend

Julia: Julie [her main friend] comes over every weekend, and I see
her sometimes in the week. She . . . she's really nice. She's on a
Youth Training Scheme in a bank. Umm . . . she doesn't really go
out that much. I remember I was . . . I was very upset the other
week when I asked her to come out with me and she went out to
Sally's with her friends. [pauses] . . . But she only gets about £5 a
week to go out with. She only goes out once a week. But lately she
can't afford it, so I've got to wait 'till she can, and then we're both
going to go out together!'
   Julia: Well, I'm more honest with my friends now, 'cause of that
. . . you know when you don't want to be rude to anyone . . . I'll tell
them what I think! And there was one . . . she was . . . she was
really 'bitchy' and I couldn't stand her at one time . . . and we had
this row once, I said, 'I don't really want to know you', and she
'phones me up now and then and if she says anything, I say it back
. . . 'cause you can find some people are really bitchy to you and
that's why, I just thought, 'I've had enough of this'. That's how they
really used me last year because I was so quiet. [long pause]
   Julia: Oh. We're [talking about her long standing boyfriend] not

as close as we used to be, 'cause I want more freedom. He . . . he just messes around with jobs, he don't really stay in 'em. He . . . you could call him a bum! That's all he is. I was just staying in . . . I mean, I do everything he said, and I just thought, 'What am I doing, if I'm going to do this for the rest of my life. It's not worth going on!' [long pause] I was just fed-up!

I: You said you really wanted it to last, last year.

Julia: Yeah, well, I . . . I was just stupid then! [laughs] I don't mind it lasting with him now, but I just want as much freedom . . . I mean one of them has just got married, not married . . . engaged, last year . . . and I thought, 'Oh!' . . . she . . . they were always having rows, her and her boyfriend. I don't know how they could get engaged! And then one of my other friends is getting engaged in August, she's only 16 [pauses] . . . they all thought I was going to get engaged, but I'm not now. [laughs, pauses] I thought I'd get married when I'm about 21 . . . Yeah! I mean she [talking about her friend Julie] doesn't let a boy tie her down or anything like that, she's not stupid [pauses] . . . she's just waiting for the right one! She don't want . . . she don't get upset over a boy, if he doesn't turn up to see her.

Julia's talk about her parents

Julia: Now . . . we [talking about her mother] were really close then but we were still the 'mother and daughter' type and then she thought that I wasn't really working for my exams, which was true, and we were rowing all the time, but we row now and then but . . . we really get on better with each other . . . I've got a lot more confidence . . . We're more like 'friends' than 'mother and daughter' now.

I: Have you got a similar sort of relationship with him [talking about Julia's father] as last year – I mean, do you still cheek him a lot?

Julia: Well it's not really 'cheek', we're only messing around. I mean, I can get away with 'murder' whereas my sister, he'll just shout at and he's . . . he's only ever hit me once in my life and that was when I was really young . . . [but] he's not really fussed about family life . . . he just gets on with what he's doing.

Julia's 'talk about herself'

[Julia is describing herself in the third person as if she were a very close friend of Julia's:]

Julia: She can be a bit mouthy sometimes by upsetting me, 'cause she's a bit forward. She doesn't really go out much, I wish she'd hang round with me a bit more. [long pause] Umm . . . I know she's fed up at home, 'cause she's always staying in with no money, that's why she's got to look for another Saturday job. [long pause] She's a really good friend [long pause] . . . Easy to talk to, and understanding. [long pause] Umm . . . she's kind, not really too rude, [pauses] . . . can't think . . . She can be too mouthy . . . always leaves her bedroom in a mess. [long pause] And sometimes she's too lazy.

[The issue of significant change was taken up by Julia, in response to a question concerning what she had gained most satisfaction from in the last year:]

Julia: That's a hard question. I have to think about that one. Because I'm closer with my friends, 'cause I can really speak to them, instead of just being quiet. [very long pause] I suppose 'cause I'm standing on my own two feet, I'm satisfied that I've gained that. I can do things myself – independence – confidence. I feel better. [very long pause] It just happened. I was so fed-up at home. The rows . . . and then the past year . . . it's been great! No rows at all – well, some, not that many.

[Of particular interest was how far Julia could account for the change away from her first interview self-characterization of 'soft':]

Julia: I don't know, I just got so depressed 'cause of staying in every day, and people don't really notice me that . . . I just . . . I just said, 'Oh I've got to get confidence up if I don't . . . I'll be like this for the rest of my life' and I'm certainly not going to stay like it. I don't know really, it was just something on the spur of the moment.

I: Was it a sudden decision?

Julia: Yeah! It was just . . . 'cause I was staying in, I thought, 'Oh', it was one night when . . . I said, 'Oh, I'm not staying in any more', so I just got up and I walked out of the house. I thought, 'I've had enough', and I stayed over my friend's then, I just . . . told them at my house, 'You'll see me when I come back!' She [mother] wasn't really worried – she knows what I'm like. 'Cause you can find some people are really bitchy to you and that's why, I just thought, 'I've had enough of this'. That's how they really used me last year because I was so quiet. [long pause]

2 What is 'maturity' for John and Julia?

Several propositions about development – becoming an adult – can be generated from the interviews.

1) *There is a need for paid work (or academic/training success) with relatively long term security.* This serves a variety of functions, some common to all individuals, such as the enjoyment and freedom that money can bring. The importance of employment for 'identity consolidation' is clear from the interviews, and is central to the writings of both Erikson and Havighurst.

Related functions of the (potential) world of work are nicely summarized by Allport when he talks of the need 'for an extension of the sense of self'. This can serve other developmental needs; for example, helping to cope with more generalized insecurity, as was the case for John.

Nevertheless, it is within the world of work and training that the 'gendered subjectivity' discussed by Hollway becomes particularly profound. Differences in employment preference and placement may be best understood with reference to the gendered opportunity structure. Relatively poorly qualified young women typically name 'nursery nursing' or some other work 'involving people' as an ideal, and might find an outlet in retailing, where there is, ostensibly, a people focus. Boys' choices tend towards the instrumental – apprenticeships are much desired, although they more usually find themselves in some unskilled or semi-skilled occupation.

An emphasis on social processes (Havighurst on 'an active learner interacting with an active social environment') suggests that it would be an appropriate accommodation to develop aspirations that reflect not only general social pressures from parents and school, but also particular opportunities. Girls will 'prefer' jobs in which there is a strong element of social supportiveness (as reported by Griffin 1985). This is a 'style' that is encouraged (amply demonstrated in the gender identity literature), and it is one that is appropriate for the opportunities that the labour market affords them. Moreover, declining youth employment and the introduction of training schemes do not appear to mitigate against stereotyped aspirations. Unemployment and unemployment schemes 'serve to reproduce, rather than disrupt, the sexual division of labour', comments Horne (1986) with respect to both paid and upaid labour.

2) *There is a profound transformation of the adolescent-parent relationship*. Our research suggests that this can take different forms – a separation from the parents, or a new-found closeness, as was the case for John, but it is necessarily predicated on a change in status from being experienced as 'child' to being experienced as 'adult'. Julia may have felt less close to her mother, but 'We're more like friends than "mother and daughter" now'. Honess and Lintern (1990) and Youniss and Smollar (1990) provide substantial empirical support for this proposition. The task identified by Havighurst – 'achieving emotional independence from parents' – is potentially misleading. What is important is that new forms of relating need to be developed.

John's interview, and that of other boys in our sample, also suggests that better father–son relationships may be fostered because they share an increasingly common language in respect of 'men's work' and 'men's concerns'.

3) *Sexual relationships become increasingly regular and relatively routine*. Both Julia and John had experience of a relatively stable heterosexual relationship, and for both the developmental task appears to have been giving themselves some freedom from these regular relationships. In these regards, the developments suggested by our three authors appeared to have been satisfactorily achieved.

An ostensibly different picture is suggested by Griffin (1985) and Lees (1986), who discuss the negative side of heterosexual relations for girls. However, Lees's analysis suggests that, ironically, it is a steady heterosexual relationship that is often the only available solution for girls to overcome what she argues are problems that derive from the inequitable structure of sexual power relations.

In the case of Julia, however, a new-found self-assertion is the central theme of her transition. This is very clearly reflected in her coping with the boys at school (although, it must be noted, on their terms), and her disentanglement from the long-standing boyfriend – 'I can tell him what to do instead of him telling me what to do'. Boyfriends did not feature as her central concern; this, as we have seen, was to find work and earn money.

4) *There is a need to 'fit in' to society, and accept what you cannot change*. This is reflected in the concern to sort out and establish one's own immediate world, giving oneself room to manoeuvre without worrying about the bigger issues. This might be

seen as a form of agenda-setting and is consistent with Coleman's 'focal theory' (see Coleman and Hendry 1990). Our interviews with young people prior to their leaving school produced many more 'idealistic' ideas. Thus the task identified by Havighurst – 'desiring and achieving socially acceptable behaviour' – may be partly driven by the demands of the leaving transition.

5) *Relatively enduring psychological problems tend to come into sharper focus or fade in importance.* However, the change from school to work can aid their resolution.

Such problems may be central or relatively peripheral for the transition to adulthood, but will reflect personal histories. Examples from our research which were alleviated in the school-leaving transition are: worries over one's physical prowess (would I let a mate down if he was in trouble?); worries over others' opinions (e.g. John's description of the 'glaring eyes') and low self-confidence (e.g. Julia: 'They really used me last year because I was so quiet').

3 What is the 'self'?: a conceptual framework for integrating self and social identity

The task in this section is to show how the concepts of self and social identity are but two sides of the same coin, and that both must be considered within the same theoretical framework if we are to account properly for the development of self within a particular context. First, it is necessary to draw a distinction between 'the concept of self', and the 'reality of selves' in a discussion of the proposition that selves might be understood as linguistic or 'social constructions'.

A radical constructionist position is that selves are exclusively constituted through social processes, i.e. they are nothing more than social constructions. A most thorough treatment of the argument that selves are socially constructed is to be found in the work of Harré (1983; 1987). Related accounts may be found in Gergen and Shotter (1988). In essence, Harré argues that 'the organisation of mind is a cultural artefact based on the learning of a local concept of self' (1987: 48).

From the constructionist perspective, therefore, 'self' is an important *concept* that is learned by all persons, but selves (unlike persons) are not real, they do not have substance. Rather, self-talk and self-understanding are something learned within a language community, they are 'the heart of a *theory* learnt by all persons'.

A better-known tradition that has much influenced the constructionists (see Shotter 1984) is 'symbolic interactionism', which
draws on the work of G. H. Mead (1934). It is particularly
important to appreciate that Mead's key ideas carry different
emphases for an analysis of self and social context. First, he argues
that self is a reflected entity, and mind a social product which
implies a form of social determinism. However, second, Mead's
writings also stress that self involves a dynamic, self-reflexive
process, realized in the dialectic between the 'I' and the 'me'. Both of
these propositions are interwoven in Strauss (1977):

> Identity as a concept is fully as elusive as is everyone's sense of
> his (her) own personal identity. But whatever else it may be,
> identity is connected with the fateful appraisals made of oneself –
> by oneself and by others. Everyone presents himself to others
> and to himself and sees himself in the mirrors of their judgments.

4 How is the 'self' developed

Of particular interest is the way in which emerging trends in the
psychoanalytic and cognitive accounts of the development of self
are compatible with the foregoing in respect of their increasing
emphasis on the primary role of relationships. Consider, first, new
developments in psychoanalysis: Wolf argues that the increasingly
theoretical and abstract nature of Freud's work gave it an 'exper-
ience-distant status, far from its subjective origins. *The Self had no
place in it'* (1987: 261, italics mine). Nevertheless, developments in
psychoanalysis, particularly object relations theory (1971 e.g.
Winnicot) and, more recently, Kohut's 'self psychology' (1977)
provide some of the most important clinical developments which
lead to 'self' as a central psychoanalytic concept.

These developments emphasize the adequacy of the caretaking
environment with respect to allowing the emergence of the child's
fragile 'self'. Within Kohut's 'self psychology', it is the primary
caretakers who provide the 'selfobject' functions for the child and
the key processes here are 'mirroring' and 'idealization'. Wolf (1987)
stresses that the selfobject is intersubjective, it is 'the inner experience of those relationships that evoke and maintain the feeling of
selfhood'. A detailed review of this caretaker/child relationship is
provided by Pines (1987) in the context of the 'mirroring process'.
This is an important review because it clarifies the common ground

between analysts and developmental psychologists. Moreover, the 'mirror' is the central metaphor in both the psychoanalytic and symbolic interactionist accounts of the development of self.

For the 'self psychoanalysts', the importance of the child's sense of personal continuity cannot be overemphasized. As we have seen, continuity in respect of gender constancy, for example, is a central feature of cognitive accounts of self development. Of particular interest with respect to self constancy is the work of Chandler *et al.* (1987), who demonstrate that the form of children's justifications for self and other continuity do change with age. However, the work of Chandler *et al.* ties these changes more closely to the traditional Piagetian paradigm: pre-operational children justify continuity on the basis of simple inclusion of specific features; concrete-operational children refer to essential, central features, and later to material cause and effect relations between past and present; and formal-operational children provide accounts where present self is seen to be logically related to past self. Most important, however, is when formal-operations children achieve constructionist accounts, where meanings are 'made', rather than 'found'. Such children are seen as providing 'narratives' on self, where 'the self is a narrative centre of gravity'.

This provides an important bridge between the cognitive traditions, and the more constructivist perspectives discussed above. This is so because an emphasis on narrative brings 'the self' into the *public* domain. This argument is summarised by MacIntyre:

> To be the subject of a narrative that runs from one's birth to one's death is to be accountable for the actions and experiences that compose a narratable life. It is to be open to be asked to give a certain kind of account of what one did or what happened to one; the other aspect of narrative selfhood is correlative: I am not only accountable, I am one who can also ask others for an account. I am part of their story as they are part of mine.
>
> (MacIntyre 1981: 202–3)

MacIntyre's orientation still sustains the importance of continuity and distinctness (central themes for cognitive-developmental researchers), but it stresses the publicly negotiated nature of identity i.e. 'identity' becomes an ability – an ability to account for oneself *to others*.

Overall, the theoretical ideas introduced so far stress the development of self in and through relations with others, and within particular social contexts. A basis for an integrative framework for bringing together this body of ideas, with practical implications, can be found in Harré and Secord's (1972) analysis of social life as the blocking or exercise of personal powers ('strengths' is preferred here) and the succumbing to, or overcoming of, personal liabilities ('vulnerabilities' is preferred here). This framework allows us to characterize young persons' development as either enhanced or limited by particular social contingencies.

The author's scheme (see Table 4.4) allows a description of both person and environment characteristics, and it is assumed that particular features of such are key features of self in particular contexts. For any one individual, the person/environment 'transactions' are in particular forms e.g. 'circumstances' – the vulnerability of being easily distracted may be overcome by an individual given a quiet place to work, but if the bedroom is shared by younger siblings a quiet place may not be available. Hence, the vulnerability may not be overcome; 'interpersonal network' – 'I feel I could do well in my biology, but the teacher says it's just a waste of time because I haven't got the head for it.' Hence, the strength may not be exercised; 'subculture' – different 'coping' patterns are relatively strongly expressed in different communities. These can be understood, for example, in terms of local labour market opportunities.

The principal message to emerge here is that individual (psychological) factors must be understood as an active accommodation to a particular set of social conditions (circumstances, interpersonal network, and broader subculture). By the same token, social factors, such as experiences in school, must be seen as facilitating or hindering, but not determining individual experiences.

5 How is the 'self' to be measured?: assessing the self-concept – who are you?

The review of work on the 'self-concept' has shown the importance of self-report questionnaires, particularly the widely used 'Tell me about yourself' or 'Who are you?' questions. This sharpens an important conceptual and methodological issue: Can we equate the 'self-concept' with the 'concept of self'? The answer must be 'No'. The concept of self does allow the important fact, rightly

Table 4.4 Enabling conditions for action

Personal Enabling Conditions

Strengths (Blocked or expressed)	Vulnerabilities (Prone to or mastered)
Academic confidence	Severe worries about jobs
Physical attractiveness	Bad temper
Determination	Feelings of isolation

Social/External Enabling Conditions
(Affecting blocking and expressing of strengths and succumbing to, and mastery of, vulnerabilities)

Circumstances	Interpersonal network	Subculture
Lack of money	Relationship	Marriage pressure
Teacher quality	with parents	Working mothers
Sharing bedroom	with girl/boyfriend	Local unemployment

Note: The examples are *general* categories of the responses given by the 15-year-olds in the author's research study

emphasized by the social constructionists, that individuals' sense of self does vary between cultures and epochs. Thus a sense of self may, at times, involve a very low level of self-awareness, rendering questions such as 'Tell me about yourself' virtually meaningless. This varying level of self-awareness is not confined to distant or obscure cultures. Our own research indicates that children in a relatively prosperous South Wales economy employed 60 per cent more self-reflections and were more sensitive to others' appraisals than their counterparts in a relatively depressed community not more than forty miles away (Honess and Edwards 1990).

This suggests that the way children and adults talk about themselves can be just as informative as the content of what they talk about. Simple questionnaires do not allow for different styles of response. For example, consider Bertaux's work (ed. Bertaux 1981) which suggests that females provide more detail in describing their lives – they remember more, in particular, they describe webs of contradiction and complexity, which contrast with males' relatively consistent, and 'self-willed' accounts. It appears that there are different relations to life revealed in the form of telling, the act of telling. In a similar vein, an analysis of the lives of John and Julia is much aided by interview scripts in which contradictions, hesitations, and responses to interviewer challenges are available. These give a distinctive sense of John and Julia's style of telling – which would be lost with a simple questionnaire approach.

Moreover, even within relatively 'self-conscious' cultures, it can be argued (Turner 1987) that 'in many cases *who I am* is little more than *where I fit*'. Hence, John's statements about washing-up, and going out with his mates, for example – activities in which he feels comfortable – tell us as much about his sense of self as do direct self-reflexive statements such as 'I'm a great worrier' and 'I am not a defeatist', and so on. Finally, Turner argues that the emphasis on eliciting the self-conscious 'self-concept' has drawn attention away from the exploration of self-in-situation 'in which discovery and recognition of self occur'. This is a point we shall return to below in respect of teacher–pupil relationships, where we shall argue that the teacher's task is not to find and measure 'selves', but to help *construct* them.

6 Does it make any difference to the practitioner?

Practical issues relating to the development of self in the school context focus on personal development and careers counselling. These matters are no longer seen to be the province of specialist staff because almost all teachers in the state sector are required to produce Records of Achievement for all secondary pupils. The author has been engaged in preparatory training with teachers in respect of these new requirements. Teachers' worries relate to the new form of relationship that these tasks appear to require, e.g. 'What if we disagree with the pupil?', and to the concern that they may not be able to 'find out about' certain pupils because e.g. 'It might be difficult to find anything positive', or because 'Some pupils have little ability to talk about themselves'.

A discussion of 'interviewing skills' is not relevant for present purposes, but a brief summary of how our transactional model (see Table 4.4) may help in constructing counselling/careers interviews for individuals is relevant. In our own research, we conducted individual interviews with 150 young people towards the end of their fifth year of secondary school – at age 15. These lasted about forty minutes, and covered five broad areas (the full schedule is available on request from the author): job hopes – in respect of realistic expectations, family and school support, work experience and so on; time organization – details of a typical day, degree of planning in day-to-day life as well as in the longer term; coming-year expectations in all areas of life; description of relationships with important figures, especially with mother and father; direct self-descriptions using a variety of different prompts.

The school children were specifically probed about likely support and difficulties, and encouraged to talk about themselves (an unusual experience for some) in different contexts using different prompts. The experience for the interviewees appeared to be a positive one. All 150 readily agreed to be contacted after they had left school, and at the follow-up interview (six to nine months after they had left school), approximately one-third of those interviewed clearly recalled the first interview and had found it very helpful in thinking about their futures. The remainder reported they had found it helpful in some respects or had quickly forgotten it. An interview more closely tied to their needs, rather than one designed for research purposes, should prove even more valuable. This more participative approach focusing on the young person's needs is outlined below.

The new transactional framework that has been introduced in this paper describes social life as the blocking or exercising of personal strengths, and the overcoming of or succumbing to personal vulnerabilities. This is entirely appropriate given that careers/counselling interviews are generally oriented towards the facilitation of individual action. It is helpful for both the interviewer and interviewee to construe strengths and vulner-abilities as reflecting different pathways which are more or less accessible to the individual.

The social enabling conditions (circumstances, interpersonal network and subculture) orient the interviewer and interviewee to a wider frame than is usual. In talking about such concerns, the enabling and constraining features of the social environment in relation to the 'pathways' for possible action will be elaborated. Moreover, as might be expected from the transactional model which stresses the contingent nature of personal and social con-ditions, in talking about such social factors there are inevitably further 'personal' conditions elicited (and vice versa for talking about personal factors). This necessary and inevitable blurring of the personal and social allows the interviewer to become more of a participant in the interview through providing details of various options and requirements for particular career lines.

The wider framing also serves the important objective of allowing individuals to talk about themselves in a variety of different contexts. This opportunity invariably allows many more personal qualities to be elicited than a set of narrow questions that focus on skills that are elicited only in the context of questions directly concerned with employment or subject choice. In our research, young people talked about themselves quite differently in different contexts. For example, some individuals readily integrated qualities from non-school situations with school situations, whereas others did not. This broader frame for considering 'self-development', coupled with an emphasis on negotiation and joint construction, significantly overcomes the worries expressed by many teachers.

CONCLUSIONS

There are important conceptual distinctions to be drawn: the need to distinguish the *concepts* of self and identity from the hypothetical *reality* of 'selves' or 'identities'; the need to distinguish the *concept of self* from the *self-concept*; the need to avoid equating *self-esteem* with the *self-concept*.

The most pressing theoretical issue is the need to avoid equating 'self' or 'identity' with either individualized accounts or exclusively social accounts of action. The most telling practical implication is that selves are not to be found, but are constructed in the process of social interaction. As Haimes (1987) puts it, the self becomes an ability, 'the ability to give an account of one's life and ask others for an account of their part in one's life'.

REFERENCES

Aboud, F. (1984) 'Social and cognitive bases of ethnic identity constancy', *Journal of Genetic psychology* 145: 217–29.

Aboud, F. and Ruble, D. (1987) 'Identity constancy in children: developmental processes and implications', in T. Honess and K. Yardley (eds), *Self and Identity: Perspectives Across the Lifespan*, London: Routledge & Kegan Paul.

Allport, G. (1955) *Becoming: Basic considerations for a Psychology of Personality*, New Haven, CT: Yale University Press.

——(1964) *Pattern and Growth in Personality*, New York: Holt, Rinehart & Winston.

Bem, S. (1981) 'Gender schema theory: a cognitive account of sex typing', *Psychological Review* 88: 345–64.

Bertaux, D. (ed.) (1981) *Biography & Society*, Beverly Hills, CA: Sage.

Bosma, H. and Jackson, S. (eds) (1990) *Coping and Self-Concept in Adolescence*, New York: Springer Verlag.

Chandler, M., Boyes, M., Ball, L. and Hala, S. (1987) 'The conservation of selfhood: children's changing conceptions of self-continuity', in T. Honess and K. Yardley (eds), *Self and Identity: Perspectives Across the Lifespan*, London: Routledge & Kegan Paul.

Coleman, J. C. and Hendry, L. (1990) *The Nature of Adolescence*, 2nd edn, London: Routledge.

Erikson, E. (1950) *Childhood and Society*, New York: Norton.

——(1968) *Identity: Youth and Crisis*, London: Faber.

Gergen, K. and Shotter, J. (eds) (1988) *Texts of Identity*, London: Sage.

Griffin, C. (1985) *Typical Girls?*, London: Routledge & Kegan Paul.

Grotevant, H. D., Thorbecke, W. L. and Myer, M. L. (1982) 'An extension of Marcia's identity status interview into the interpersonal domain', *Journal of Youth and Adolescence* 11: 33–47.

Haimes, E. (1987) 'Now I know who I really am: identity change and redefinitions of the self in adoption', in T. Honess and K. Yardley (eds) *Self and Identity: Perspectives Across the Lifespan*, London: Routledge & Kegan Paul.

Harré, R. (1983) *Personal Being*, Oxford: Blackwell.

——(1987) 'The social construction of selves', in K. Yardley and T. Honess (eds), *Self and Identity: Psychosocial Perspectives*, Chichester: Wiley.

Harré, R. and Secord, P. (1972) *The Explanation of Social Behaviour*, Oxford: Blackwell.

Havighurst, R. (1953) *Human Development and Education*, New York: Longman.

——(1956) 'Research on the developmental task concept', *School Review* 64: 215–23.

——(1972) *Developmental Tasks and Education*, 3rd edn, New York: David McKay.

Hollway, W. (1989) *Subjectivity and Method in Psychology*, London: Sage.

Honess, T. (1989a) 'A longitudinal study of school leavers' employment experiences, time structuring and self-attributions as a function of local opportunity structure', *British Journal of Psychology* 80: 45–77.

——(1989b) 'Personal and social enabling conditions for the sixteen-year-old school leaver: a transactional model for understanding the school leaving transition', *Research Papers in Education* (National Foundation for Educational Research) 4: 28–52.

——(1989c) 'School leavers' changing identifications with different reference groups and their representation of the social category "school leaver" ', *British Journal of Educational Psychology* 59: 59–65.

Honess, T. and Edwards, A. (1987) 'Qualitative and case study work with adolescents', in T. Honess and K. Yardley (eds), *Self and Identity: Perspectives Across the Lifespan* London: Routledge & Kegan Paul.

——(1990) 'Selves-in-Relation: school leavers' accommodation to different interpersonal and situational demands', in H. Bosma and S. Jackson (eds) *Coping and Self-Concept in Adolescence*, New York: Springer Verlag.

Honess, T. and Lintern, F. (1990) 'Relational and systems methodolgies for analysing parent–child relationships: an exploration of conflict, support and independence in adolescence and post-adolescence', *British Journal of Social Psychology* 29: 331–47.

Horne, J. (1986) 'Continuity and change in the state regulation and schooling of unemployed youth', in L. Barton and S. Walker (eds) *Youth Unemployment and Schooling*, Milton Keynes: Open University Press.

Josselson, R. (1987) *Finding Herself: Pathways to Identity Achievement in Woman*, San Francisco: Jossey-Bass.

Kohlberg, L. (1966) 'A cognitive-developmental analysis of children's sex role concepts and attitudes', in E. Maccoby (ed.) *The Development of Sex Differences*, Stanford, CA: Stanford University Press.

Kohut, H. (1977) *The Restoration of the Self*, New York: International Universities Press.

Kuhn, D., Nash, S. and Brucken, L. (1978) 'Sex role concepts of two- and three-year-olds', *Child Development* 49: 445–51.

Lees, S. (1986) *Losing Out*, London: Hutchinson.

MacIntyre, A. (1981) *After Virtue: A Study in Moral Theory*, London: Duckworth.

McGuire, W. (1984) 'Search for the self: going beyond self-esteem and the reactive self', in R. A. Zucker *et al.* (eds) *Personality and the Prediction of Behavior*, New York: Academic Press.

McGuire, W. and McGuire, C. (1987) 'Developmental trends and gender differences in the subjective experience of self' in T. Honess and K. Yardley (eds) *Self and Identity: Perspectives Across the Lifespan*, London: Routledge & Kegan Paul.

McGuire, W., McGuire, C. and Winton, W. (1979) 'Effects of household sex composition on the salience of one's gender in the spontaneous self-concept', *Journal of Personality and Social Psychology*, 36, 511–20.

Marcia, J. E. (1966) 'Development and validation of Ego Identity Status', *Journal of Personality and Social Psychology* 3: 551–8.

——(1980) 'Identity in Adolescence', in J. Adelson (ed.) *Handbook of Adolescent Psychology*, New York: Wiley.

Mead, G. H. (1934) *Mind, Self and Society*, Chicago: University of Chicago Press.

Offer, D., Ostrov, E. and Howard, K. (1981) *The Adolescent: A Psychological Self-Portrait*, New York: Basic Books.

Pines, M. (1987) 'Mirroring and child development: psychodynamic and psychological interpretations', in T. Honess and K. Yardley (eds), *Self and Identity: Perspectives Across the Lifespan*, London: Routledge & Kegan Paul.

Ruble, D. and Stangor, C. (1986) 'Stalking the elusive schema: insights from developmental and social-psychological analyses of gender schemas', *Social Cognition* 4: 227–61.

Ruble, D., Balaban, T. and Cooper, J. (1981) 'Gender constancy and the effects of sex-typed televised toy commercials', *Child Development* 52: 667–73.

Semaj, L. (1980) 'The development of racial evaluations and preference: a cognitive approach', *Journal of Black Psychology* 6: 59–79.

Shotter, J. (1984) *Social Accountability and Selfhood*, Oxford: Blackwell.

Siffge-Krenke, I. (1990) 'Developmental processes in self-concept and coping behaviour', in H. Bosma and S. Jackson (eds) *Coping and Self-Concept in Adolescence*, New York: Springer Verlag.

Simmons, R. (1987) 'Self-esteem in adolescence', in T. Honess and K. Yardley (eds) *Self and Identity: Perspectives Across the Lifespan*, London: Routledge & Kegan Paul.

Slaby, R. and Frey, L. (1975) 'Development of gender constancy and attention to same-sex models', *Child Development* 46: 849-56.

Strauss, A. (1977) *Mirrors and Masks: The Search for Identity*, London: Martin Robertson.

Turner, R. (1987) 'Articulating self and social structure' in K. Yardley and T. Honess (eds) *Self and Identity: Psychosocial Perspectives*, Chichester: Wiley.

Wolf, E. (1987) 'Some comments on the selfobject concept', in K. Yardley and T. Honess (eds) *Self and Identity: Psychosocial Perspectives*, Chichester: Wiley.

Winnicott, D. W. (1971) *Playing and Reality*, London: Tavistock.

Wylie, R. C. (1979) *The Self-Concept: Theory and Research on Selected Topics*, Lincoln, NB: University of Nebraska Press.

——(1987) 'Mothers' attributions to their young children', in T. Honess and K. Yardley (eds) *Self and Identity: Perspectives Across the Lifespan*, London: Routledge & Kegan Paul.

Youniss, J. and Smollar, J. (1990) 'Self through relationship development', in H. Bosma and S. Jackson (eds) *Coping and Self-Concept in Adolescence*, New York: Springer Verlag.

Chapter 5

The peer group

Phillida Salmon

A survey of literature on the peer group, over the last ten years or so, shows a complex and in some ways a surprising situation. Many of the preoccupations of the 1970s are no longer evident, while other, new concerns have become salient. In particular, there is a clear perception, in much recent research, that young people form part of the social world at large. This means not merely that adolescent groupings reflect wide socio-cultural diversity. Beyond this, the processes and functions of peer groups are inseparable from those of the wider society. Yet in many texts of developmental psychology the account offered is still that of documenting the natives. Young people, in these accounts, are characterized in entirely generic terms; they represent a species which is apparently classless, raceless and ungendered. 'The adolescent', in such texts, treads the universal path to adulthood, through group membership, friendships and (hetero)sexual encounters.

Such extraordinary generalizations, which sweep aside major social differences, stem from a view of human beings as essentially separable from their social structures. This view has, of course, been characteristic of psychological research until quite recently, and, at least as far as the 1980s, it has governed much of the work on young people's peer groups. One aspect which seems striking now about such work is its pervasive individualism. A frequent concern has been with the attributes of particular group members: socio-metric stars and isolates, leaders and followers, conformers and independents. The processes examined have been defined intrapersonally, as in conformity studies, or at best interpersonally, as in socio-metric work. The function of groups has also generally been conceived in individualized terms: as facilitating the acquisition by their members of the personal characteristics associated with 'normal' adult social adjustment. In recent versions of this line of work, the currency has been that of 'social competence'.

An individualistic orientation does of course still inform some current research, just as it continues to dominate even quite recent academic texts. But the concern of this chapter will be with work which locates the peer groups of young people within their social context, and relates their ways of functioning to those of the wider society. In establishing the beginnings of such work, the ethnographic and longitudinal study of Paul Willis, *Learning to Labour* (1977), was certainly seminal. This study broke new ground in a number of ways, and showed how fertile it could be to examine the functions of adolescent groupings as essentially social and cultural, rather than merely personal. Willis's most distinctive contribution is his analysis of the crucial socio-cultural role served by their peer group, for 'the lads', a group of twelve non-academic, working-class white boys living in Birmingham. It is through their group membership that these young men come to establish their own distinctive stance: a stance of a particularly macho kind which entails resistance towards 'the establishment' across both school and factory shop floor. This analysis avoids the usual conceptual segregation of young people within some special realm of their own. Willis shows the essential continuity for his subjects of the institutions of work and education, both of which relegate young working-class males to a similar low status. Nor is the peer group, in this study, viewed in terms which divorce it from the wider world. Its function, for its adolescent members, is integral with their position, their engagement, in society; it carries an essentially social stance.

Though Willis's classic study differs strikingly from traditional peer group research, it shares one common feature with that research in that its subjects are male and white. For the young men in *Learning to Labour* their race and gender constitute a social identity which is marked by explicit racism and sexism. In the vast bulk of conventional research, however, the gender bias – let alone that of race – goes unacknowledged. Most studies have examined white boys' groups but proceeded to generalize their findings to all young people. The universalized accounts in academic texts are in fact disguised portraits of white male adolescents. No doubt there are many reasons for the male bias in peer group studies, which echoes a similar tendency in research on 'normal' adults. Some writers, in considering this bias, have justified it on the grounds that peers have greater developmental significance for boys than for girls. Because most adult male lives are lived outside the worlds of home and school, so runs the argument, boys are obliged to learn masculine roles through their participation in boys' groups. Girls, on the other hand, have direct access to the adult female sphere through their close proximity to their mothers' lives; therefore their need of peers is less.

One of the assumptions underpinning this argument is that the worlds and the lives of children and young people are qualitatively different from those of adults. This assumption cannot easily stand against the evidence of studies such as that of Willis. Boys still at school, in that research, speak as experienced and streetwise members of a society which is undeniably the one we know as adults. And where researchers have begun to counter the traditional male bias by making girls the focus of their study, the outcomes are, in this, altogether similar.

In a pioneering feminist study, Sue Sharpe (1976) offers an account based on a survey of fourth-form girls in the Ealing district of London. Drawing on wide-ranging material, she fleshes out the social and cultural realities of young female working-class lives in the early 1970s – realities which, as she remarks, tend to be disregarded within the contemporary popular ideology of equal opportunities. Girls' experience, from this study, emerges as far from homogeneous; both class and race affect, in complex ways, their life constraints and possibilities. But in varying degrees all share the double-bind predicament carried by female gender. Sharpe argues that pressures operate on girls at every stage and in every context of their lives. Family unbringing works to discourage independence in the interest of developing 'proper femininity'. The organization of schooling, though ostensibly open, reinforces gender divisions, while its curriculum teaches girls not to achieve in high status subjects, but to acquire the skills needed for low status 'women's work'. And when they enter the occupational structure, young women cannot but encounter some measure of discrimination.

The girls Sharpe talks to have, inevitably, assimilated many of the stereotyped attitudes and expectations towards their own gender which are endemic in their contemporary culture. Feminist ideas, if encountered at all, have had little impact. For the huge majority of these working-class girls, 'finding true love with Mr Right' remains the primary goal in life. Within this context, the concerns and goals of formal education have minimal relevance, and school is valued only for the friends to be met there. Yet, just as for 'the lads' of Willis's study, there is an underlying continuity between school life and work life; in both spheres the same processes operate to the disadvantage of girls and women – processes of sexual segregation and the division of labour. Within the life predicament of these working-class girls, friends offer a basic and essential support and affirmation. For despite the constant and conflicting pressures of their gender, many of these subjects do find pleasure and confidence in being female, and this, as Sharpe suggests, makes a strong basis for their sense of gender solidarity.

A decade later, another important feminist study, *Typical Girls?* (Griffin, 1985) echoes and develops many of Sharpe's conclusions. The young working-class women studied by Christine Griffin are seen first in the fifth forms of Birmingham schools and, two years on (Griffin, 1987), over their first two years in the local job market. Through her analysis of their family lives, school experience, work and leisure, Griffin discusses the meaning of gender for these young women. Though the study was set up as a female version of *Learning to Labour*, these girls' groups do not parallel those of 'the lads'; their situation is considerably more complicated. The significance of their peers is no less for young women than for young men, but the predicament in which their female gender places them renders their friendships more vulnerable, less continuous and less integral with their future lives than those of male youth.

Most girls, as Griffin documents, spend much time, both in and out of school, in the same-sex friendship groupings: 'hanging around in a group of all girls together'. However, lack of money, domestic and family responsibilities, and a dearth of local provision greatly restrict access to youth leisure facilities, which, in any case, are likely to be dominated by young men and to entail the probability of harassment. Instead, these young women usually meet after school in each other's homes, generally the bedroom, to play records, try out clothes and make-up, and discuss school and teachers, boys and sex. The groups involved are typically small and emotionally intense. There may be 'best friends', pairs of girls who, as Griffin describes, not only go everywhere together arm in arm, but also dress identically, with the same clothes, shoes and hairstyles. Such friendship pairs may last for years. However, the composition of friendship groups is generally much less stable,

particularly after those involved have left school, with its guar-
anteed daily contacts. A major reason for this instability, so
Griffin argues, lies in the demands of compulsory heterosexuality.
The constant and relentless pressure, both social and financial, to
'get a man' – to make the transition to 'normal' adult femininity –
carries its cost for female solidarity. Unlike young men, whose
peer group status is unaffected, or even enhanced, by 'going
steady', young women, when they acquire a regular boyfriend, find
it increasingly hard to keep up their female friendships. Faced
with a boyfriend who expects to monopolize her leisure time, a
young woman has to work very much against the grain if she is to
maintain contact with her peer group. It is, as Griffin suggests, the
dislocating effects of heterosexual relations on female friendships
which act, for girls, to forestall the close cultural connections, so
notable in Willis's gang of 'lads', between friendship groupings,
attitudes to school and job expectations, and subsequent destina-
tions in the labour market.

A central feature of studies such as those of Willis, Sharpe and
Griffin is their locating of young people's friendships within a
material world. For the peer groups of girls and boys do not, of
course, exist in a vacuum but are grounded in social, economic and
political realities. A recent compilation of research papers, entitled
The Social World of the Young Unemployed (White 1988) examines young people not as some special segregated population, but
within an economic context structured by high youth unemployment. In one of these studies, Claire Wallace, working in the Isle of
Sheppey, analyses her interviews with a number of young men and
women, first at 16 years old and then a year later. In this
predominantly working-class area, unemployment is high, and
more than half these young people are without regular work; this
creates a situation of unwanted material dependence on parents,
with whom relations are often difficult. Despite this, both young
men and young women view this period of their lives as one of
engagement, before settling down, in traditional peer group leisure
pursuits: discos, music, fashions, and so on. Given the lack of
material resources, reality, of course, is not so easy. But for girls the
constraints are additionally narrow. Young men living in the family
home are usually free to come and go as they please, and are not
expected to contribute to domestic work. Daughters, on the other
hand, are generally subject to 'oppressive social and sexual control',
and have far less freedom to organize their own lives. Their leisure

time is further curtailed by the domestic responsibilities they almost universally carry.

The more grounded, more differentiating approach of contemporary work has necessarily thrown into relief certain features of peer groups which remained invisible within the abstract and homogenizing studies of earlier research. Locating young people in a socio-economic world calls attention, not merely to their vast diversity, but also to the uglier and less benign aspects of adolescent group life. Within a society structured by power, conflict and inequality, the young themselves cannot but reproduce these features within their own relations. One aspect which forms the topic of a proliferating line of research is that of bullying in school. This research has been reviewed recently by Peter Smith (1989). As he illustrates, studies of bullying have typically examined three kinds of question: its incidence, the characteristics of bullies, victims and bullying behaviour, and the development of intervention strategies. Smith notes that the incidence of bullying is widespread, and that it markedly increases from primary to secondary schooling. 'Bullies' have been characterized in terms of temperamental attributes such as impulsiveness or quick temper, or as lacking social skills; 'victims', on their side, are seen as withdrawn or underassertive. In both British and Scandinavian research much work has gone into developing strategies of intervention: folders of advice for parents; booklets and discussion packs for teachers; role play and bully courts for the use of pupils.

What is strikingly absent in this line of work is any reference to the wider social relations which must inevitably inform the interactions of secondary school pupils. Bullying is viewed as a purely local phenomenon: a function of the personal attributes of individual young people, to be dealt with in terms of particular school institutions. Yet it is unarguably the case that racist, sexist and classist kinds of oppression are present, even sometimes endemic, in the peer groups of young people. The mockery, abuse and harassment suffered by many secondary school pupils cannot be adequately understood without reference to wider social inequalities and injustices. That young people themselves may adopt an explicitly oppressive ideology, particularly when facing the prospect of economic hardship, is borne out in a study conducted by Michael Billig and Ray Cochrane (1987). These researchers focus, over a three-year period, from 1979 to 1982, on two different groups of male and female fifth formers in the West

Midlands. From questionnaires, small group discussion and participant observation, Billig and Cochrane trace changes in the social and political views held by young people over this period. Their findings show a marked increase, over the three years, in support for fascist ideologies. Whereas for the 1979 sample, only a small group of male skinheads adopt such views, by 1982, sympathy with these views has more than doubled, and is felt across a much wider spectrum of young men and women. Consciously facing the likelihood of unemployment on leaving school, these young people relate economic decline to the need for the repatriation of ethnic minorities. Their general political ignorance, apathy and alienation allow them, so these writers suggest, to opt for a simplistic and racist solution to a complex socio-economic problem.

The link between economic recession and inter-racial group hositility among the young is also made by David Milner, whose anlaysis of children and race is a classic. Writing in 1983, he concludes that one of the consequences of the then current depression will be to throw issues of racism into sharper relief. As people compete for a diminishing supply of jobs, housing and material goods, social divisiveness is likely to increase. White people will be encouraged to externalize the blame for hardships on Black people; the problem will come to be articulated in racial terms. In this way the enduring strain of racism in our society stands to be increasingly mobilized.

In the pioneering book *Children and Race* (1973), which drew together his own work and that of others, Milner powerfully demonstrated the significance of race in children's lives. Writing ten years later, in *Children and Race: Ten Years On* (1983), he examines evidence from the intervening period and its meaning for the original issues. As he argues, there have been major changes between 1973 and 1983 in the ethnic and cultural populations in question, and in the economic and social status of ethnic minority groups. On one level, positive attitudinal shifts are apparent. In the early 1970s, Black children typically showed a 'white orientation', paralleled by the skin bleaching and hair straightening which James Baldwin and Malcolm X have documented. Ten years later, Blackness has far more positive connotations for Black children and adolescents. In this, Milner believes the Rastafarian movement has been hugely influential. Its celebration of Blackness, through its distinctive reggae music, clothes and lifestyle, has provided a powerful cultural identity for Black youth. Low-achieving Black pupils, for instance, in a study conducted by Troyna (1979) are able to express strong in-group identity; Rasta offers these pupils a group focus, a distinctive voice, and a positive way of defining their common situation. Despite these hopeful straws in the wind, Milner draws, in 1983, generally pessimistic conclusions – conclusions which unfortunately seem all too well borne out from the perspective of 1990.

Children and young people live in a society which is structured by racism, and which is permeated by racist attitudes. One consequence of such attitudes, in research itself, must be the neglect of friendship and affiliation among ethnic and cultural minorities. There have been studies of inter-relations between white and Black groups, and of attitudes among young white people towards their Black contemporaries. But as yet scarcely any attention has been paid to the peer groupings of Black youngsters in their own right. Troyna's study, cited above, is exceptional. Another rare contribution is made by Mary Fuller (1984), who set out to examine, within a small group of Black girls in a London comprehensive school, the double disadvantage of race and gender. From interviews with eight girls aged between 15 and 16, Fuller describes a very distinctive subculture. Theirs is not just a school-based grouping; in defining their identity these girls draw on their shared experience of life in the West Indies, as well as on their understanding of racial and sexual discrimination. As Fuller emphasizes, this identity is strongly positive, and involves a firm rejection of the negative stereotyping of girls and Black people. These girls' view of themselves entails a definite commitment to achievement in the job market via the acquisition of educational qualifications. Their distinctive stance towards school is, however, complex. Their high level of academic success is the outcome of private application to work set in class or as homework. But in the classroom itself, they conspicuously abjure the role of 'good pupil', distancing themselves from teachers and, while avoiding sanctionable misdemeanours, putting up a smokescreen of bored and irritating behaviour, which allows them to retain the friendship of other, less academically-oriented Black girls.

It is interesting to consider the implications of Fuller's study in relation to another, burgeoning line of work on the peer group in the setting of school This is the study of collaborative learning. Against the traditional assumption that the friendships of young people are irrelevant, if not downright inimical, to education, making learning collaborative rests on the idea that friends may be a potential educational resource. The conceptual roots of much of this work derived from Piagetian notions, taken further by Doise and Mugny (1984), of the significance of peers in promoting intellectual development. Vygotsky's model, with its emphasis on proximal zones and the importance of cognitive conflict, has also served to underpin some studies, such as those of Slavin (1987). In a recent overview of this line of research, Helen Cowie and Joan Rudduck (1990) offer a strongly positive message. They believe that, given experience and support on the part of teachers and peers, 'pupils can develop the qualities which will help them to solve problems, to complete tasks and to interact effectively with others'.

The use of collaborative methods in the classroom presupposes an uncomplicated relation between teachers and their official business, on the one hand, and the subcultures of pupil groupings on the other. Consideration of studies such as Fuller's suggest that reality may not always be so simple. The stance of certain pupil groups is, perhaps, deeply incompatible with the wholehearted public commitment to classroom learning which is entailed in collaborative modes. Quite apart from this, racist, sexist or classist divisions may undermine groupings which are set up on educational grounds by teachers. Nor does the positive and affirming ethos of collaborative learning sit comfortably alongside the hidden curriculum of school: the multiple subtle messages which tell certain groups of pupils of their own low status.

That the friendships of pupils cannot necessarily be enlisted and put to work for the official curriculum of school is certainly suggested by a study carried out a few years ago by the present writer, together with Hilary Claire (Salmon and Claire, 1984). This study, done in the setting of two London comprehensive schools, involved working with four individual teachers, each committed to a philosophy of collaborative learning but working, to varying extents, against the grain of the wider school ethos. The outcomes are mixed. In the case of three second-year groups certain benefits, both social and educational, do seem to accrue from the pupils' experience of collaborative learning modes. Whether these gains, from a single isolated classroom, can be maintained in the wider school setting, or, over time, in the altered subcultures of older adolescents, is open to doubt. Certainly for the fifth-year group of boys with whom we worked, all but one of whom is Black, the meaning of collaborative learning, in the Social Studies class, is much more complicated.

> It seems that these boys had a generally negative perception of school, and saw it as having failed to provide them with qualifications they urgently needed. They also seemed to feel considerable personal distance from teachers. Their peers, though evidently a source of social support, were not felt to contribute to classroom learning. Classroom learning itself was seen as imposed rather than undertaken. Finally, this group of boys seemed to have assimilated, from their particular educational history, a very low image of themselves as school learners. In the light of these attitudes, it does not seem surprising that the take-up by this group of Islay's collaborative learning opportunities was so limited,[1] or that their encounter with her philosophy failed to tip the balance against the accumulated weight of attitudes derived from five years of traditional teaching.
>
> (Salmon and Claire 1984: 91)

In working with young people, no intervention can hope to be effective if it fails to take account of, and indeed to work with, their own attitudes, beliefs and values – in the broadest sense, their culture. Gemma Moss (1989), in a recent study, *Un/Popular Fictions*, sets out to intervene against sexist attitudes among secondary students in Bristol, taking popular fiction as the ground of her curriculum. She shows how, in using the genre of romantic fiction, girls are able to pose questions of social identity. So far from being trapped in cultural stereotypes, they can, with support, deploy fictional forms to examine the meaning of power, difference and gender. Moss argues that rather than devising anti-sexist strategies, presented from a fixed position, teachers should support girls in using the cultural forms with which they are already familiar. Although such forms inevitably contain built-in kinds of sexist oppression, they are diverse rather than homogenous. In focusing on their inherent contradictions, as Moss shows, it is sometimes possible to open up spaces for questioning cultural stereotypes, within the context of the peer group.

An eloquent proponent of the cultural studies approach to intervention is Philip Cohen, whose own research shows the fertility of this approach to young people. From his starting point that 'the youth question is never not an issue of class, gender and ethnicity', Cohen seeks to articulate the meaning of these social categories, and their interactions, for the adolescent groups with whom he works. What emerges from his analysis is the sheer complexity of classist, sexist and racist attitudes – a complexity which is vastly underestimated by many anti-racist and anti-sexist initiatives.

Some ethnic attributes may be idealised because of their positive class and gender associations, while others are denigrated. Most typically, of course, many White working-class boys discrimi-nate positively in favour of Afro-Caribbean subcultures as exhibiting a macho, proletarian style, and against Asian Cultures as 'effeminate' and 'middle-class'. Such boys experience no sense of contradiction in wearing dreadlocks, smoking ganja and going to reggae concerts while continuing to assert that 'Pakis stink'. Split perceptions linking double standards of gender, ethnicity and class are increasingly the rule . . . Sexist imagery may at one moment add injury to racist insult, and in the next, unite White and Black boys in displays of male chauvinism; the shared experience of sexism may in one setting bring girls together, and in another polarise them through the operation of a racial double standard.

(Cohen 1988: 85)

In a project entitled *No Kidding* (personal communication) Cohen describes his work with a group of unemployed boys, all active members of the National Front, who have carried out a number of vicious attacks on Black families living in their neighbourhood. Abjuring informational or moralistic exhortations, Cohen encour-ages this group, over a series of weekly discussions, to talk out their racisim to the point where its limited repertoire of meanings becomes exhausted. At this point, some group members begin to reflect on and revise their beliefs, and to develop alternative ways of making sense of their personal and collective histories.

The cultural studies approach to intervention is based on a commitment to taking seriously and engaging with, rather than ignoring and bypassing, the popular cultural forms of adolescence. Young people, however socially or economically constrained, have, so Cohen insists, access to a wide range of cultural resources. For this reason, what is offered in education or in training needs to be seen by young men and women as 'really useful knowledge', knowledge which can be put to the service of their own agendas. In a further project (1989) Cohen introduces a group of 16-year-olds about to leave school to techniques of photomontage and the construction of photo stories. In using these techniques, often playfully, to explore themes in their shared experience, this group of young men and women begin to look beyond 'common sense' and to unearth new, shared meanings in their present and future lives.

Unfortunately, the subcultures of young people's peer groups still often go disregarded, undermining the potential usefulness of the research concerned. This has long been the case where what is in question is delinquent behaviour. How differently this topic may appear if adolescent perceptions are taken into account is clear from a study by Nicholas Emler and Stephen Reicher (1987), who look at the meaning of delinquency for a Scottish sample. Over 400 boys and girls aged between 12 and 15 and living in Dundee in the early 1980s were asked to report on their own involvement in law-breaking activities. A third of the sample were retested after eighteen months and, additionally, forty-nine 15-year-olds kept a diary about any delinquencies they engaged in. These writers do not, unfortunately, make any clear differentiation in their analysis between boys and girls, for whom the meaning of delinquency is surely unlikely to be identical. But what emerges from their study is the essentially collective nature of delinquent acts. As against the traditional image of the young law-breaker as a social isolate acting alone and in secret, the acts of vandalism, theft and aggression reported by these young people are typically well publicized and committed in company. Of paramount importance to those involved is their reputation in the peer group.

> The point of being delinquent was to be seen being so, and to have one's toughness observed by one's peers; without an audience and the attendant prospect of wider social visibility much of the point would have been lost.
>
> (Emler and Reicher 1987: 87)

The perspective on delinquency offered in Emler and Reicher's study contrasts in a number of ways with the traditional view. Not only have delinquents typically been defined in terms of individual rather than social processes; they have also nearly always been pathologized. And as several recent writers have remarked, youth itself has often been characterized in this way. Discussing contemporary approaches to youth unemployment, Mungham suggests that in much research the long-existing perception of adolescence as problematic has become heightened into a sense of moral panic. Workless young people, as 'the nation's rotting seed corn', are seen as carriers of potential disorder and subversion. Yet in reality, 'The young remain as they have always been in contemporary Britain: a battleground for moralists and soothsayers, but having, for themselves, precious little power and leverage on the social system' (1982:40).

Even where peer group research avoids clearly pathologizing assumptions, it is, apparently, often premissed on a deficiency model. Commenting on work concerned with the Youth Opportunities Programme, Williamson (1982) argues that trainees are typically viewed as 'a lumpen, uneducated, unmotivated, undisciplined and culturally inadequate class'. To be an unemployed teenager is to be seen as socially deficient, occupationally naïve and culturally inept. This argument is taken further in a study by Paul Atkinson and colleagues (1982), who analyze social and life skills courses as one form of compensatory education. By definition, these writers argue, such courses addressed to young people must define them as culturally deprived. In stigmatizing their dress or demeanour, their accent or their dialect, training in social and life skills altogether neglects the rich stock of cultural resources in any youth peer group.

If there is one sphere in which such perspectives on the young have been particularly dominant, it is probably that traditional topic in peer group research – conformity. As Nick Hopkins argues in a thoughtful analysis (1989), the conventional understanding of peer group conformity is embedded in an essentially individualistic model of adolescence itself. Adolescents are seen as susceptible to influence from their peers by virtue of their failure to develop an adequate sense of self. The group enters the scene as an 'unhealthy' source of pressure on those who are already developmentally inadequate. In much health education research, as Hopkins shows, these assumptions have led to a view of teenage drinking as the outcome, in vulnerable individuals, of yielding to peer group pressures which distort their capacity for rational judgement. Yet so far from being normless and anomic units, to be buffeted about by any passing breeze, young men and women are fundamentally members of groups, each with its own specific culture, its own definition of what constitutes appropriate behaviour. Their drinking, essentially a group activity, possesses ideological coherence; it has its own, qualitatively distinct meaning as a social practice.

Given that adolescent drinking takes its significance from the subculture of a particular teenage group, it cannot, as Hopkins insists, be globally defined. Drinking practices among young people can be understood only by reference to the very specific, very differentiated group contexts in which they take place. By drawing on the work of Willis, on the one hand, and that of Dorn (1983) on the other, Hopkins sketches two qualitatively distinctive worlds, in which drinking and getting drunk have quite different meanings for young men and women. In these two worlds gender and class, as well as the material environment and the available ideological resources, affect the youth cultures that come to be developed. For 'the lads' in Willis's study drinking derives its significance from the social world of the traditional working-men's club. The forms it takes, and the meanings it has for the young men involved, fit within a 'rough, tough, aggressive masculinity'. This drinking culture is very different from that of a girls' group studied by Dorn, in a working-class area of London during the late 1970s. Despite locally high youth unemployment, an expanding service sector, as Dorn describes, offers girls a relative, if temporary, economic equality with boys. One group of young women working in this sector has developed a culture which stresses their independence, as wage earners on a par with young men. Their drinking practices, as an integral part of this culture, are different from those of other girls' groups observed by Dorn. Not only is their presence in bars not dependent on boyfriends; they are also full participants, in mixed groups, in the buying of rounds. Nor does getting drunk leave them vulnerable to sexist moral censure.

As psychology at large begins to acknowledge the shaping of human experience and behaviour by socio-cultural forms, so research on the peer group is likely to become transformed. Studies of young people's friendship groupings which ignore the significance of cultural and subcultural factors will, perhaps, become a thing of the past. For it is clear that the practices and experience of young men and women in their own social groups cannot ultimately be divorced from the wider material and socio-cultural contexts of which they form part.

NOTE

1 Islay was one of the teachers with whom we worked.

REFERENCES

Atkinson, P., Rees, T. L., Shone, D. and Williamson, H. (1982) 'Social and lifeskills: the latest case of compensatory education', in T. L. Rees and P. Atkinson (eds) *Youth Unemployment and State Intervention*, London: Routledge.

Billig, M. and Cochrane, R. (1987) 'Adolescents and politics', in H. McGurk (ed.) *What Next?*, London: ESRC.

Cohen, P. (1988) 'The perversions of inheritance', in P. Cohen and H. S. Bains (eds) *Multi-Racist Britain*, Basingstoke and London: Macmillan.

Cohen, P. (1989) *Really Useful Knowledge: Photography and Cultural Studies in the Transition from School*, London: Trentham Books.

Cowie, H. and Rudduck, J. (1990) 'Learning from one another: the challenge', in H. C. Foot, M. J. Morgan and R. H. Shute (eds) *Children Helping Children*, London: John Wiley & Sons.

Doise, W. and Mugny, G. (1984) *The Social Development of the Intellect*, London and New York: Pergamon.

Dorn, N. (1983) *Alcohol, Youth and the State*, London: Croom Helm.

Emler, N. and Reicher, S. D. (1987) 'Adolescent delinquency', in H. McGurk (ed.) *What Next?*, London: ESRC.

Fuller, M. (1984) 'Black girls in a London comprehensive', in M. Hammersley and P. Woods (eds) *Life in School*, Milton Keynes: Open University Press.

Griffin, C. (1985) *Typical Girls? Young Women from School to the Job Market*, London and Boston: Routledge & Kegan Paul.

Griffin, C. (1987) 'Broken transitions: from school to the scrap heap', in P. Allatt, T. Keil, A. Bryman and B. Blytheway (eds) *Women and the Life Cycle: Transitions and Turning Points*, London: Macmillan.

Hopkins, N. (1989) ' "Peer group pressure": questioning the assumptions', Conference paper, British Psychological Society, Strathclyde.

Milner, D. (1973) *Children and Race*, London: Ward Lock.

——(1983) *Children and Race: Ten Years On*, London: Ward Lock International.

Mungham, G. (1982) 'Workless youth as a moral panic', in T. L. Rees and P. Atkinson (eds) *Youth Unemployment and State Intervention*, London: Routledge.

Salmon, P. and Claire, H. (1984) *Classroom Collaboration*, London: Routledge & Kegan Paul.

Sharpe, S. (1976) *Just Like a Girl: How Girls Learn to be Women*, Harmondsworth: Penguin.

Slavin, R. (1987) 'Developmental and motivational perspectives on co-operative learning: a reconciliation', *Child Development* 58: 1161-7.

Smith, P. K. (1989) 'The silent nightmare: bullying and victimisation in school peer groups', Conference paper, British Psychological Society, London.

Troyna, B. (1979) 'Race and streaming: a case study', *Educational Review* 30: 59-65.

Wallace, C. (1988) 'Between the family and the state: young people in transition', in M. White (ed.) (1988) *The Social World of the Young Unemployed*, London: Policy Studies Institute.

White, M. (ed.) (1988) *The Social World of the Young Unemployed*, London: Policy Studies Institute.

Williamson, H. (1982) 'Client responses to the Youth Opportunities Programme', in T. L. Rees and P. Atkinson (eds) *Youth Unemployment and State Intervention*, London: Routledge.

Willis, P. (1977) *Learning to Labour*, London: Saxon House.

Chapter 6

Juvenile delinquency

David P. Farrington

DEFINITION AND SCOPE

Juvenile delinquency covers a multitude of sins. As defined by English criminal law, it includes acts as diverse as theft, burglary, robbery, violence, vandalism, fraud, drug use and various kinds of heterosexual and homosexual acts. The focus in this chapter is on delinquency in England (and Wales), with some reference to the United States, since most research is American. At the time of writing (January 1991), the age boundaries for juvenile delinquency in English law were between 10 and 16 inclusive, but the current Criminal Justice Bill proposes to raise the upper age limit to 17. In most states of the United States, the upper age limit is 17, while the lower age limit can be as low as 7. Of course, there are no sharp cut-off points for the occurrence of behaviour, and acts such as stealing and vandalism can be committed before age 7.

There are many problems in using legal definitions of delinquency. For example, the boundary between what is legal and what is illegal may be poorly defined and subjective, as when school bullying gradually escalates into criminal violence. Legal categories may be so wide that they include acts which are behaviourally quite different, as when robbery ranges from armed bank hold-ups carried out by gangs of masked men, to thefts of small amounts of money perpetrated by one schoolchild on another. Legal definitions rely on the concept of intent, which is difficult to measure reliably and validly, rather than the behavioural criteria preferred by social scientists. Also, legal definitions change over time. However, their main advantage is that, because they have been adopted by most delinquency researchers, their use makes it possible to compare and summarize results obtained in different projects.

Within the scope of a single chapter, it is obviously impossible to review everything that is known about juvenile delinquency. (For more detailed reviews, see Rutter and Giller 1983; Wilson and Herrnstein 1985.) I will be very selective in focusing on some of the more important and replicable findings obtained in some of the more methodologically adequate studies. I will refer especially to knowledge gained in the Cambridge Study in Delinquent Development, a prospective longitudinal survey of over 400 London males from age 8 to age 32 (Farrington and West 1990). However, similar results have been obtained in similar studies elsewhere in England (e.g. Kolvin *et al.* 1988), in the United States (e.g. McCord, 1979; Robins 1979), in the Scandinavian countries (e.g. Pulkkinen 1988; Wikstrom 1987), and in New Zealand (e.g. Moffitt and Silva 1988a). Most research is on males.

METHODS OF MEASUREMENT

Delinquency is commonly measured using either official records of arrests or convictions or self-reports of offending. Other measures are less satisfactory. For example, victims can be asked to report on offenders (Hindelang 1981). However, such reports can only be made for offences where there was some personal contact between the offender and victim (e.g. rape), and victims' assessments (e.g. about the age of the offender) may be inaccurate. Also, victim reports provide information about the total number of offences, not about the total number of different offenders who committed them.

The main problem with official records of offending is that the vast majority of delinquent acts are undetected. This would not be so important if offenders who were officially recorded were a random sample of all offenders, but unfortunately there are likely to be some biases in official processing. Official records reflect the behaviour of police and courts as well as that of delinquents, and it may be hard to disentangle these different elements. Also, records are kept for the benefit of agency personnel rather than researchers, and they may not include key information that is needed (e.g. the date on which the offence was committed).

The most important alternative method of measuring delinquency is to use a self-report survey, in which juveniles are asked to say whether they have committed certain acts during a specified period such as the last year. The main problem with self-report surveys is that juveniles may conceal or exaggerate their delinquencies or fail to remember them. More trivial acts (such as stealing small amounts of money from home) tend to be over-represented in such surveys. Also, the most delinquent juveniles may be missing from the sample interviewed, because they are in the most transient living arrangements, incarcerated, the most difficult to find, the most unco-operative, or the most likely to be missing from school.

The advantages and disadvantages of official records and self-reports are to some extent complementary. In general, official records include the worst offenders and the worst offences, while self-reports include more of the normal range of delinquent activity. Self-reports have the advantage of including undetected offences, but the disadvantages of concealment and forgetting. The key issue is whether the same results are obtained with both methods. For example, if official records and self-reports both show that more boys than girls commit offences, it is likely that gender is related to delinquent behaviour (rather than to any biases in measurement).

Incidence of delinquency

In England and Wales, the number of persons found guilty in court or officially cautioned by the police for indictable (more serious) offences constitutes the major measure of official juvenile offending. In 1989, the most recent year with available figures, about 23,900 male and 2,500 female juveniles were found guilty in court, while 57,800 male and 15,000 female juveniles were cautioned (Home Office 1990: Table 5.22).

Unfortunately, the usefulness of the Home Office figures as an index of juvenile offending has declined dramatically since 1985. In a chapter quoting 1984 Criminal Statistics, Farrington (1987a: 39) was still able to say that 'most arrests lead to an officially recorded conviction or caution', but this is no longer true. Since 1985, police forces have increasingly begun to use informal (unrecorded) warnings and to take no further action with apprehended juveniles whom they believe to be guilty (see e.g. Barclay 1990), thereby eliminating them from the official records. The gap between the number of apprehended juvenile delinquents and the number officially recorded gets wider every year, making the official figures since 1985 useless as an indication of trends in juvenile offending.

Other changes since 1985 have also tended to reduce the number of recorded juvenile offenders. The introduction in 1986 of the

Police and Criminal Evidence Act 1984, which provided increased safeguards for accused persons, caused a marked decrease in the number of detected offenders (see e.g. Irving and MacKenzie 1989). The introduction in 1986 of the Crown Prosecution Service, which transferred responsibility for the prosecution of offenders from the police to lawyers, caused a decrease in the number of persons prosecuted. Most recently, the Criminal Justice Act 1988 downgraded the offence of unauthorized taking of a motor vehicle from the indictable to the summary category, thereby eliminating about 25,000 (mostly young) offenders from the official crime statistics.

These changes caused the number of 10- to 13-year-old males found guilty or cautioned to decrease by 40 per cent between 1985 and 1989, from 32.3 to 19.4 per 1,000 population (Home Office 1990: Table 5.22). The corresponding decrease for 14- to 16-year-old males was 31 per cent (from 81.3 to 56.1). Females decreased even more; 60 per cent for 10 to 13-year-olds (from 10.5 to 4.2 per 1,000 population) and 36 per cent for 14- to 16-year-olds (from 20.2 to 13.0). These are remarkable decreases in official delinquency during a four-year time period. In contrast, the number of recorded crimes in England and Wales did not decrease between 1985 and 1989. On the contrary, they increased slightly (by 6 per cent, from 72.6 to 76.8 per 1,000 population; Home Office 1990: Table 2.2). However, recorded juvenile offending became less important as a fraction of all offending; 30 per cent of all recorded offenders were juveniles in 1985, but only about 20 per cent in 1989.

In order to monitor trends in juvenile offending, it is a pity that the Home Office does not record arrests, as is the custom in the United States. American juvenile arrest rates for index (more serious) offences peaked in 1974 (at 25.7 males and 6.0 females arrested per 1,000 population) and have since declined by about 20–25 per cent (to 19.1 males and 4.8 females per 1,000 in 1989; Federal Bureau of Investigation 1990: 269). During the same time period, recorded index crimes in the United States increased by 17 per cent (from 48.5 per 1,000 population in 1974 to 56.6 in 1988; Federal Bureau of Investigation 1975; 1989).

Self-reports of delinquency reveal many more offences, but not so many more offenders, than official records. In the Cambridge Study, the 400 males admitted a total of 342 burglaries between ages 15 and 18, but only thirty-five led to convictions (Farrington 1983a). Similarly, they admitted 423 unauthorized takings of vehicles, but again only thirty-five led to convictions. Bearing in mind the fact that the probability of detection and conviction was greater for burglary and unauthorized taking than for most offences, it seems likely that the official records of convictions underestimate the true number of offences committed by a factor of at least ten. In the case of some offences, such as shoplifting (Buckle and Farrington 1984), the underestimation is probably by a factor of at least a hundred.

The discrepancy between official records and self-reports in identifying offenders in the Cambridge Study was much less. For example, between ages 15 and 18, 11 per cent admitted burglary and 7 per cent were convicted of burglary (including 5 per cent admitting and convicted). Similarly, 15 per cent admitted unauthorized taking and 6 per cent were convicted of this offence (including 5 per cent admitting and convicted). Hence, official records and self-reports agreed quite well in estimating the prevalence of serious offending.

There was more discrepancy between the two measures in estimating the prevalence of less serious offences. For example, 39 per cent admitted shoplifting between ages 10 and 14, and 16 per cent between ages 15 and 18, but the corresponding proportions convicted of shoplifting were 3 per cent and 2 per cent respectively (Farrington 1989; this was before the widespread use of police cautioning in London). As many as 89 per cent of the boys admitted at least one offence between ages 10 and 14, and 67 per cent between ages 15 and 18; but the corresponding proportions convicted were 11 per cent and 20 per cent respectively. Other English self-report studies also indicate that the majority of boys (Willcock 1974; Belson 1976) and even girls (Campbell 1981) have committed at least one minor delinquency, although only a small minority have committed more serious acts such as burglary.

Versatility and continuity in delinquency

While the acts included under the heading of delinquency are heterogeneous, it nevertheless makes sense to investigate the characteristics of delinquents. This is because juvenile delinquents are predominantly versatile rather than specialized (e.g. Klein 1984; Farrington *et al.* 1988). In other words, people who commit one type of offence have a significant tendency also to commit other types. For example, Farrington (1991a) found that forty-three out of fifty convicted violent offenders in the Cambridge Study also had convictions for non-violent offences.

In addition, there is considerable continuity between juvenile and adult offending. In the Cambridge Study, nearly three-quarters of those convicted as juveniles (age 10–16) were reconvicted between ages 17 and 24, and nearly half of the juvenile offenders were reconvicted between ages 25 and 32 (Farrington and West 1990). The males first convicted at the earliest ages tended to become the most persistent offenders, in committing large numbers of offences at high rates over long time periods. Furthermore, this continuity over time did not merely reflect continuity in police reaction to crime. Farrington (1989) showed that, for ten specified offences, the significant continuity between offending in one age range and offending in a later age range held for both self-reports and official convictions. The overlap between juvenile delinquency and adult crime means that research on adults often has valid implications for juveniles.

Delinquency and anti-social behaviour

Just as offenders are versatile in their types of offending, they are also versatile in their anti-social behaviour generally. Table 6.1 shows some of the predictors and correlates of official and self-reported delinquency in the Cambridge Study. The eighty-five official juvenile delinquents (20.7 per cent of the sample) were those who were found guilty in court for offences normally recorded in the Criminal Record Office and committed between ages 10 and 16 inclusive. The majority of these offences were of theft, burglary or taking vehicles. The eighty self-reported delinquents (19.6 per cent of those interviewed) were those who admitted the greatest number of different acts (at least twenty-one) out of thirty-eight enquired about at ages 14 and 16 (West and Farrington 1973: 151–5). Because the percentages of convicted and self-reported delinquents are almost identical, all the percentages in Table 6.1 are directly comparable.

Each predictor or correlate was dichotomized into the 'worst' quarter versus the remainder. For example, the ninety-two boys who got into trouble most (according to peers and teachers at age 8–10) were contrasted with the remaining 319. Table 6.1a shows that nearly half (45 per cent) of troublesome boys were convicted as juveniles (in comparison with 14 per cent of the remaining 319; chi-squared = 39.4, 1 d.f., p ‹ .001; significance level indicated by

Table 6.1 Relationships with official and self-reported delinquency

Variable at age/source (N)	% convicted† (20.7)		% self-reported† (19.6)	
(a) Child problem behaviour				
Troublesome 8–10 TP(92)	44.6	(5.0)***	34.1	(2.8)***
Dishonest 10 P(88)	37.5	(3.8)***	30.7	(2.5)**
Lies frequently 12–14 MT (122)	41.0	(5.0)***	36.1	(3.9)***
Aggressive 12–14 T(134)	35.1	(3.4)***	33.1	(3.3)***
Bullies 14 B(71)	38.0	(3.0)***	29.6	(2.0)*
(b) Teenage anti-social behaviour				
Heavy drinker 18 B(78)	33.3	(2.2)**	34.6	(2.8)***
Heavy smoker 18 B(104)	31.7	(2.2)**	30.8	(2.4)**
Drug user 18 B(122)	33.6	(2.7)***	31.1	(2.6)***
Heavy gambler 18 B(87)	34.5	(2.5)**	32.2	(2.4)**
High sexual activity 18 B (164)	36.0	(4.6)***	32.3	(4.1)***
(c) Physical measures				
Small 8–10 S(73)	31.5	(2.1)*	20.8	(1.1)
Small 18 S(59)	32.2	(2.0)*	20.3	(1.0)
Tattooed 18 B(35)	54.3	(5.4)***	48.6	(4.6)***
(d) Impulsivity				
Lacks conc./restless 8–10 T(82)	32.9	(2.3)**	28.4	(1.9)*
High daring 8–10 MP(121)	38.8	(4.2)**	34.7	(3.5)***
Lacks conc./restless 12–14 T(107)	42.1	(4.8)***	36.4	(3.7)***
High daring 12–14 T(53)	49.1	(4.9)***	39.6	(3.3)***
High impulsivity 18 B(105)	29.5	(1.9)*	31.4	(2.5)***
(e) School problems				
Low intelligence 8–10 S(103)	32.0	(2.3)**	28.4	(2.0)*
Low attainment 11 R(90)	33.3	(2.6)***	31.1	(2.4)**
High delinquency school 11 R(77)	36.4	(2.6)***	20.8	(1.1)
Frequently truants 12–14 T(73)	49.3	(5.7)***	37.0	(3.1)***
Left school 15 B(248)	28.6	(4.2)***	28.2	(5.9)***
No exams taken by 18 B(197)	34.0	(5.6)***	29.4	(3.8)***
(f) Family influences				
Poor parental child-rearing 8 M(96)	33.3	(2.8)***	28.4	(1.9)*
Poor parental supervision 8 M(74)	31.1	(2.2)**	37.0	(3.2)***
Low parent int. in education 8 M(63)	31.7	(2.2)*	33.3	(2.4)**
Separated from parents 10 M(90)	33.3	(2.4)**	30.0	(2.2)**
Poor relation with parents 18 B(86)	37.2	(2.9)***	31.4	(2.3)**
(g) Anti-social influences				
Convicted parent 10 R(104)	37.5	(3.4)***	33.7	(2.9)***
Delinquent sibling 10 R(46)	41.3	(3.2)***	37.0	(2.8)**
Sibling behaviour problems 8 M(138)	29.0	(2.7)***	26.3	(2.1)**
Delinquent friends 14 B(101)	42.6	(4.8)***	54.5	(13.9)***
(h) Socio-economic factors				
Low family income 8 M(93)	34.4	(2.6)***	28.0	(1.9)*
Low SES family 8–10 M(79)	26.6	(1.5)	30.4	(2.1)*
Poor housing 8–10 I(151)	26.5	(1.7)*	26.7	(2.0)**
Large family size 10 MR(99)	33.3	(2.5)***	27.3	(1.8)*
Unstable job record 18 B(92)	40.2	(3.7)***	33.7	(2.8)***
Unskilled manual job 18 B(62)	45.2	(4.1)***	35.5	(2.8)**

†Odds ratio in parentheses; * p < .05; ** p < .01; *** p < .001
Data Source: B = Boy; I = Interviewer; M = Mother; P = Peer; R = Records; S = Test; T = Teacher.
Notes: conc. = concentration, int. = interest, SES = socio-economic status

asterisks). The odds ratio for this relationship was 5.0, showing that the odds of conviction (the ratio of convicted to unconvicted boys) were five times as great for troublesome boys as for the remainder. Similarly, one-third (34 per cent) of those who were troublesome at age 8–10 became juvenile self-reported delinquents at age 14–16 (in comparison with 15 per cent of the remainder; odds ratio = 2.8, chi-squared = 14.5, p < .001). In general, factors that were significantly related to convictions tended also to be significantly related to self-reported delinquency.

West and Farrington (1977) argued that delinquency (which is dominated by crimes of dishonesty) is only one element of a larger syndrome of anti-social behaviour which arises in childhood and usually persists into adulthood. Hence, valid implications about juvenile delinquency can often be drawn from research on child anti-social behaviour or conduct disorder. Table 6.1a shows that delinquents tended to be troublesome and dishonest in their primary schools, tended to be aggressive and frequent liars at age 12–14, and tended to be bullies at age 14. By age 18, delinquents tended to be anti-social in a wide variety of respects, including heavy drinking, heavy smoking, using prohibited drugs and heavy gambling. In addition, they tended to be sexually promiscuous, often beginning sexual intercourse under age 15, having several sexual partners by age 18, and usually having unprotected intercourse.

These results are entirely consistent with those obtained in numerous other studies. For example, in a St Louis survey of black males, Robins and Ratcliff (1980) found that juvenile delinquency tended to be associated with truancy, precocious sex, drinking and drug use. In Philadelphia, Spivack et al. (1986) discovered that troublesome behaviour in kindergarten (age 3–4) predicted later police contacts; and Ensminger et al. (1983) in Chicago showed that teachers' ratings of aggressiveness in the first grade (age 6) predicted self-reported offending at age 15.

NATURAL HISTORY OF OFFENDING

The prevalence of offending increases to a peak in the teenage years and then decreases in the twenties. This pattern is seen both cross-sectionally and longitudinally (Farrington 1986a). The peak age of official offending for English males was 15 until 1987, but it increased to 18 in 1988 as a result of a decrease in detected juvenile shoplifting offenders (Barclay 1990). The peak age for females was 14 until 1985 but then increased to 15. In England and Wales in 1989, the rate of findings of guilt or cautions of males for indictable offences increased from seven per 1,000 at age 10, to sixty-four at age 15, and a peak of seventy at age 18; then decreased to fifty-six at age 20, and twenty-eight at age 25–29 (Home Office 1990: Table 5.23). The corresponding figures for females were one per 1,000 at age 10, a peak of fifteen at age 15, eleven at age 18, nine at age 20, and five at age 25–29.

These figures do not exactly show the prevalence of offending (the number of different offenders), since a minority of offenders are convicted or cautioned more than once a year. However, prevalence varies with age in much the same way as these rates vary. The cumulative or lifetime prevalence of convictions is much greater than most people realize. On the basis of 1977 statistics, Farrington (1981) estimated that 44 per cent of English males and 15 per cent of females would be convicted of standard list (non-traffic) offences during their lifetimes. Up to age 16, the corresponding figures were 12 per cent of males and 2 per cent of females. These estimates were later verified by a longitudinal follow-up of a 1953 birth cohort in official records (Home Office Statistical Bulletin 1985). During the 1980s, conviction rates have been falling, as mentioned earlier.

In the Cambridge Study, the rate of convictions increased to a peak at age 17 and then declined (Farrington 1990a). It was seventeen per 1,000 males at age 10, sixty-eight at age 13, 168 at age 17, 101 at age 22, and forty-two at age 30. The median age for most types of offences (burglary, robbery, theft of and from vehicles, shoplifting) was 17, while it was 20 for violence and 21 for fraud. While the cumulative prevalence of convictions was high (37 per cent up to age 32), it was nevertheless true that only 5 per cent of the sample accounted for nearly half of all the convictions (Farrington and West 1990). In the Philadelphia cohort study of Wolfgang et al. (1987), the arrest rate increased to a peak at age 16 and then declined, and there was a similar concentration of offending in a small proportion of the sample.

Self-report studies also show that the most common types of offending decline from the teens to the twenties. In the Cambridge Study, the prevalence of burglary, shoplifting, theft of and from vehicles, theft from slot machines and vandalism all decreased from the teens to the twenties, but the same decreases were not seen for theft from work, assault, drug abuse and fraud (Farrington 1989). For example, burglary (since the last interview) was admitted by 13 per cent at age 14, 11 per cent at age 18, 5 per cent at age 21, and 2 per cent at both ages 25 and 32. In their American National Youth Survey, Elliott *et al.* (1989) found that self-reports of the prevalence of offending increased from age 11–13 to a peak at 15–17 and then decreased by 19–21.

Many theories have been proposed to explain why offending peaks in the teenage years (see Farrington 1986a). For example, offending has been linked to testosterone levels in males, which increase during adolescence and early adulthood and decrease thereafter, and to changes in physical abilities or opportunities for crime. The most popular explanation focuses on social influence. From birth, children are under the influence of their parents, who generally discourage offending. However, during their teenage years, juveniles gradually break away from the control of their parents and become influenced by their peers, who may encourage offending in many cases. After age 20, offending declines again as peer influence gives way to a new set of family influences hostile to offending, originating in spouses and cohabitees.

Gender

In general, boys commit delinquent acts more frequently and seriously than girls, as extensive literature reviews show (e.g. Hindelang *et al.* 1981; Visher and Roth 1986). In England and Wales in 1989, the male:female ratio for findings of guilt or cautions for indictable offences was 4.6:1 at age 10–13 and 4.3:1 at age 14–16 (Home Office 1990: Table 5.22). However, this ratio was much higher for serious offences such as burglary (about 17:1 at both ages).

Other surveys of official records yield similar results. In his national English longitudinal survey of over 5,000 children born in one week of 1946, Wadsworth (1979) reported that 12.9 per cent of males and 2.2 per cent of females were convicted or cautioned for indictable offences up to age 20, giving a gender ratio of 5.9:1 for prevalence. In the longitudinal follow-up in records of national samples born in 1953, 1958 and 1963, the percentages of males convicted of standard list (non-traffic) offences as juveniles was 13.4 per cent, 13.9 per cent and 12.2 per cent respectively (Home Office Statistical Bulletin 1985). The corresponding percentages of females were 1.9 per cent, 2.2 per cent and 2.3 per cent respectively, giving gender ratios of 7.1:1, 6.6:1 and 5.3:1. Ouston (1984), in her follow-up of over 2,300 London children born in 1959-60, found that 29 per cent of the boys and 6 per cent of the girls were convicted or cautioned for an offence up to age 17-18. The gender ratio for cumulative prevalence in this study was therefore 4.8:1.

Self-reported delinquency surveys generally yield much lower male:female ratios. For example, both Campbell (1981) and Riley and Shaw (1985) reported ratios of only 1.3:1 in English projects. However, most of the acts included in these surveys were relatively trivial. The gender ratio was higher for more serious acts such as burglary (15:1 in the largest survey reported by Campbell) and carrying a weapon intending to use it (about 3:1 in both surveys).

Numerous explanations of gender differences in delinquency have been proposed. For example, they may have a biological foundation. Maccoby and Jacklin (1974) pointed out that gender differences in aggressiveness are found very early in life, before any differential reinforcement of aggression in boys and girls. Furthermore, they argued that males were more aggressive than females in all human societies for which evidence was available, that similar gender differences in aggressiveness were found in sub-human primates as in humans, and that aggression was related to levels of sex hormones such as testosterone (which are much higher in males). It seems obvious that, because on average males are bigger and stronger than females, males will be better able to commit offences that require physical strength.

Not all offences are linked to aggression or physical strength, of course. Another possible explanation is that boys and girls are socialized differently by their parents. Generally, girls are supervised more closely, and girls stay at home more. Hence, if they behave in a socially disapproved fashion, their parents are more likely to notice this and react to it. Adults are generally more tolerant of incipient delinquency in boys than in girls, and they may encourage boys to be tough and take risks. On the theory that the strength of the conscience depends on the reinforcement of appropriate behaviour and the punishment of socially disapproved acts, it follows that girls will develop a stronger conscience and will be less likely to commit delinquent acts than boys.

The gender ratio can also be explained by reference to sex roles, social habits and opportunities. Boys are more likely than girls to spend time hanging around on the street at night, especially in groups, and therefore are more likely to commit acts such as burglary and violence, which may often arise in this social situation. Girls are more likely than boys to spend time shopping, and so it is not surprising that shoplifting is the most common female offence. Boys have more interest in cars and weapons and more knowledge about how to use them, and so are more likely to commit car thefts and robberies. Later on in life, women have more opportunity to commit minor frauds because they are more likely to be collecting welfare benefits, and men are more likely to have the opportunity to steal from employers.

Biological factors

Studies of twins and adopted children suggest that there is some kind of genetic influence on offending (for reviews see Wilson and Herrnstein 1985; Eysenck and Gudjonsson 1989). This is indicated by the greater concordance (similarity) of monozygotic (identical) than dizygotic (fraternal) twins in offending. It might be argued that identical twins behave more like each other because they are treated more similarly in their social environment, not because of their greater genetic similarity. Against this, however, identical twins reared apart are as similar in many respects (e.g. intelligence, personality, attitudes) as identical twins reared together (Bouchard *et al.* 1990). Also, the offending of adopted children is more similar to that of their biological parents than to that of their adoptive parents (e.g. Mednick *et al.* 1983; see also Cloninger *et al.* 1982), again suggesting some kind of genetic influence.

Numerous psycho-physiological and biochemical factors have also been linked to offending, through the key theoretical construct of arousal. Offenders have a low level of arousal according to their low alpha (brain) waves on the EEG, or according to autonomic nervous system indicators such as heart rate, blood pressure, or skin conductance, or they show low autonomic reactivity (e.g. Venables and Raine 1987). For example, adult offenders showed low adrenalin levels at age 13 (Magnusson 1988) and aggressive juveniles tended to have low adrenalin levels (Olweus 1987). All these researchers focus on impulsivity as a key intervening construct. The causal links between low autonomic arousal, consequent sensation-seeking, and offending are brought out explicitly in Mawson's (1987) theory of transient criminality.

Heart rate was measured in the Cambridge Study at age 18.

While a low heart rate correlated significantly with convictions for violence (Farrington, 1987b), it did not significantly relate to delinquency in general. Other physical measures taken in this research showed that relatively small boys at ages 8–10 and 18 were significantly more likely to be convicted as juveniles than others (Table 6.1c). This may reflect the influence of poor nutrition. However, height was not related to self-reported delinquency. In addition, being tattooed was highly related to offending in the Cambridge Study, with a very high odds ratio for both convictions (5.4) and self-reported delinquency (4.6). While the meaning of this result is not entirely clear, tattooing may reflect risk-taking, daring and excitement-seeking.

Numerous pre-natal and peri-natal factors also predict a child's anti-social behaviour, including pregnancy and birth complications (e.g. Szatmari et al. 1986), low birth weight (e.g. Breslau et al. 1988), and teenage parenting (e.g. Brooks-Gunn and Furstenberg, 1986). Also, stressful life events are related to anti-social behaviour (e.g. Novy and Donahue 1985; Werner 1989).

Personality and impulsivity

One of the best-known theories linking personality and offending was proposed by Eysenck (1977). He viewed offending as essentially rational behaviour, and assumed that a person's delinquent tendency varied inversely with the strength of the conscience, which was essentially a conditioned anxiety response that was built up in a process of classical conditioning. Eysenck concluded that delinquents tended to be those who had not built up strong consciences, because they were constitutionally poor at building up conditioned responses. He also linked conditionability to his dimensional theory of personality, predicting that those who were high on extraversion (E), neuroticism (N) and psychoticism (P) would tend to have the weakest consciences and hence that they were the most likely to be delinquents.

Farrington et al. (1982) reviewed studies relating Eysenck's personality dimensions to official and self-reported delinquency. They concluded that high N (but not E) was related to official offending, while high E (but not N) was related to self-reported offending. High P was related to both, but this could have been a tautological result, since many of the items on the P scale are connected with anti-social behaviour or were selected in the light of their ability to discriminate between prisoners and non-prisoners. In the Cambridge Study, those high on both E and N tended to be juvenile self-reported but not official delinquents. However, when individual items of the personality questionnaire were studied, it was clear that the significant relationships were caused by the items measuring impulsivity (e.g. doing things quickly without stopping to think). Hence, it was concluded that the major contribution of research inspired by the Eysenck theory was to identify the correlation between impulsivity and offending.

This link is also shown in Table 6.1d. In the Cambridge Study, official and self-reported delinquents tended to be lacking in concentration, restless and daring at school. Farrington *et al.* (1990) developed a combined measure of hyperactivity–impulsivity–attention deficit (HIA) at age 8–10 and showed that it significantly predicted juvenile convictions independently of conduct problems at age 8–10. Hence, it might be concluded that HIA is not merely another measure of anti-social tendency. Other studies have also concluded that hyperactivity and conduct disorder are different constructs (e.g. Blouin *et al.* 1989). Similar constructs to HIA, such as sensation-seeking, are also related to delinquency (e.g. White *et al.* 1985), and low self-control is the central construct of Gottfredson and Hirschi's (1990) theory.

Intelligence and cognitive factors

Loeber and Dishion (1983) and Loeber and Stouthamer-Loeber (1987) extensively reviewed the predictors of male delinquency. They concluded that poor parental child-management techniques, offending by parents and siblings, low intelligence and educational attainment, and separations from parents were all important predictors. Longitudinal (and indeed cross-sectional) surveys have consistently demonstrated that children with low intelligence are disproportionally likely to become delinquents.

In the Cambridge Study, about one-third (32 per cent) of the boys scoring 90 or less on a non-verbal intelligence test (Raven's Progressive Matrices) at age 8–10 were convicted as juveniles, twice as many as among the remainder (Table 6.1e). Low non-verbal intelligence was highly correlated with low verbal intelligence (vocabulary, word-comprehension, verbal reasoning) and with low school attainment, and all of these measures predicted juvenile convictions to much the same extent. In addition to their poor school performance, delinquents tended to be frequent truants, to leave school at the earliest possible age (which was then 15) and to take no school examinations. Low non-verbal intelligence was especially characteristic of the juvenile recidivists (who had an average IQ of 89) and those first convicted at the earliest ages (10–13). Furthermore, low intelligence and attainment predicted juvenile self-reported delinquency almost as well as juvenile convictions, suggesting that the link between low intelligence and delinquency was not caused by the less intelligent boys having a greater probability of being caught. Similar results have been obtained in other projects (e.g. Wilson and Herrnstein 1985).

The key explanatory factor underlying the link between intelligence and delinquency is probably the ability to manipulate abstract concepts. People who are poor at this tend to do badly in intelligence tests such as the Matrices and in school attainment, and they also tend to commit offences, mainly because of their poor ability to foresee the consequences of their offending and to appreciate the feelings of victims (i.e. their low empathy). Certain family backgrounds are less conducive than others to the development of abstract reasoning. For example, lower-class, poorer parents tend to live for the present and to have little thought for the future, and tend to talk in terms of the concrete rather than the abstract. A lack of concern for future consequences, which is a central feature of Wilson and Herrnstein's (1985) theory, is also linked to the concept of impulsivity.

Modern research is studying not just intelligence but also detailed patterns of cognitive and neuro-psychological deficit. For example, in a New Zealand longitudinal study of over 1,000 children from birth to age 15, Moffitt and Silva (1988b) found that self-reported delinquency was related to verbal, memory and visual-motor integration deficits, independently of low social class and family adversity. Neuro-psychological research might lead to important advances in knowledge about the link between brain functioning and delinquency. For example, the 'executive functions' of the brain, located in the frontal lobes, include sustaining attention and concentration, abstract reasoning and concept formation, anticipation and planning, self-monitoring of behaviour, and inhibition of inappropriate or impulsive behaviour (Moffitt 1990). Deficits in these executive functions are conducive to low measured intelligence and to delinquency.

School influences

It is clear that the prevalence of delinquency varies dramatically between different secondary schools, as Power *et al.* (1967) showed more than twenty years ago in London. However, what is far less clear is how much of this variation should be attributed to differences in school climates and practices, and how much to differences in the composition of the student body.

In the Cambridge Study, Farrington (1972) investigated the effects of secondary schools on offending by following boys from their primary schools to their secondary schools. The best primary school predictor of official delinquency in this study was the rating of troublesomeness at age 8–10 by peers and teachers. The secondary schools differed dramatically in their official delinquency rates, from one school with twenty-one court appearances per hundred boys per year to another where the corresponding figure was only 0.3. However, it was very noticeable that the most troublesome boys tended to go to the high delinquency-rate schools, while the least troublesome boys tended to go to the low delinquency-rate schools. Furthermore, it was clear that most of the variation between schools in their delinquency rates could be explained by differences in their intakes of troublesome boys. The secondary schools themselves had only a very small effect on the boys' offending.

Table 6.1e shows that the boys who went to high delinquency-rate secondary schools at age 11 tended to be convicted but not self-reported delinquents. One possible explanation of this unusual result is that the police were more likely to apprehend and prosecute boys from these schools than similarly badly behaved boys who went to low delinquency-rate schools, possibly because of different police policies in different areas.

The most famous study of school effects on offending was also carried out in London, by Rutter *et al.* (1979). They studied twelve comprehensive schools, and again found big differences in official delinquency rates between them. High delinquency rate schools tended to have high truancy rates, low ability pupils, and low social class parents. However, the differences between the schools in delinquency rates could not be entirely explained by differences in the social class and verbal reasoning scores of the pupils at intake (age 11). Therefore, they must have been caused by some aspect of the schools themselves or by other, unmeasured factors.

In trying to discover which aspects of schools might be encouraging or inhibiting offending, Rutter *et al.* (1979) developed a measure of 'school process' based on school structure, organization and functioning. This was related to school misbehaviour, academic achievement and truancy independently of intake factors. However, it was not significantly related to delinquency independently of intake factors. The main school factors that were related to delinquency were a high amount of punishment and a low amount of praise given by teachers in class. Unfortunately, it is difficult to know whether much punishment and little praise are causes or consequences of anti-social school behaviour, which in turn is probably linked to offending outside school.

Family influences

Loeber and Stouthamer-Loeber (1986) completed an exhaustive review of family factors as correlates and predictors of juvenile conduct problems and delinquency. They found that poor parental supervision or monitoring, erratic or harsh parental discipline, marital disharmony, parental rejection of the child, and low parental involvement with the child (as well as anti-social parents and large family size) were all important predictors.

In the Cambridge Study, West and Farrington (1973) found that harsh or erratic parental discipline, cruel, passive or neglecting parental attitude, poor supervision, and parental conflict, all measured at age 8, all predicted later juvenile convictions. Table 6.1f shows that poor parental child-rearing behaviour (a combination of discipline, attitude and conflict), poor parental supervision and low parental interest in education all predicted juvenile convictions and self-reported delinquency. Poor parental child-rearing behaviour was related to early rather than later offending (Farrington 1986b) and was not characteristic of those first convicted as adults (West and Farrington 1977).

Other studies also show the link between family factors and delinquency. In a Birmingham survey, Wilson (1980) concluded that the most important correlate of convictions, cautions and self-reported delinquency was lax parental supervision. In their national survey of juveniles aged 14–15 and their mothers, Riley and Shaw (1985) found that poor parental supervision was the most important correlate of self-reported delinquency for girls, and that it was the second most important for boys (after delinquent friends).

In agreement with the hypothesis that being physically abused as a child foreshadows later violent offending (Widom 1989), harsh parental discipline and attitude at age 8 significantly predicted later violent as opposed to non-violent offenders in the Cambridge Study (Farrington 1978). However, more recent research showed that it was equally predictive of violent and frequent offending (Farrington 1991a).

Broken homes and early separations also predict delinquency. Table 6.1f shows that, in the Cambridge Study, both permanent and temporary (more than one month) separations before age 10 predicted convictions and self-reported delinquency, provided that they were not caused by death or hospitalization, and similar results were obtained by Wadsworth (1979). However, homes broken at an early age were not unusually criminogenic.

Criminal, anti-social and alcoholic parents also tend to have delinquent sons, as Robins (1979) found. In the Cambridge Study, the concentration of offending in a small number of families was remarkable. West and Farrington (1977) discovered that less than 5 per cent of the families were responsible for about half the criminal convictions of all family members (fathers, mothers, sons and daughters). West and Farrington (1973) showed that having convicted mothers, fathers and brothers by a boy's tenth birthday significantly predicted his own later convictions. Furthermore, convicted parents and delinquent siblings predicted self-reported as well as official delinquency (Table 6.1g). Unlike most early precursors, convicted parents were related less to offending of early onset (age 10–13) than to later offending (Farrington 1986b). Also, convicted parents predicted which juvenile offenders went on to become adult criminals and which recidivists at age 19 continued offending (West and Farrington 1977).

These results are concordant with the psychological theory (e.g. Trasler 1962) that offending occurs when the normal social learning process, based on rewards and punishments from parents, is disrupted by erratic discipline, poor supervision, parental disharmony and unsuitable (anti-social or criminal) parental models. However, some part of the link between criminal parents and delinquent sons may reflect genetic influences.

Peer influences

The reviews by Zimring (1981) and Reiss (1988) show that delinquent acts tend to be committed in small groups (of two or three people, usually) rather than alone. In the Cambridge Study, most officially-recorded juvenile and young adult offences were committed with others, but the incidence of co-offending declined steadily with age from 10 onwards. Burglary, robbery and theft from vehicles were particularly likely to involve co-offenders, who tended to be similar in age and sex to the Study males and lived close to their homes and to the locations of the offences. The Study males were most likely to offend with brothers when they had brothers who were similar in age to them (Farrington and West 1990).

The major problem of interpretation is whether young people are more likely to commit offences while they are in groups than while they are alone, or whether the high prevalence of co-offending merely reflects the fact that, whenever young people go out, they tend to go out in groups. Do peers tend to encourage and facilitate offending, or is it just that most kinds of activities out of the home (both delinquent and non-delinquent) tend to be committed in groups? Another possibility is that the commission of offences encourages association with other delinquents, perhaps because 'birds of a feather flock together' or because of the stigmatizing and isolating effects of court appearances and institutionalization. It is surprisingly difficult to decide among these various possibilities, although most researchers argue that peer influence is an important factor. For example, the key construct in Sutherland and Cressey's (1974) theory is the number of persons in a child's social environment with norms and attitudes favouring delinquency.

There is clearly a close relationship between the delinquent activities of a young person and those of his friends. Both in the United States (Hirschi 1969) and in England (West and Farrington 1973), it has been found that a boy's reports of his own offending are significantly correlated with his reports of his friends' delinquency (Table 6.1g). In the American National Youth Survey of Elliott et al. (1985), having delinquent peers was the best independent predictor of self-reported offending in a multi-variate analysis. However, the major problem of interpretation is that, if delinquency is a group activity, delinquents will almost inevitably have delinquent friends, and this result does not necessarily show that delinquent friends cause delinquency. The very high odds ratio in Table 6.1g for the link between delinquent friends and self-reported delinquency suggests that both measures may reflect the same underlying construct.

Delinquent peers are likely to be most influential where they have high status within the peer group and are popular. However, studies both in the United States (Roff and Wirt 1984) and in England (West and Farrington 1973) show that delinquents are usually unpopular with their peers. It seems paradoxical for offending to be a group phenomenon facilitated by peer influence, and yet for offenders to be largely rejected by other adolescents (Parker and Asher 1987). However, it may be that offenders are popular in anti-social groups and unpopular in pro-social groups.

Socio-economic deprivation

Most delinquency theories assume that delinquents disproportionally come from lower-class social backgrounds, and aim to explain why this is so. For example, Cohen (1955) proposed that lower-class boys found it hard to succeed according to the middle-class standards of the school, partly because lower-class parents tended not to teach their children to delay immediate gratification in favour of long-term goals. Consequently, lower-class boys joined delinquent subcultures by whose standards they could succeed. Cloward and Ohlin (1960) argued that lower-class children could not achieve universal goals of status and material wealth by legitimate means and consequently had to resort to delinquency.

Generally, the social class or socio-economic status (SES) of a family has been measured primarily according to rankings by sociologists of the occupational prestige of the family breadwinner. Persons with professional or managerial jobs are ranked in the highest class, while those with unskilled manual jobs are ranked in the lowest. However, these occupational prestige scales may not correlate very highly with real differences between families in socio-economic circumstances. In general, the scales date from many years ago, when it was more common for the father to be the family breadwinner and for the mother to be a housewife. Because of this, it may be difficult to derive a realistic measure of socio-economic status for a family with a single parent or with two working parents (Mueller and Parcel 1981).

Over the years, many other measures of social class have become popular, including family income, educational levels of parents, type of housing, overcrowding in the house, possessions, dependence on welfare benefits, and family size. These may all reflect more meaningful differences between families than occupational prestige. Family size is highly correlated with other indices of socio-economic deprivation, although its relationship with delinquency may reflect child-rearing factors (e.g. less attention to each child) rather than socio-economic influences.

In many criminological research projects, delinquents and non-delinquents are matched on SES, or SES is controlled first in regression analyses. This reflects a widespread belief in the importance of SES, but of course it often prevents the correctness of this belief from being tested. Unfortunately, as Thornberry and Farnworth (1982) pointed out, the voluminous literature on the relationship between SES and offending is characterized by inconsistencies and contradictions, and some reviewers (e.g. Hindelang et al. 1981) have concluded that there is no relationship between SES and either self-reported or official delinquency.

Beginning with the pioneering self-report research of Short and Nye (1957), it was common in the United States to argue that low social class was related to official offending but not to self-reported offending, and hence that the official processing of offenders was biased against lower-class youth. However, English studies have reported more consistent links between low social class and delinquency. In the English national survey, Douglas et al. (1966) showed that the prevalence of official juvenile delinquency in males varies considerably according to the occupational prestige and educational background of their parents, from 3 per cent in the highest category to 19 per cent in the lowest. Also, Wadsworth (1979) reported that offending increased significantly with increasing family size in this survey. Similar results were reported by Kolvin et al. (1988) in their follow-up of Newcastle children from birth to age 33, and by Ouston (1984) in her longitudinal survey in London.

Numerous indicators of SES were measured in the Cambridge Study, both for the man's family of origin and for the man himself as an adult, including occupational prestige, family income, housing, employment instability and family size. Most of the measures of occupational prestige (based on the Registrar General's scale) were not significantly related to delinquency. However, in a reversal of the American results, low SES of the family when the boy was aged 8–10 significantly predicted his later self-reported but not official delinquency. More consistently, low family income, poor housing and large family size predicted official and self-reported delinquency (Table 6.1h).

Socio-economic deprivation of parents is usually related to offending by sons. However, when the sons grow up, their own socio-economic deprivation can be related to their own offending. In the Cambridge Study, official and self-reported delinquents tended to have unskilled manual jobs and an unstable job record at age 18. Also, between ages 15 and 18, the boys were convicted at a higher rate when they were unemployed than when they were employed (Farrington *et al.* 1986b), suggesting that unemployment in some way causes crime, and conversely that employment may lead to desistance from offending.

Ethnic origin

Most research on ethnic origin has compared blacks (Afro-Caribbeans) and whites. In London, blacks are far more likely to be arrested than whites, especially for violent offences and particularly for robbery. For example, of those arrested for robbery in 1987, 41 per cent were white, 54 per cent were black, 2 per cent were Asian and 3 per cent were other or not known (Home Office Statistical Bulletin 1989). These figures can be compared with the estimated resident population of London aged 10 or over, which was 85 per cent white, 5 per cent black, 5 per cent Asian, and 5 per cent other or not known. The comparison of these figures gives a black:white ratio for robbery of 22:1. This ratio is increasing over time, since it was only 11:1 in 1977. The comparable American ratio for index arrests for robbery was 10:1 in 1988, and this has stayed constant since 1976 (Federal Bureau of Investigation 1990). The American black:white ratio in 1988 for all violent arrests was 5:1, and for all index arrests was 3:1.

It might be argued that police arrests reflect bias against blacks. However, the black:white ratio based on victim reports of the offender's appearance seems, if anything, even higher. For example, in 1985 (the last year for which this information was compiled), London robbery victims said that their offender(s) were white in 19 per cent of cases, non-white in 56 per cent, mixed in 7 per cent and not known in the remaining 18 per cent (Home Office Statistical Bulletin 1989). Making the plausible assumption that very few of the non-whites were not black, the black:white ratio corresponding to these figures is about 50:1. The discrepancy between the 50:1 ratio from victims and the 22:1 ratio from arrests may mean that the average black robber commits twice as many robberies as the average white robber, or that white robbers are twice as likely to be arrested as black robbers. From reports in the United States by victims of personal crimes (rape, robbery, assault, and theft from a person), Hindelang (1981) calculated that eighty-five of these crimes per year were committed by every hundred black males aged 18–20. The comparable figure for white males of this age was 15, yielding a black:white ratio of 5:1, very similar to the figure for all violent arrests.

Longitudinal surveys yield lower black:white ratios, at least for prevalence. This is because prevalence ratios are constrained by the maximum of 100 per cent, whereas ratios like those above, based on numbers of offences, have no such constraint. In the first Philadelphia cohort study of Wolfgang et al. (1972), 50 per cent of black males and 29 per cent of white males had police records for non-traffic offences by the eighteenth birthday. The comparable figures for the second cohort were 42 per cent and 23 per cent (Tracy et al., 1985). Up to age 30, 69 per cent of black males and 38 per cent of white males in the first cohort had police records for non-traffic offences (Wolfgang et al. 1987). Clearly, if 38 per cent of whites are arrested, the maximum possible black:white ratio is 100/38 or 2.6:1. Extensive reviews of the prevalence of official offending by Gordon (1976), Hindelang et al. (1981) and Visher and Roth (1986) show consistent black:white differences averaging about 3:1 over the majority of offences.

The most reliable English survey figures on ethnicity and crime are probably those obtained in Ouston's (1984) follow-up of over 2,000 Inner London children. Ouston found that 39 per cent of black males were convicted or cautioned as juveniles, in comparison with 28 per cent of white males. There are no comparable figures for Asians (originating in India, Pakistan or Bangladesh). However, studies elsewhere in England suggest that they have a lower crime rate than whites. For example, Mawby et al. (1979) calculated the annual rate of convictions and cautions in Bradford per hundred juveniles as 3.2 for Asians and 6.3 for others (mostly whites).

Differences between blacks and whites in self-reported offending are much less than differences in official offending, as Williams and Gold (1972) pointed out in their national American survey. Probably the most extensive self-reported offending figures have been obtained in the 'Monitoring the Future' project. In this, nationally representative samples of American high school students are interviewed each year, and usually about 400 of the 3,000 respondents were black. Over the ten years 1976–85, black:white prevalence ratios are close to 1:1 for most offences (Jamieson and Flanagan 1987). Even for robbery using a weapon, the black:white ratio was only 1.7:1, since it was admitted by an average of 3.9 per cent of blacks and 2.3 per cent of whites. Similar results were obtained in the National Youth Survey (Huizinga and Elliott 1987). There seem to be no published large-scale English comparisons of blacks, whites and Asians on self-reported offending.

To explain why black:white ratios in self-reports are much smaller than in official records, Williams and Gold (1972) suggested that blacks and whites were treated differently by the police and the courts, and there is some evidence of ethnic bias in the treatment of juveniles in Philadelphia (Thornberry 1973) and London (Landau 1981). However, the differing results may be a function of the comparison of official offence rates and self-reported prevalence (Reiss 1975). Also, the fact that victim reports of offenders reveal substantial black:white ratios suggests that the differences between blacks and whites are not entirely attributable to bias in official processing.

A plausible explanation for the discrepancy between official and self-report figures is that self-report instruments are differentially invalid by ethnicity. In a validity check, Hindelang et al. (1981) found that the percentage of officially-recorded offences which were not self-reported was 10 per cent for white males but 33 per cent for black males. Similarly, Huizinga and Elliott (1986) discovered in the National Youth Survey that black males underreported arrests more than white males (39 per cent versus 19 per cent). It is possible that black males are more likely to be falsely arrested. Also, black males, and especially those who are the most serious offenders, are likely to be under-represented in samples interviewed, because they are differentially institutionalized, uncooperative or difficult to locate.

The weight of evidence indicates that Afro-Caribbeans are more likely to commit offences – especially violent crimes – than whites, both in England and in the United States. Most theories proposed to explain black–white differences suggest that ethnicity in itself is not an important causal factor, but that blacks and whites differ on known precursors of offending such as low family income, poor parental child-rearing behaviour or low intelligence. Rutter et al. (1975b) outlined the socio-economic deprivation suffered by black families, especially in regard to poorer-quality housing and lower-status jobs. Wilson and Herrnstein (1985) commented on socio-economic deprivation and also proposed that, partly because of the high proportion of black single-parent female-headed households, parental control and supervision were poor in black families. Gordon (1976; 1987) suggested that black-white differences in the prevalence of offending reflected black-white differences in intelligence. In testing these and other theories, it is important to determine whether observed ethnic differences in offending hold independently of these known precursors. For example, Ouston (1984) showed that her black-white differences in official offending did not hold independently of differences in social class or school attainment.

In general, research on the link between ethnicity and offending has paid too little attention to ethnic groups other than whites and blacks. Results obtained with Orientals in the United States and with Asians in England suggest that minorities (even those suffering socio-economic deprivation) can be less delinquent than the majority white population, and it is important to establish why this is so. The low offending rate of Japanese-Americans has often been attributed to their closely knit family system, characterized by strong parental control (e.g. Voss 1966), and a similar explanation was proposed by Batta et al. (1975) and Mawby et al. (1979) for the low offending rate of Asians in England. Hence, different child-rearing techniques might explain low offending rates by different ethnic groups as well as high ones.

Continuity influences

Delinquency rates vary systematically with area of residence. The classic studies by Shaw and McKay (1969) in Chicago and other American cities showed that juvenile delinquency rates (based on where offenders lived) were highest in inner city areas characterized by physical deterioration, neighbourhood disorganization and high residential mobility. A large proportion of all offenders came from a small proportion of areas, which tended to be the most deprived. Furthermore, these relatively high delinquency rates persisted over time, despite the effect of successive waves of immigration and emigration in changing the demographics of the population in different areas. Shaw and McKay concluded that variations in offending rates reflected variations in the social values and norms to which children were exposed, which in turn reflected the degree of social disorganization of an area.

Later work has tended to cast doubt on the consistency of offending rates over time. Bursik and Webb (1982) tested Shaw and McKay's cultural transmission hypothesis using more recent data in Chicago and more sophisticated quantitative methods. They concluded that the distribution of delinquency was not stable after 1950, but reflected demographic changes. Variations in delinquency rates in different areas were significantly correlated with variations in the percentage of non-whites, the percentage of foreign-born whites, and the percentage of overcrowded households. The greatest increase in offending in an area occurred when blacks moved from the minority to the majority. These results suggested that Shaw and McKay's ideas – about community values which persisted despite successive waves of immigration and emigration – needed revising. It was necessary to take account both of the type of area and of the type of people living in the area (e.g. Simcha-Fagan and Schwartz 1986).

Similar ecological studies have been carried out in England (for a review see Baldwin 1979). Wallis and Maliphant (1967) in London showed that official delinquency rates correlated with rates of local authority renting, the percentage of land used industrially or commercially, population density, overcrowded households, the proportion of non-white immigrants and the proportion of the population aged under 21. Power *et al.* (1972) carried out a similar study in one working-class London borough and found that official delinquency rates varied with rates of overcrowding and fertility and with the social class and type of housing of an area.

In Wallis and Maliphant's (1967) project, it was generally true that delinquency rates were higher in the inner city, and it is important to investigate why this is so. One of the most significant studies of inner city and rural areas is the comparison by Rutter *et al.* (1975a) of 10-year-old children in Inner London and in the Isle of Wight. They found a much higher incidence of conduct disorder in their Inner London sample. These results are relevant to delinquency, because of the link between conduct disorder in children and offending in juveniles and adults. Rutter *et al.* (1975b) investigated factors that might explain this area difference. They found that four sets of variables – family disorder, parental deviance, social disadvantage and school characteristics – were correlated with conduct disorder in each area, and concluded that the higher rates of disorder in Inner London were at least partly caused by the higher incidence of these four adverse factors.

Reiss (1986) pointed out that a key question was why crime rates of communities changed over time, and to what extent this was a function of changes in the communities or in the individuals living in them. Answering this question requires longitudinal research in which both communities and individuals are followed up. The best way of establishing the impact of the environment is to follow people who move from one area to another, thus using each person as his or her own control. In the Cambridge Study, Osborn (1980) found that moving out of London led to a significant decrease in convictions and self-reported offending, possibly because moving out led to a breaking up of offending groups. Rutter (1981) showed that the differences between Inner London and the Isle of Wight held even when the analyses were restricted to children reared in the same area by parents reared in the same area. This result suggests that the movement of problem families into problem areas cannot be the whole explanation of area differences in delinquency.

Clearly, there is an interaction between individuals and the communities in which they live. Some aspect of an inner city neighbourhood may be conducive to offending, perhaps because the inner city leads to a breakdown of community ties or neighbourhood patterns of mutual support, or perhaps because the high population density produces tension, frustration or anonymity. There may be many inter-related factors. As Reiss (1986) argued, high crime areas often have a high concentration of single-parent female-headed households with low incomes, living in low-cost, poor housing. The weakened parental control in these families – partly caused by the fact that the mother had to work and left her children unsupervised – meant that the children tended to congregate on the streets. In consequence, they were influenced by a peer subculture that often encouraged and reinforced offending.

Situational influences

While most delinquency researchers have aimed to explain the development of offending people, some have tried to explain the occurrence of offending events. As already mentioned, delinquents are predominantly versatile rather than specialized. Hence, in studying delinquents, it seems unnecessary to develop a different theory for each different type of offence. In contrast, in trying to explain why offences occur, the situations are so diverse and specific to particular crimes that it probably is necessary to have different explanations for different types of offences.

The most popular theory of offending events suggests that they occur in response to specific opportunities, when their expected benefits (e.g. stolen property, peer approval) outweigh their expected costs (e.g. legal punishment, parental disapproval). For example, Clarke and Cornish (1985) outlined a theory of residential burglary which included such influencing factors as whether a house was occupied, whether it looked affluent, whether there were bushes to hide behind, whether there were nosy neighbours, whether the house had a burglar alarm and whether it contained a dog. Several other researchers have also proposed that offending involves a rational decision in which expected benefits are weighed against expected costs (e.g. Wilson and Herrnstein 1985).

In the Cambridge Study, the most common reasons given for offending were rational ones, suggesting that most property crimes were committed because the offenders wanted the items stolen (West and Farrington 1977). Also, a number of cross-sectional surveys have shown that low estimates of the risk of being caught were correlated with high rates of self-reported offending (e.g. Erickson *et al.* 1977). Unfortunately, the direction of causal influence is not clear in cross-sectional research, since committing delinquent acts may lead to lower estimates of the probability of detection as well as the reverse. Farrington and Knight (1980) carried out a number of studies, using experimental, survey, and observational methods, that suggested that stealing involved risky decision-making. Hence, it is plausible to suggest that opportunities for delinquency, the immediate costs and benefits of delinquency, and the probabilities of these outcomes all influence whether people offend in any situation.

EXPLAINING DELINQUENCY

One of the greatest problems in interpreting results is that all possibly causal factors tend to be inter-correlated. People living in criminal areas tend to be socio-economically deprived, tend to use erratic methods of child-rearing and to have poor supervision, tend to have children who are impulsive and who have low school attainment, and so on. The explanation, prevention and treatment of delinquency requires some disentangling of the mass of inter-correlations, but this is very difficult to achieve convincingly.

A first step is to establish which factors predict delinquency independently of other factors. In the Cambridge Study, it was generally true that each group of influences shown in Table 6.1 (e.g. family influences or school problems) predicted offending independently of each other group (Farrington 1990b). Farrington and Hawkins (1991) reported that the independent predictors of convictions between ages 10 and 20 included troublesomeness, convicted parents, high daring, low school attainment, poor housing and poor parental child-rearing. Hence, it might be concluded that anti-social influences, impulsivity, school problems, socio-economic deprivation and family factors, despite their inter-correlations, all contribute independently to the development of delinquency.

Some of the most important theories of delinquency (Cohen 1955; Cloward and Ohlin 1960; Trasler 1962; Hirschi 1969; Sutherland and Cressey 1974; Eysenck 1977; Wilson and Herrnstein 1985; Clarke and Cornish 1985; Gottfredson and Hirschi 1990) have already been mentioned in this chapter. The modern trend is to try to achieve increased explanatory power by integrating propositions derived from several earlier theories (e.g. Elliott *et al.*, 1985; Hawkins and Weis 1985; Pearson and Weiner 1985). My own theory of delinquency (Farrington 1991b) is also integrative, and it distinguishes explicitly between the development of anti-social tendencies and the occurrence of delinquent acts.

My theory proposes that the major factors fostering anti-social tendencies are impulsivity, a poor ability to manipulate abstract concepts, low empathy, a weak conscience, internalized norms and attitudes favouring delinquency, and long-term motivating influences such as the desire for material goods or status with peers. The major factors that influence whether anti-social tendencies are translated into delinquent acts are short-term situational influences such as boredom, frustration, alcohol consumption, opportunities to offend, and the perceived costs and benefits of delinquency.

PREVENTION AND TREATMENT

Methods of preventing or treating delinquency should be based on theories about causes. In this section, implications about prevention and treatment are drawn from some of the likely causes of delinquency listed above. The implications reviewed here are those for which there is some empirical justification, especially in randomized experiments. The effect of any intervention on delinquency can be demonstrated most convincingly in such experiments (Farrington 1983b; Farrington *et al.* 1986a).

If low intelligence and school problems are causes of offending, then any programme that leads to an increase in school success should lead to a decrease in offending. One of the most successful delinquency prevention programmes was the Perry pre-school project carried out in Michigan by Schweinhart and Weikart (1980). This was essentially a 'Head Start' programme targeted on disadvantaged black children, who were allocated (approximately at random) to experimental and control groups. The experimental children attended a daily pre-school programme, backed up by weekly home visits, usually lasting two years (covering ages 3–4). The aim of the programme was to provide intellectual stimulation, to increase cognitive abilities and to increase later school achievement.

More than 120 children in the two groups were followed up to age 15, using teacher ratings, parent and youth interviews, and school records. As demonstrated in several other Head Start projects, the experimental group showed gains in intelligence that were rather shortlived. However, they were significantly better in elementary school motivation, school achievement at 14, teacher ratings of classroom behaviour at 6 to 9, self-reports of classroom behaviour at 15 and self-reports of offending at 15. Furthermore, a later follow-up of this sample by Berrueta-Clement *et al.* (1984) showed that, at age 19, the experimental group was more likely to be employed, more likely to have graduated from high school, more likely to have received college or vocational training, and less likely to have been arrested. Hence, this pre-school intellectual enrichment programme led to decreases in school failure and to decreases in delinquency.

Impulsivity and other personality characteristics of offenders might be treated using the set of techniques variously termed 'cognitive-behavioural interpersonal social skills training' (e.g. Michelson 1987). For example, the methods used by Ross to treat juvenile delinquents (see Ross *et al.* 1988; Ross and Ross 1988) are solidly based on some of the known individual characteristics of delinquents: impulsivity, concrete rather than abstract thinking, low empathy and egocentricity.

Ross believes that delinquents can be taught the cognitive skills in which they are deficient, and this can lead to a decrease in their offending. His reviews of delinquency rehabilitation programmes (Gendreau and Ross 1979; 1987) show that those which have been successful in reducing offending have generally tried to change the offender's thinking. Ross carried out his own 'Reasoning and Rehabilitation' programme in Canada, and found (in a randomized experiment) that it led to a significant decrease in re-offending for a small sample in a nine-month follow-up period. His training is carried out by probation officers, but he believes that it could be carried out by parents or teachers.

Ross's programme aims to modify the impulsive, egocentric thinking of delinquents, to teach them to stop and think before acting, to consider the consequences of their behaviour, to conceptualize alternative ways of solving interpersonal problems, and to consider the impact of their behaviour on other people, especially their victims. It includes social skills training, lateral thinking (to teach creative problem solving), critical thinking (to teach logical reasoning), value education (to teach values and concern for others), assertiveness training (to teach non-aggressive, socially appropriate ways to obtain desired outcomes), negotiation skills training, interpersonal cognitive problem solving (to teach thinking skills for solving interpersonal problems), social perspective training (to teach how to recognize and understand other people's feelings), role playing and modelling (demonstration and practice of effective and acceptable interpersonal behaviour).

If poor parental supervision and erratic child-rearing behaviour are causes of delinquency, it seems likely that parent training might succeed in reducing offending. The behavioural parent training developed by Patterson (1982) is one of the most hopeful approaches. His careful observations of parent–child interaction showed that parents of anti-social children were deficient in their methods of child-rearing. These parents failed to tell their children how they were expected to behave, failed to monitor the behaviour to ensure that it was desirable, and failed to enforce rules promptly and unambiguously with appropriate rewards and penalties. The parents of anti-social children used more punishment (such as scolding, shouting or threatening), but failed to make it contingent on the child's behaviour.

Patterson attempted to train these parents in effective child-rearing methods, namely noticing what a child is doing, monitoring behaviour over long periods, clearly stating house rules, making rewards and punishments contingent on behaviour, and negotiating disagreements so that conflicts and crises did not escalate. His treatment was shown to be effective in reducing child stealing over short periods in small-scale studies.

If having delinquent friends causes offending, then any programme which reduces their influence or increases the influence of pro-social friends could have a reductive effect on offending. Several studies show that school children can be taught to resist peer influences encouraging smoking, drinking and marijuana use. For example, Telch et al. (1982) employed older high school students to teach younger ones to develop counter-arguing skills to resist peer pressure to smoke, using modelling and guided practice. This approach was successful in decreasing smoking by the younger students, and similar results were reported by Botvin and Eng (1982). Murray et al. (1984) used same-aged peer leaders to teach students how to resist peer pressures to begin smoking, and Evans et al. (1981) used films. These techniques, designed to counter anti-social peer pressures, could help to decrease offending.

CONCLUSIONS

A great deal has been learned in the last twenty years, particularly from longitudinal surveys, about the causes of delinquency and crime. Offenders differ significantly from non-offenders in many respects, including intelligence, personality (especially impulsivity), family background, peer influence, socio-economic status, and area of residence. These differences are often present before, during and after criminal careers.

It is plausible to suggest that there is an 'anti-social personality' that arises in childhood and persists into adulthood, with numerous different behavioural manifestations, including offending. This idea has been popularized by Robins (1979). The anti-social male adult generally fails to maintain close relationships with anyone else, performs poorly in his jobs, is involved in crime, fails to support himself and his dependants without outside aid, and tends to change his plans impulsively and to lose his temper in response to minor frustrations. As a child, he tended to be restless, impulsive, and lacking in guilt, performed badly in school, truanted, ran away from home, was cruel to animals or people, and committed delinquent acts. A similar pattern is seen in the Cambridge Study (Farrington and West 1990). The typical delinquent – a male property offender – tends to be born in a low-income, large-sized family and to have criminal parents. When he is young, his parents supervise him rather poorly, use harsh or erratic child-rearing techniques, and are likely to be in conflict and to separate. At school, he tends to have low intelligence and attainment, is troublesome, hyperactive and impulsive, and often truants. He tends to associate with friends who are also delinquents.

After leaving school, the delinquent tends to have a low-status job record punctuated by periods of unemployment. His deviant behaviour tends to be versatile rather than specialized. He not only commits property offences such as theft and burglary but also engages in violence, vandalism, drug use, excessive drinking, reckless driving, and sexual promiscuity. His likelihood of offending reaches a peak during his teenage years and then declines in his twenties, when he is likely to get married or cohabit with a woman.

Research is needed on methods of preventing and treating this anti-social personality syndrome. Some hopeful techniques were reviewed in the previous section, but the most that can be said about them is that they warrant large-scale testing. In order to advance knowledge about the causes, prevention and treatment of delinquency, my colleagues and I have argued (Farrington 1988; Farrington et al., 1986a; Tonry et al. 1991) that a new generation of longitudinal studies on offending and anti-social behaviour is needed, including testing of the effects of experimental interventions on the natural history of delinquency and crime.

Because of the link between delinquency and numerous other social problems, any measure that succeeds in reducing delinquency will have benefits that go far beyond this. Any measure that reduces delinquency will probably also reduce alcohol abuse, drunk driving, drug abuse, sexual promiscuity, family violence, truancy, school failure, unemployment, marital disharmony and divorce. It is clear that problem children tend to grow up into problem adults, and that problem adults tend to produce more problem children. Major efforts to tackle the problems of anti-social personality and delinquency are urgently needed.

REFERENCES

Baldwin, J. (1979) 'Ecological and areal studies in Great Britain and the United States', in N. Morris and M. Tonry (eds) *Crime and Justice*, vol. 1, Chicago: University of Chicago Press.

Barclay, G. C. (1990) 'The peak age of known offending by males', *Home Office Research Bulletin* 28: 20–23.

Batta, I. D., McCulloch, J. W. and Smith, N. J. (1975) 'A study of juvenile delinquency amongst Asians and half-Asians', *British Journal of Criminology* 15: 32–42.

Belson, W. A. (1976) *Juvenile Theft*, London: Harper & Row.

Berrueta-Clement, J. R., Schweinhart, L. J., Barnett, W. S., Epstein, A. S. and Weikart, D. P. (1984) *Changed Lives*, Ypsilanti, MI: High/Scope.

Blouin, A. G., Conners, C. K., Seidel, W. T. and Blouin, J. (1989) 'The independence of hyperactivity from conduct disorder: methodological considerations', *Canadian Journal of Psychiatry* 34: 279–82.

Botvin, G. J. and Eng. A. (1982) 'The efficacy of a multicomponent approach to the prevention of cigarette smoking', *Preventive Medicine* 11: 199–211.

Bouchard, T. J., Lykken, D. T., McGue, M., Segal, N. L. and Tellegen, A. (1990) 'Sources of human psychological differences: the Minnesota study of twins reared apart', *Science* 250: 223–8.

Breslau, N., Klein, N. and Allen, L. (1988) 'Very low birthweight: behavioral sequelae at nine years of age', *Journal of the American Academy of Child and Adolescent Psychiatry* 27: 605–12.

Brooks-Gunn, J. and Furstenberg, F. F. (1986) 'The children of adolescent mothers: physical, academic, and psychological outcomes', *Developmental Review* 6: 224–51.

Buckle, A. and Farrington, D. P. (1984) 'An observational study of shoplifting', *British Journal of Criminology* 24: 63–73.

Bursik, R. J. and Webb, J. (1982) 'Community change and patterns of delinquency', *American Journal of Sociology* 88: 24–42.

Campbell, A. (1981) *Girl Delinquents*, Oxford: Blackwell.

Clarke, R. V. and Cornish, D. B. (1985) 'Modelling offenders' decisions: a framework for research and policy', in M. Tonry and N. Morris (eds) *Crime and Justice*, vol. 6, Chicago: University of Chicago Press.

Cloninger, C. R., Sigvardsson, S., Bohman, M. and von Knorring, A. (1982) 'Predisposition to petty criminality in Swedish adoptees. II. Cross-fostering analysis of gene–environment interaction', *Archives of General Psychiatry*, 39: 1242–7.

Cloward, R. A. and Ohlin, L. E. (1960) *Delinquency and Opportunity*, New York: Free Press.

Cohen, A. K. (1955) *Delinquent Boys*, Glencoe, IL: Free Press.

Douglas, J. W. B., Ross, J. M., Hammond, W. A. and Mulligan, D. G. (1966) 'Delinquency and social class', *British Journal of Criminology* 6: 294–302.

Elliott, D. S., Huizinga, D. and Ageton, S. S. (1985) *Explaining Delinquency and Drug Use*, Beverly Hills, CA: Sage.

Elliott, D. S., Huizinga, D. and Menard, S. (1989) *Multiple Problem Youth*,

New York: Springer Verlag.

Ensminger, M. E., Kellam, S. G. and Rubin, B. R. (1983) 'School and family origins of delinquency', in K. T. Van Dusen and S. A. Mednick (eds) *Prospective Studies of Crime and Delinquency*, Boston: Kluwer-Nijhoff.

Erickson, M., Gibbs, J. P. and Jensen, G. F. (1977), 'The deterrence doctrine and the perceived certainty of legal punishment', *American Sociological Review*, 42: 305–17.

Evans, R. I., Rozelle, R. M., Maxwell, S. E., Raines, B. E., Dill, C. A., Guthrie, T. J., Henderson, A. H. and Hill, P. C. (1981) 'Social modelling films to deter smoking in adolescents: results of a three-year field investigation', *Journal of Applied Psychology* 66: 399–414.

Eysenck, H. J. (1977) *Crime and Personality*, 3rd edn, London: Routledge & Kegan Paul.

Eysenck, H. J. and Gudjonsson, G. H. (1989) *The Causes and Cures of Criminality*, New York: Plenum.

Farrington, D. P. (1972) 'Delinquency begins at home', *New Society* 21: 495–7.

—— (1978) 'The family backgrounds of aggressive youths', in L. Hersov, M. Berger and D. Shaffer (eds) *Aggression and Antisocial Behaviour in Childhood and Adolescence*, Oxford: Pergamon.

—— (1981) 'The prevalence of convictions', *British Journal of Criminology* 21: 173–5.

—— (1983a) 'Offending from 10 to 25 years of age', in K. T. Van Dusen and S. A. Mednick (eds) *Prospective Studies of Crime and Delinquency*, Boston: Kluwer-Nijhoff.

—— (1983b) 'Randomized experiments on crime and justice', in M. Tonry and N. Morris (eds) *Crime and Justice*, vol. 4, Chicago: University of Chicago Press.

—— (1986a) 'Age and crime', in M. Tonry and N. Morris (eds) *Crime and Justice*, vol. 7, Chicago: University of Chicago Press.

—— (1986b) 'Stepping stones to adult criminal careers', in D. Olweus, J. Block and M. R. Yarrow (eds) *Development of Antisocial and Prosocial Behavior*, New York: Academic Press.

—— (1987a) 'Epidemiology', in H. C. Quay (ed.) *Handbook of Juvenile Delinquency*, New York: Wiley.

—— (1987b) 'Implications of biological findings for criminological research', in S. A. Mednick, T. E. Moffitt and S. A. Stack (eds) *The Causes of Crime: New Biological Approaches*, Cambridge: Cambridge University Press.

—— (1988) 'Advancing knowledge about delinquency and crime: The need for a coordinated program of longitudinal research', *Behavioral Sciences and the Law* 6: 307–31.

—— (1989) 'Self-reported and official offending from adolescence to adulthood', in M. W. Klein (ed.) *Cross-national Research in Self-reported Crime and Delinquency*, Dordrecht, Netherlands: Kluwer.

—— (1990a) 'Age, period, cohort, and offending', in D. M. Gottfredson and R. V. Clarke (eds) *Policy and Theory in Criminal Justice: Contribution in Honour of Leslie T. Wilkins*, Aldershot: Avebury.

—— (1990b) 'Implications of criminal career research for the prevention of offending', *Journal of Adolescence* 13: 93–113.

—— (1991a) 'Childhood aggression and adult violence: early precursors and later life outcomes', in D. J. Pepler and K. H. Rubin (eds) *The Development and Treatment of Childhood Aggression*, Hillsdale, NJ: Erlbaum.

—— (1991b) 'Explaining the beginning, progress and ending of antisocial behavior from birth to adulthood', in J. McCord (ed.) *Advances in Criminological Theory*, vol. 3: *Crime Facts, Fictions and Theory*. New Brunswick, NJ: Transaction.

Farrington, D. P. and Hawkins, J. D. (1991) 'Predicting participation, early onset, and later persistence in officially recorded offending', *Criminal Behaviour and Mental Health* 1: 1–33.

Farrington, D. P. and Knight, B. J. (1980) 'Four studies of stealing as a risky decision', in P. D. Lipsitt and B. D. Sales (eds) *New Directions in Psycholegal Research*, New York: Van Nostrand Reinhold.

Farrington, D. P. and West, D. J. (1990) 'The Cambridge Study in Delinquent Development: a long-term follow-up of 411 London males', in H. J. Kerner and G. Kaiser (eds) *Criminality: Personality, Behaviour and Life History*, Berlin: Springer Verlag.

Farrington, D. P., Biron, L. and LeBlanc, M. (1982) 'Personality and delinquency in London and Montreal', in J. Gunn and D. P. Farrington (eds) *Abnormal Offenders, Delinquency, and the Criminal Justice System*, Chichester: Wiley.

Farrington, D. P., Loeber, R. and Van Kammen, W. B. (1990) 'Long-term criminal outcomes of hyperactivity–impulsivity–attention deficit and conduct problems in childhood', in L. N. Robins and M. Rutter (eds) *Straight and Devious Pathways from Childhood to Adulthood*, Cambridge: Cambridge University Press.

Farrington, D. P., Ohlin, L. E. and Wilson, J. Q. (1986a) *Understanding and Controlling Crime*, New York: Springer Verlag.

Farrington, D. P., Snyder, H. N. and Finnegan, T. A. (1988) 'Specialization in juvenile court careers', *Criminology* 26: 461–87.

Farrington, D. P., Gallagher, B., Morley, L., St Ledger, R. J. and West, D. J. (1986b) 'Unemployment, school leaving, and crime', *British Journal of Criminology* 26: 335–56.

Federal Bureau of Investigation (1975) *Crime in the United States, 1974*, Washington, DC: US Department of Justice.

—— (1989) *Crime in the United States, 1988*, Washington, DC: US Department of Justice.

—— (1990) *Age-specific Arrest Rates and Race-specific Arrest Rates for Selected Offenses 1965–1988*, Washington, DC: US Department of Justice.

Gendreau, P. and Ross, R. R. (1979) 'Effective correctional treatment: bibliotherapy for cynics', *Crime and Delinquency* 25: 463–89.

—— (1987) 'Revivification of rehabilitation: evidence from the 1980s', *Justice Quarterly* 4: 349–407.

Gordon, R. A. (1976) 'Prevalence: the rare datum in delinquency measurement and its implications for the theory of delinquency', in M. W. Klein

(ed.) *The Juvenile Justice System*, Beverly Hills, CA: Sage.
—— (1987) 'SES versus IQ in the race–IQ–delinquency model', *International Journal of Sociology and Social Policy* 7: 30–96.
Gottfredson, M. and Hirschi, T. (1990) *A General Theory of Crime*, Stanford, CA: Stanford University Press.
Hawkins, J. D. and Weis, J. G. (1985) 'The social development model: an integrated approach to delinquency prevention', *Journal of Primary Prevention* 6: 73–97.
Hindelang, M. J. (1981) 'Variations in sex–race–age–specific incidence rates of offending', *American Sociological Review* 46: 461–74.
Hindelang, M. J., Hirschi, T. and Weis, J. G. (1981) *Measuring Delinquency*, Beverly Hills, CA: Sage.
Hirschi, T. (1969) *Causes of Delinquency*, Berkeley, CA: University of California Press.
Home Office (1990) *Criminal Statistics, England and Wales, 1989*, London: HMSO.
Home Office Statistical Bulletin (1985) *Criminal Careers of Those Born in 1953, 1958 and 1963*, London: Home Office Statistical Department.
—— (1989) *Crime Statistics for the Metropolitan Police District by Ethnic Group, 1987: Victims, Suspects and Those Arrested*, London: Home Office Statistical Department.
Huizinga, D. and Elliott, D. S. (1986) 'Reassessing the reliability and validity of self-report measures', *Journal of Quantitative Criminology* 2: 293–327.
—— (1987) 'Juvenile offenders: prevalence, offender incidence, and arrest rates by race', *Crime and Delinquency* 33: 206–23.
Irving, B. and MacKenzie, I. (1989) *Police Interrogation*, London: Police Foundation.
Jamieson, K. M. and Flanagan, T. J. (eds) (1987) *Sourcebook of Criminal Justice Statistics, 1986*, Washington, DC: Bureau of Justice Statistics.
Klein, M. W. (1984) 'Offence specialization and versatility among juveniles', *British Journal of Criminology* 24: 185–94.
Kolvin, I., Miller, F. J. W., Fleeting, M. and Kolvin, P. A. (1988) 'Social and parenting factors affecting criminal-offence rates: findings from the Newcastle Thousand Family Study (1947–1980)', *British Journal of Psychiatry* 152: 80–90.
Landau, S. (1981) 'Juveniles and the police', *British Journal of Criminology*, 21: 27–46.
Loeber, R. and Dishion, T. (1983) 'Early predictors of male delinquency: a review', *Psychological Bulletin* 94: 68–99.
Loeber, R. and Stouthamer-Loeber, M. (1986) 'Family factors as correlates and predictors of juvenile conduct problems and delinquency', in M. Tonry and N. Morris (eds) *Crime and Justice*, vol. 7, Chicago: University of Chicago Press.
—— (1987) 'Prediction', in H. C. Quay (ed.) *Handbook of Juvenile Delinquency*, New York: Wiley.
Maccoby, E. E. and Jacklin, C. N. (1974) *The Psychology of Sex Differences*, Stanford, CA: Stanford University Press.

Magnusson, D. (1988) *Individual Development from an Interactional Perspective*, Hillsdale: NJ: Erlbaum.

Mawby, R. I., McCulloch, J. W. and Batta, I. D. (1979) 'Crime amongst Asian juveniles in Bradford', *International Journal of the Sociology of Law* 7: 297–306.

Mawson, A. R. (1987) *Transient Criminality*, New York: Praeger.

McCord, J. (1979) 'Some child-rearing antecedents of criminal behaviour in adult men', *Journal of Personality and Social Psychology*, 37: 1477–86.

Mednick, S. A., Gabrielli, W. F. and Hutchings, B. (1983) 'Genetic influences on criminal behavior: evidence from an adoption cohort', in K. T. Van Dusen and S. A. Mednick (eds) *Prospective Studies of Crime and Delinquency*, Boston: Kluwer-Nijhoff.

Michelson, L. (1987) 'Cognitive-behavioral strategies in the prevention and treatment of antisocial disorders in children and adolescents', in J. D. Burchard and S. N. Burchard (eds) *Prevention of Delinquent Behavior*, Beverly Hills, CA: Sage.

Moffitt, T. E. (1990) 'The neuropsychology of juvenile delinquency: a critical review', in M. Tonry and N. Morris (eds) *Crime and Justice*, vol. 12, Chicago: University of Chicago Press.

Moffitt, T. E. and Silva, P. A. (1988a) 'IQ and delinquency: a direct test of the differential detection hypothesis', *Journal of Abnormal Psychology* 97: 330–3.

—— (1988b) 'Neuropsychological deficit and self-reported delinquency in an unselected birth cohort', *Journal of the American Academy of Child and Adolescent Psychiatry* 27: 233–40.

Mueller, C. W. and Parcel, T. L. (1981) 'Measures of socio-economic status: alternatives and recommendations', *Child Development* 52: 13–30.

Murray, D. M., Luepker, R. V., Johnson, C. A. and Mittelmark, M. B. (1984) 'The prevention of cigarette smoking in children: a comparison of four strategies', *Journal of Applied Social Psychology* 14: 274–88.

Novy, D. M. and Donahue, S. (1985) 'The relationship between adolescent life stress events and delinquent conduct including conduct indicating a need for supervision', *Adolescence*, 20: 313–21.

Olweus, D. (1987) 'Testosterone and adrenalin: aggressive antisocial behavior in normal adolescent males', in S. A. Mednick, T. E. Moffitt, and S. A. Stack (eds) *The Causes of Crime: New Biological Approaches*, Cambridge: Cambridge University Press.

Osborn, S. G. (1980) 'Moving home, leaving London, and delinquent trends', *British Journal of Criminology* 20: 54–61.

Ouston, J. (1984) 'Delinquency, family background, and educational attainment', *British Journal of Criminology* 24: 2–26.

Parker, J. G. and Asher, S. R. (1987) 'Peer relations and later personal adjustment: are low accepted children at risk?', *Psychological Bulletin* 102: 357–89.

Patterson, G. R. (1982) *Coercive Family Process*, Eugene, OR: Castalia.

Pearson, F. S. and Weiner, N. A. (1985) 'Toward an integration of

criminological theories', *Journal of Criminal Law and Criminology* 76: 116–50.
Power, M. J., Benn, R. T. and Morris, J. N. (1972) 'Neighbourhood, schools and juveniles before the courts', *British Journal of Criminology* 12: 111–32.
Power, M. J., Alderson, M. R., Phillipson, C. M., Shoenberg, E. and Morris, J. N. (1967) 'Delinquent schools?', *New Society* 10: 542–3.
Pulkkinen, L. (1988) 'Delinquent development: theoretical and empirical considerations', in M. Rutter (ed.) *Studies of Psychosocial Risk*, Cambridge: Cambridge University Press.
Reiss, A. J. (1975) 'Inappropriate theories and inadequate methods as policy plagues: self-reported delinquency and the law', in N.J. Demerath, O. Larson and K. F. Schuessler (eds) *Social Policy and Sociology*, New York: Academic Press.
—— (1986) 'Why are communities important in understanding crime?', in A. J. Reiss and M. Tonry (eds) *Communities and Crime*, Chicago: University of Chicago Press.
—— (1988) 'Co-offending and criminal careers', in M. Tonry and N. Morris (eds) *Crime and Justice*, vol. 10, Chicago: University of Chicago Press.
Riley, D. and Shaw, M. (1985) *Parental Supervision and Juvenile Delinquency*, London: HMSO.
Robins, L. N. (1979) 'Sturdy childhood predictors of adult outcomes: replications from longitudinal studies', in J. E. Barrett, R. M. Rose and G. L. Klerman (eds) *Stress and Mental Disorder*, New York: Raven Press.
Robins, L. N. and Ratcliff, K. S. (1980) 'Childhood conduct disorders and later arrest', in L. N. Robins, P. J. Clayton and J. K. Wing (eds) *The Social Consequences of Psychiatric Illness*, New York: Brunner/Mazel.
Roff, J. D. and Wirt, R. D. (1984) 'Childhood aggression and social adjustment as antecedents of delinquency', *Journal of Abnormal Child Psychology* 12: 111–26.
Ross, R. R. and Ross, B. D. (1988) 'Delinquency prevention through cognitive training', *New Education* 10: 70–75.
Ross, R. R., Fabiano, E. A. and Ewles, C. D. (1988) 'Reasoning and rehabilitation', *International Journal of Offender Therapy and Comparative Criminology* 32: 29–35.
Rutter, M. (1981) 'The city and the child', *American Journal of Orthopsychiatry*, 51: 610–25.
Rutter, M. and Giller, H. (1963) *Juvenile Delinquency*, Harmondsworth: Penguin.
Rutter, M., Maughan, B., Mortimore, P. and Ouston, J. (1979) *Fifteen Thousand Hours: Secondary Schools and their Effects on Children*, London: Open Books.
Rutter, M., Cox, A., Tupling, C., Berger, M. and Yule, W. (1975a) 'Attainment and adjustment in two geographical areas: I. The prevalence of psychiatric disorder', *British Journal of Psychiatry* 126: 493–509.
Rutter, M., Yule, B., Quinton, D., Rowlands, O., Yule, W. and Berger, M.

(1975b) 'Attainment and adjustment in two geographical areas: III. Some factors accounting for area differences', *British Journal of Psychiatry* 126: 520–33.

Schweinhart, L. J. and Weikart, D. P. (1980) *Young Children Grow Up*, Ypsilanti, MI: High/Scope.

Shaw, C.R. and McKay, H. D. (1969) *Juvenile Delinquency and Urban Areas*, rev. edn, Chicago: University of Chicago Press.

Short, J. F. and Nye, F. I. (1957) 'Reported behavior as a criterion of deviant behavior', *Social Problems* 5: 207–13.

Simcha-Fagan, O. and Schwartz, J. E. (1986) 'Neighborhood and delinquency: an assessment of contextual effects', *Criminology* 24: 667–703.

Spivack, G., Marcus, J. and Swift, M. (1986) 'Early classroom behaviors and later misconduct', *Developmental Psychology* 22: 124–31.

Sutherland, E. H. and Cressey, D. R. (1974) *Criminology*, 9th edn, Philadelphia, PA: Lippincott.

Szatmari, P., Reitsma-Street, M. and Offord, D. R. (1986) 'Pregnancy and birth complications in antisocial adolescents and their siblings', *Canadian Journal of Psychiatry* 31: 513–6.

Telch, M. J., Killen, J. D., McAlister, A. L., Perry, C. L. and Maccoby, N. (1982) 'Long-term follow-up of a pilot project on smoking prevention with adolescents', *Journal of Behavioral Medicine* 5: 1–8.

Thornberry, T. P. (1973) 'Race, socio-economic status, and sentencing in the juvenile justice system', *Journal of Criminal Law and Criminology*, 64: 90–98.

Thornberry, T. P. and Farnworth, M. (1982) 'Social correlates of criminal involvement: further evidence on the relationship between social status and criminal behavior', *American Sociological Review* 47: 505–18.

Tonry, M., Ohlin, L. E. and Farrington, D. P. (1991) *Human Development and Criminal Behavior*, New York: Springer Verlag.

Tracy, P. E., Wolfgang, M. E. and Figlio, R. M. (1985) *Delinquency in Two Birth Cohorts*, Washington, DC: National Institute of Juvenile Justice and Delinquency Prevention.

Trasler, G. B. (1962) *The Explanation of Criminality*, London: Routledge & Kegan Paul.

Venables, P. H. and Raine, A. (1987) 'Biological theory', in B. J. McGurk, D. M. Thornton and M. Williams (eds) *Applying Psychology to Imprisonment*, London: HMSO.

Visher, C. A. and Roth, J. A. (1986) 'Participation in criminal careers', in A. Blumstein, J. Cohen, J. A., Roth and C. A. Visher (eds) *Criminal Careers and 'Career Criminals'*, vol. 1, Washington DC: National Academy Press.

Voss, H. L. (1966) 'Socio-economic status and reported delinquent behaviour', *Social Problems* 13: 314–24.

Wadsworth, M. (1979) *Roots of Delinquency*, London: Martin Robertson.

Wallis, C. P. and Maliphant, R. (1967) 'Delinquent areas in the county of London: ecological factors' , *British Journal of Criminology* 7: 250–84.

Werner, E. E. (1989) 'High-risk children in young adulthood: a longitudinal study from birth to 32 years', *American Journal of Orthopsychiatry*

59: 72-81.
West, D. J. and Farrington, D. P. (1973) *Who Becomes Delinquent?*, London: Heinemann.
—— (1977) *The Delinquent Way of Life*, London: Heinemann.
White, H. R., Labouvie, E. W. and Bates, M. E. (1985) 'The relationship between sensation seeking and delinquency: a longitudinal analysis', *Journal of Research in Crime and Delinquency* 22: 197-211.
Widom, C. S. (1989) 'The cycle of violence', *Science* 244: 160-6.
Wikstrom, P. O. (1987) 'Patterns of crime in a birth cohort', Stockholm: University of Stockholm Department of Sociology (report).
Willcock, H. D. (1974) *Deterrents and Incentives to Crime among Boys and Young Men aged 15-21 Years*, London: Office of Population Censuses and Surveys.
Williams, J. R. and Gold, M. (1972) 'From delinquent behavior to official delinquency', *Social Problems* 20: 209-29.
Wilson, H. (1990) 'Parental supervision: a neglected aspect of delinquency', *British Journal of Criminology* 20: 203-35.
Wilson, J. Q. and Herrnstein, R. J. (1985) *Crime and Human Nature*, New York: Simon and Schuster.
Wolfgang, M. E., Figlio, R. M. and Sellin, T. (1972) *Delinquency in a Birth Cohort*, Chicago: University of Chicago Press.
Wolfgang, M. E., Thornberry, T. P. and Figlio, R. M. (1987) *From Boy to Man, from Delinquency to Crime*, Chicago: University of Chicago Press.
Zimring, F. E. (1981) 'Kids, groups and crime: some implications of a well-known secret', *Journal of Criminal Law and Criminology* 72: 867-85.

Chapter 7

The home and the school

Maurice Chazan

INTRODUCTION

Issues relating to the links between home and school have been
debated for a very long time, but it is during the last three decades
that the role and influence of parents (or their caretakers) in the
education of their children have become a particular focus for
concern. The burgeoning literature on parental participation in
education, the attention given to the home in governmental reports
on education published during this period, and various legislative
measures have all shown an increasing recognition of first, the
importance of the role of home and family in the educational
process; second, parental rights; and third, the need for the
influence of parents to be made effective through real power.

Parental participation, rights and powers have been well covered
in recent publications, though these have given more attention to
pupils of primary school age than to those at the secondary stage,
perhaps indicating that the parents of younger children have more
opportunities to engage in close contact with school than do the
parents of older pupils. While the growth in volume of publications
of this kind testifies to a real increase in interest in fostering a
partnership between home and school, it cannot be assumed that it
necessarily reflects the extent of general changes in attitudes and
practices on the part of teachers and parents.

So many references to parents have been made by official reports
on education that only examples of these references can be given
here. The Newsom Report (CACE 1963), dealing with the education of pupils aged 13–16 of average and less than average ability,
showed its concern about the harmful effects of pupils returning
home to an empty house, when both parents were at work, and
about the disadvantages that schools might suffer when located in

slum areas. However, it was the Plowden Report (CACE 1967a; b), covering primary education, that gave prominence to participation by parents in the educational process. The Plowden Committee highlighted the interaction between home and school; the association between parental encouragement and educational performance, irrespective of occupational background; and the need for parents to have information not only about their own children's progress but also about general school policy and activities. The Report included a number of recommendations encouraging schools to have a well-planned programme for contact with pupils' homes. About ten years later, the Warnock Report on special educational needs (DES 1978) devoted a chapter to 'Parents as Partners' and stressed throughout its pages that the successful education of children with special needs was dependent upon the full involvement of their parents. The Warnock Committee asserted that parents of children with special needs required three principal forms of support – information, advice and practical help – at as early a stage as possible. The Elton Report (DES 1989a), on discipline in schools, underlined the importance of the home in ensuring acceptable standards of behaviour in school, a point which had been made strongly by the Newsom Report twenty-five years previously.

Official reports on aspects of the school curriculum have also recognized the role of parents in advancing scholastic progress. For example, the Bullock Report (DES 1975), which considered all aspects of teaching the use of English in school, considered that there was room for many more initiatives designed to encourage parents to take part in the life of the school, and to co-operate with teachers in fostering language development and reading skills. However, the Report cautioned that much thought needed to be given to the nature of parents' involvement in school. The Cockcroft Report (DES 1982), on the teaching of mathematics, highlighted the value of schools explaining their approaches to the subject, and discussing pupils' progress with their parents.

It is noteworthy that committees of enquiry set up by the government to consider educational issues have tended, in addition to taking into account available research findings, to commission research projects designed to throw light on questions relevant to their terms of reference. Projects established in this way have included some on parental attitudes and home–school links. For example, the Plowden Committee carried out, in 1964, a national survey of parental attitudes and circumstances related to school and pupil characteristics (see DES 1967b); and the Warnock Committee commissioned a research project on services for parents of handicapped children under five (see DES 1978; ed. Laing 1979). As the Plowden Report pointed out, research contributes much to progress within the educational system, particularly if findings are related to practice and effectively disseminated. However, it must be borne in mind that the study of such questions as the relationship between socio-economic status and educational attainment, or the relative influence of home and school on children's development, is fraught with difficulties. For instance, many of the concepts involved – such as social class – are subject to a variety of definitions; perceptions and attitudes are not easy to measure; and both home and school influences are often subtle and difficult to assess in precise terms. Further, any association which is established statistically (for example, between low socio-economic status and reading difficulties) does not necessarily imply a causal relationship. This does not mean that research bearing on home and school is without value, but rather indicates that research findings should always be interpreted with due caution.

As Docking (1990) points out, the Education Acts of 1980, 1981, 1986 and 1988, in making schools more publicly accountable, have given parents more statutory rights and political power, both in regard to the education of their own children and in decision making. Parents have been given new or increased rights, *inter alia*, in relation to special educational needs, the curriculum, choice of school, information and school government. However, in practice parents do not always use their rights and powers effectively.

As mentioned above, much has been written about the relationship between home and school (see, for example, ed. Bastiani 1987; 1988; ed. Wolfendale 1989; Docking 1990 for useful overviews of the literature). It is impossible, therefore, within the confines of a single chapter to deal comprehensively with the many facets of the topic that merit attention. This chapter will focus on selected aspects, briefly covering the different roles and perceptions of parents and teachers; the association between home background and educational achievement; the developing role of parents as school governors; ways of improving home–school relationships; and efforts to effect change in families. The discussion will relate mainly to policy and practice in England and Wales.

ROLES AND PERCEPTIONS OF PARENTS AND TEACHERS

As parents increasingly take on a relatively formal teaching role at times, it is necessary to be aware that parents and teachers carry out their educational functions from different frames of reference. It is desirable that, in working together, teachers and parents should understand each other's viewpoints, attitudes and perceptions.

Similarities and differences in the role of parents and teachers

There are many similarities in the role of parents and teachers but, in thinking of them as partners, the differences should not be overlooked. It is the function of both parents and teachers to be responsible for the physical care and safety of the children in their charge; to develop their social skills; to provide stimulation; to encourage positive attitudes to learning and exploration; and to exercise firm and consistent, while reasonable, control. However, the parent–child relationship is inevitably a closer and more intense one than the teacher–child relationship. The child looks to the parents to provide a continuous experience of warmth, affection and acceptance, while teachers have to adopt a less emotional and more objective stance. The main educational role of parents is the provision of a stable and caring home background in which the child receives appropriate stimulation, and is encouraged by the interest shown in his/her education and development. It is easy for this interest to become excessive or wrongly directed. The emotional bond between parent and child, while conducive to informal and incidental learning, may well interfere with effective learning in more formal situations. It is not uncommon for parents to become angry and even hostile when, in trying to teach their child directly, they are faced with apparent slowness of understanding or reaction, whereas most teachers are able to deal with failures in learning tasks with more tolerance. Further, their professional training gives teachers more confidence in helping children to acquire specific skills and knowledge, while parents often feel insecure as educators. It is particularly important for professionals promoting, for example, reading programmes involving parental participation (see pp. 181–2) to be fully aware of the difficulties some parents may have in adopting the teaching role demanded by such programmes.

As Becher *et al.* (1981) state, it is natural that parents' responsibilities for supporting their own children and the schools' responsibilities for the care of all children will sometimes give rise to situations which are not easy to reconcile: these differences in perspective between schools and parents could well be acknowledged and built upon.

Parental views on participation in education

Parents differ greatly in their views on the kind of schooling which their children receive, as well as on the extent to which they should be involved in their children's education. However, most parents (especially those with children in primary schools) take a favourable view of schools (CACE 1967a; Chazan *et al.* 1976), though they often have criticisms to make of certain aspects of schooling, particularly in regard to the school's failure to let them know how their child is progressing, which is the parents' main concern (Docking 1990). Parents tend to feel less competent in relation to the school curriculum as their children grow older (Cyster *et al.* 1980), and parents of secondary school pupils have more diverse expectations from school (Tomlinson 1984).

Research findings indicate that most parents are interested in their children's education and progress: the stereotype of the apathetic, uninterested parent is not supported by the evidence (Johnson and Ransom 1983; Tomlinson 1984; ed. Wolfendale 1989). However, many do not feel that they have a role to fulfil *vis-à-vis* the school. They may prefer to help their children at home rather than help at school (Tizard *et al.* 1981), or they may be too overwhelmed by their own problems to consider participation in school activities. Their feeling that they have no special part to play in the life of the school should not be interpreted as a lack of interest in their child's education.

Teachers' perceptions of parental involvement in education

A wide range of attitudes towards parental contact exists among school staff at all levels. Docking (1990) points out that parents may be seen by schools as customers, partners or problems. As customers they are viewed in a variety of ways, ranging from clients in need of expert advice to consumers with a right to determine policy matters. As partners, they may be seen as legitimately working with teachers in the education of their own children, or in decision making. Parents may be openly regarded as problems by restricting their access or involvement, or, covertly, in the sense that they are assumed to be the cause of learning difficulties or behaviour problems in their own children. It is all to easy to blame the parents, for example, for a child's disruptive behaviour in school, even though they may be doing their best for the child in very adverse circumstances.

Many examples are now to be found of constructive co-operation between teachers and parents (see pp. 177–84). However, by no means all teachers are happy to work closely with parents. Cyster *et al.* (1980) found that some teachers were wary of parents who came to school to enquire about their child's progress, and dismissive of those who did not as being apathetic and lacking in interest in education. Tizard *et al.* (1981) report that teachers in a sample of nursery units were disappointed at the response of parents to efforts designed to increase home–school links, and, after a period, reverted to an earlier pattern of contact which relied heavily on trust and social meeting. The teachers also worried far less about gaining parental understanding of children's activities in school, though they all wanted more time to talk to parents. In a study of parents' perceptions of secondary schools, Johnson and Ransom (1980) found that teachers referred to a small minority of enthusiastic parents and a small minority of 'problem' parents: in between lay the silent majority of unknown parents who were presumed to be apathetic.

It is clear that much remains to be done to change teachers' perceptions of parents where necessary, and to make progress in modifying the mismatch of expectations sometimes evident between parents and schools, especially in minority groups (Tomlinson 1984; DES 1985).

HOME BACKGROUND AND EDUCATIONAL ACHIEVEMENT

Relative importance of home and school influences on educational achievement

Research in the 1960s tended to suggest that the home environment plays a more important part than school factors in educational achievement (e.g. Coleman *et al.* 1966; Wiseman 1967). The evidence for this conclusion did not go unchallenged (see Reynolds 1982), but some later studies too have lent support to the predominant influence of the home in determining progress at school. Tizard and Hughes (1984), for example, found that in a number of respects the home provides a more powerful learning environment than nursery schools, for children from working-class as well as middle-class backgrounds, mainly because of the large number of everyday activities involved in the home. Further, Tizard *et al.* (1988) report, on the basis of a longitudinal study of children aged 4–7 in thirty-three Inner London schools, that the strongest predictor of attainment at age 7 was the amount of 3R knowledge that the children had before they started infant school (e.g. the number of letters the children could identify at 4¾ years was the strongest predictor of reading attainment at 7 years). Factors within the home made an important contribution to pre-school children's 3R knowledge.

However, investigations during the 1970s and 1980s have concluded that there are considerable differences between schools which have an effect on pupils' attainments and behaviour, and have sought to identify which factors are of particular significance. At the primary stage, Mortimore *et al.* (1988) found that school membership made a very important contribution to the explanation of variations in the attainments of pupils aged 7–11 over three years in reading, writing and mathematics, as well as in the development of attitudes, self-concept and behaviour in school. Mortimore *et al.* assert that the school makes a far larger contribution to the explanation of progress than is made by pupils' background characteristics, sex and age. Their findings also showed that parental involvement in the life of the school was a positive influence on pupils' progress and development.

At the secondary stage, Rutter *et al.* (1979), in their study of schools in Inner London, found marked school variations in pupils' attainments and behaviour, even when allowance was made for differences in family background and personal characteristics prior to secondary transfer. Differences in outcome between schools were not related, according to Rutter and his colleagues, to such physical factors as school size or available space, nor to organizational factors. Rather, they were systematically related to the characteristics of the schools as social institutions, including the degree of academic emphasis, the ways in which teachers behaved, the amount of responsibility allowed to pupils, and school ethos or climate generally. This research has not escaped criticism (Heath and Clifford 1980; Goldstein 1980), but an overview of work on school effectiveness edited by Reynolds (1985) confirms that substantial school effects remain even after controlling for the effect of intake variables such as the type of school catchment area.

Continuities and discrepancies between home and school

As Grieve (1990) puts it, some stress the discontinuities between development at home and in the school, whereas others emphasize that there are important continuities between such developments, and that learning in school can be made easier for children if these continuities are built upon. Tizard and Hughes (1984) highlight the gap between the worlds of home and school for children from both working-class and middle-class homes, asserting that the learning experiences, the discipline and the communication requirements of those worlds are very different. While accepting that children have to adapt to a variety of situations, Tizard and Hughes consider that it is vital to bridge the home–school gap, and to integrate the two worlds, by greater parental involvement in school. Teachers need to recognize the value of knowing about children's out-of-school interests and learning, and children should be encouraged to bring to school skills and interests derived from experiences at home.

A number of studies over the years have suggested that middle-class children may be better equipped for school than those from working-class homes, since middle-class families use styles of communication more compatible with those of the school (Rutter and Madge 1976; Bernstein 1977), and in general are likely to promote skills and attitudes required for success in school (Shipman 1980). This is probably less the case at present than it was some years ago, in view of the lessening differences in attitudes and lifestyle between middle-class and working-class families.

General links between socio-economic status and educational progress

Numerous research studies have confirmed that a strong association exists between social class (as measured, for example, by the Registrar General's scale (1966)) and basic school attainments. The National Child Development Study established such an association at the ages of 7, 11 and 16 (Davie *et al.* 1972; Fogelman 1975, 1983).

At 7 years children from non-manual families were nearly a year further ahead in the basic subjects than children from skilled and semi-skilled manual families (Social Classes IIIM and IV), who were 0.7 years ahead of unskilled families (Social Class V). By the age of 11, overall differences between the classes had increased to 1.9 years and 1.1 years respectively, and results at 16 showed a continuation of patterns of attainment found earlier at the age of 16 (Fogelman 1983). In their study of nearly 2,000 pupils in primary schools, Mortimore *et al* (1988) also found a marked relationship between social class background and attainment throughout the primary years, even when account was taken of differences in parents' activities with their children, and in housing and income. Both the mother's and father's occupations were highly related to reading and mathematics scores on entry to junior school, and the father's social class was significantly associated with oral language development. Socio-economic factors were also found in this study to be strongly related to teachers' behavioural assessment of junior school pupils: far more children from manual working-class families were rated as presenting emotional and behavioural difficulties.

As Meighan (1986) points out, social class is a highly ambiguous concept, but the links between social class and educational attainment and life chances have been consistently established by research studies in the UK, no matter which definition of social class is used. In general, middle-class children have better educational life chances than working-class children, in the sense that they are more likely to gain formal academic qualifications and experience extra full-time education. Mortimore *et al.* (1988) also acknowledge that the Registrar General's broad scale neglects many important aspects of the child's home background, relationships with parents and lifestyle, but consider that the scale is associated with many aspects of inequality, including health and morbidity.

A variety of explanations have been put forward for the association between social class and educational achievement. These have included inheritance; motivation; the learning of success or failure; policies and practices within the educational system; differences in cultures between the social classes; resource provision; and the tendency of teachers to have a somewhat more favourable view of both children and parents from non-manual backgrounds. It is more plausible to look for a network of causes than for a single cause (Meighan 1986).

Effects of social disadvantage

During the 1960s and 1970s, much attention was focused, particularly in the USA and Britain, on the education of children considered to be 'socially disadvantaged' in the sense that they were members of families adversely affected by poverty, unemployment and poor housing (see Rutter and Madge 1976; ed. Marland 1980; Mortimore and Blackstone 1982 for an overview of problems arising from social disadvantage). Such families tend to be located in areas with inadequate resources and amenities, and also to provide children with limited opportunities for stimulation, although 'cultural' disadvantage can occur without 'material' disadvantage. The schools which the children attend are also prone to suffer from poor buildings and equipment, a frequently changing teaching staff, and often low morale. Much controversy has surrounded the concept of social disadvantage and the research studies exploring its effects, but in general investigations have shown socially disadvantaged children to have particularly low attainments in the basic subjects, as well as in expressive and receptive language. They are, too, often less well motivated towards school success than more advantaged children (Halsey 1973; Chazan et al. 1976; Mortimore and Blackstone 1982). Although less attention is currently being given to the education of socially disadvantaged children than two decades ago, problems associated with poverty have certainly not disappeared (Alcock 1987).

Effects of family size and birth order

Rutter and Madge (1976), in a review of the literature, state that numerous studies have demonstrated that children from large families tend to have a lower level of measured intelligence (particularly verbal ability) and lower reading attainment than those from small families (i.e. only children, or those with one or two siblings). Pupils from large families are less successful, on average, in national examinations and tend to leave school earlier. These findings apply to both boys and girls and remain valid even after controlling for birth order and social class. However, the relationship between family size, birth order and attainment is a complex one, with the intervals between births contributing to the effects on individual children.

In an analysis of the data from the National Child Development Study, Fogelman (1983) found that the difference in reading attainment between those 11-year-olds with no older children in the household, and those with three or more was equivalent to a gain of fourteen months. There was a difference of twelve months between those with no younger children in the household and those with three or more. Thus the overall difference between children with no other children under 21 in the household and those with three-plus younger and three-plus older children was equivalent to a gain of twenty-six months in the context of this analysis.

The reasons for the lower attainments of children from large families remain obscure. Among the various hypotheses put forward it has been suggested that large families are more likely to suffer from multiple disadvantage (Wedge and Prosser, 1973). However, as Rutter and Madge put it, the most plausible explanation is that children in large families receive less parental attention and less verbal stimulation from adults than those from smaller families. In some cases oldest children may suffer most, particularly if they are increasingly left to their own devices as pressures on the parents grow with the addition of other children to the family (Davie *et al.* 1972).

Effects of living in single-parent families

In discussing family situations, it is all too easy to make statements which assume that children have two natural parents at home. However, with the increasing prevalence of divorce, a growing number of children are living in single-parent families (Mitchell, 1990), and many other children live in 'atypical' family situations, such as having adoptive or foster parents. Here the effects of living in a one-parent family on educational achievement will be considered; the progress and development of adopted children has been studied by Tizard (1977), and Humphrey and Humphrey (1988) have discussed the problems of children living in foster care and other 'atypical' home situations.

Mortimore and Blackstone (1982) have reviewed relevant research on the links between educational retardation and living in one-parent families. They conclude that, on the whole, studies show that, by themselves, single-parent families (as a result of either death or divorce) show little association with educational failure, though 'broken homes' tend to be linked to emotional or behavioural difficulties. Fogelman (1983) found that children who had lived at any time in a single-parent family had statistically significant lower mean scores on tests of both reading and mathematics than children who had always been with both natural parents. However, when the details of the parental situation were taken into account (e.g. length of time of mother being alone, social class, family size and amenities in the home), the differences between children in single-parent homes and those with both parents were greatly reduced and were no longer statistically different (Essen 1979; Fogelman 1983). Indeed, one-parent families tend to be over-represented in the manual working classes, to live in poor housing and to be at a considerable disadvantage financially.

Membership of ethnic minority groups

Ethnic minority parents have a wide range of attitudes towards education in this country, as well as child-rearing practices. Some are anxious to avail themselves to the fullest extent of opportunities to integrate with the wider community, while others are critical of educational provision here and would like to set up their own schools (Tomlinson 1984). The Swann Report (DES 1985) points out that while ethnic minority pupils do not necessarily have particular educational difficulties, a proportion of those pupils do underachieve in language and other basic skills. According to the Swann Report, West Indian children on average underachieve at school, whereas Asian children show a pattern of achievement which resembles that of white children (though some subgroups such as Bangladeshis seriously underachieve). Ethnic minorities are particularly disadvantaged in social and economic terms, and a substantial part of ethnic minority underachievement, where it occurs, is the result of racial prejudice and discrimination on the part of society at large.

Mackintosh et al. (1988) suggest that the Swann picture may no longer be entirely accurate. For example, they assert that children of Pakistani origin are now obtaining rather lower scores on standard tests of attainment than West Indian children, and they report some disagreement between different studies as to whether Indian children are continuing to perform at the same level as whites or whether they have slipped back.

Children with special educational needs

As the Warnock Report (DES 1978) pointed out, the nature of the support given by parents to a child with a disability or a significant difficulty may significantly affect his/her development and progress in school. Chapman (1978), too, discussing visually impaired pupils, emphasizes that the educational progress of these children depends heavily on parental encouragement of early self-reliance, the affectionate acceptance of the child, providing security within the family and the understanding of the child's special needs. It is difficult to quantify the effects of parental attitudes on the attainments of children with special educational needs, but these attitudes seem to be strongly related to the ability of children with physical disabilities, for example, to master motor activities (Gingras *et al.* 1964; Anderson 1973). Shepperdson (1988) also found that the attainments in language and self-help skills of children with Down's syndrome were significantly related to the amount and nature of stimulation provided in the home, and that this association applied as much to teenagers as to younger children.

PARENTS AS GOVERNORS

Since the Taylor Report (DES 1977), parents have gradually been given increased influence in the governing bodies of schools. The Report of the Taylor Committee, which was established to make recommendations on school government, advised that school governing bodies should be strengthened, suggesting that one-quarter of their membership should be elected by parents. In the subsequent 1980 Education Act, it was specified only that there should be at least two parent governors in each school. This did not represent great progress in giving power to parents, but it was the first time that the right of parents to participate in school government had been recognized in law. The 1986 Education Act did strengthen the parental representation on school governing bodies, as this was increased to a quarter of the membership (the same as local authority representation).

The 1988 Education Reform Act considerably extended the range of responsibilities assigned to governors, so that most school governing bodies are now taking on significant management responsibilites (Leonard 1989). These include taking part in staff appointments, the right to demand information and explanation, major budgetary powers, the preparation of an annual report for parents and, with the head teacher, responsibility for seeing that the National Curriculum is carried out in the school.

Docking (1990) observes that although, through the school's governing body, parents now have the facility to exercise a powerful influence in decision making, problems still remain. These include difficulty in obtaining parent governors from all sections of the community, of ensuring that parent governors receive support from the head and fellow governors, and the need to provide training for carrying out the increasingly complex managerial responsibilities which governing bodies have been given (see also Sallis 1988; Kogan *et al.* 1988).

IMPROVING HOME-SCHOOL RELATIONSHIPS

As Smith (1990) observes, since the mid-1970s there has been a great increase in activities designed to foster links between home and school. Developments include 'outreach work' involving home–school liaison teachers, setting up reading schemes involving parents, and bringing parents into school to help in various ways. Obstacles to progress stem from anxieties and misunderstandings rather than lack of interest, but greater co-operation is emerging (Wolfendale 1983, 1989) and classrooms are now much more open than they were. Selected developments in improving home–school relations are briefly reviewed below.

Informal contact

Not surprisingly parents tend to prefer contact with schools to be on a relatively informal rather than a formal basis. They put most emphasis on opportunities to talk in a relaxed way with teachers about their own children's schooling and progress (Chazan *et al.* 1976). In such a situation, they feel more at ease than, for example, at a formal meeting, where they may be anxious about their own knowledge of education, their social status, or presenting their views in public.

Informal contact is, of course, easier to arrange in the case of young children, who are brought to school by their parents, than with older pupils, but some schools organize activities which give parents and teachers opportunities for informal interaction. For instance, Brind (1984) gives an account of activities developed by a primary school which included joint swimming sessions for mothers and children; various courses of interest to parents; and a monthly working lunch for the agencies involved with children and parents.

Reliance on informal contact and on parents visiting school on a casual basis may mean that some parents will be left out. These will include the parents who do not find it easy to make social contacts, as well as those who are apathetic and need encouragement to take an interest in their children's education. Sharpe (1987) found that parents with limited ability and social resources rarely took the initiative to attend a comprehensive school to discuss their child's academic work or behaviour.

Parental interest groups

There are now three main parents' organizations in England and Wales – the National Confederation of Parent–Teacher Associations (NCPTA), set up in 1956; the Advisory Council for Education (ACE), established in 1960; and the Campaign for the Advancement of State Education (CASE), which started in 1962. Docking (1990), reviewing the work and policies of parents' organizations, concludes that they no longer see their purposes in terms of supporting individual schools, but rather try to articulate the concerns of parents to those in authority. They do not always agree in their policies, but they have become more centralized and politicized, monitoring developments in education, disseminating information and pressing for changes in the law and in local authority practices. They are not so much interested in power as in exerting influence, and have had some limited success in influencing government policy on education. Woods (1988) states that parents have a complex mix of roles in relation to schooling, involving choice of school, participation in school government and contributing to the political process at local and national level. He considers that tackling consumer weakness requires radically changing (or recasting) the relationship between consumer-citizens and producers, and puts forward a scheme for a national representative body of parents, which is both government-funded and accessible to local associations of parents.

Parent–teacher associations (PTAs)

In a national survey conducted by Cyster et al. (1980) only 35 per cent of a sample of 1,401 primary schools had a parent–teacher association; 26 per cent had a less formal parents' committee of some kind; and 39 per cent were without any parent group as such. The Plowden Committee (CACE 1967a) recognized the value of PTAs where good leadership was given by the head teacher, but did not think that they were necessarily the best means of fostering close relationships between home and school, particularly as a smaller proportion of manual workers tend to go to PTA meetings than to any other type of function relating to school. Parents differ in their attitudes to PTAs: some think that they are useful and enjoyable, others consider that they become social cliques or that they are unnecessary (Chazan et al. 1976).

Making PTA activities as informal as possible seems to encourage parental participation. Edwards and Redfern (1988) illustrate this in their account of a primary school where active attempts were made to raise attendance at PTA meetings. They report that, by making meetings more informal and doing away with elections for the committee, the PTA became more attractive to a much wider range of parents; ethnic minority parents were still under-represented, but this had started to change. The greatest part of PTA time at the school was spent in organizing activities to raise much-needed funds, but social aspects were also considered important. Gregory et al. (1982) report on the reorganization of a secondary school's parents' evening system. Changes instituted included sending a welcoming letter, deformalizing procedures, providing a structure for interviews, and conducting a needs assessment survey of the parents. Attendance at parents' evenings was raised from 16 per to 68 per cent.

Templeton (1989) gives an account of a home–school council set up in a London comprehensive school in 1987, from the point of view of a participating parent. The council had seven areas of functioning: as a forum for exchange of ideas; maintaining a parent-tutor group association; advising on home–school liaison; identifying areas for closer links between parents and school staff; looking at good practices in other schools; helping to plan and monitor initiatives; and attempting to utilize more fully parents' skills. Templeton considers the establishment of the council to be an exciting venture, though it is still uncertain how widespread its effects will be.

Home visits by teachers

Parents vary in their attitudes to home visiting, but on the whole are ready to welcome a teacher to their home, particularly if their child is not in any trouble (Hannon and Jackson 1987). Teachers, however, are not generally enthusiastic about visiting homes, especially if no invitation has been issued (Chazan et al. 1976). However, as Docking (1990) points out, home visiting has been seen more recently as an integral part of programmes concerned with the educational development of all children rather than as applying to parents who do not come to school of their own accord or whose children have problems at school. Cyster et al. (1980) found that in 22 per cent of primary schools home visiting was undertaken by head teachers or assistant teachers. Home visiting by educational welfare officers or home-liaison workers of various kinds was carried out in about half of all primary schools. Hirst and Hannon (1990) evaluated a pre-school home teaching project in which two home teachers were appointed to work as a team with the head teachers and staff of five nursery schools in a dis-advantaged area. They found that home teachers, parents, head teachers and other staff all felt that the children had benefited from home visiting; progress in language development was particularly noted. Many of the parents involved became more aware of their children's learning and development, and were strongly of the view that the home visitor should be a teacher.

The comments of the Plowden Committee (CACE, 1967a) about home visiting by teachers still seem valid: namely that this should not be regarded as a universal recipe for success, but if the parents do not come near the school, some agency should go to them.

Parents in school and classroom

Most primary schools invite parents to help in various ways such as preparing materials; running clubs; assisting with school produc-tions and sports; clerical duties; supervision of meals and play-ground; the maintenance of buildings; repairing equipment; and raising funds (Docking 1990). Some schools provide a place where parents can meet, or welcome parents to help on outings and other school occasions. Mostly it is women (mothers, grandmothers, older sisters) who come to help in school hours (Edwards and Redfern 1988), but a role can be found for men too.

Thomas (1987) surveyed a hundred primary schools in North Oxfordshire, and reports an increasing trend to use extra people in the classroom. These were typically involved for one to two hours at a time; listening to pupils reading, and working with children with special needs accounted for 40 per cent of all the sessions. Involvement of parents and others in school declined as the age of the children in the class increased. Extra people were involved in classroom activities on some occasion each week in 87 per cent of the sample of classes, but the findings of this study cannot be regarded as necessarily typical of primary schools generally.

Parental involvement in school and classroom can certainly bring benefits. In particular, parents gain a better understanding of classroom practices and school policies. However, not all parents are suited to this type of involvement, and parental participation in school calls for careful preparation and organization. Problems easily arise, especially if some members of the teaching staff are reluctant to share their functions with non-professionals (see Bailey *et al.* 1982; Stierer 1985; 1988; Jowett and Baginsky 1988 for discussions of parents in school and classroom).

Partnership projects involving help at home

In recent years two projects in particular have sought to encourage and support parents in teaching skills to their children. One is the Portage programme, aimed mainly at under-fives with disabilities or developmental difficulties; the other is the paired reading scheme, designed to supplement the teaching of reading in school.

The Portage programme (Bluma *et al.* 1976) involves a home visiting teacher and the parents in a co-operative effort to help the child master specific skills. A 'curriculum guide' is provided in the form of a box containing a card for each step on a developmental checklist, and serves as a source of ideas for teacher and parents to build upon. Set up in 1969 in the United States, the scheme has attracted wide interest in Britain, and has been generally welcomed by parents. As White and Cameron (1989) state, the Portage programme supports the natural role of parents as educators and enhancers of development, and is flexible in responding to different needs and styles of teaching. The main criticisms of the programme which have been expressed are, according to White and Cameron, that it teaches isolated 'tricks' and that it is heavily reliant on the teaching situation and the structured intervention of parents.

However, parents view the service positively and value the support given (Sturmey and Crisp 1986).

Over the last ten years or so, various schemes have been developed to promote reading through 'paired reading' or allied projects (see Topping and Wolfendale 1985; Branston and Provis 1986). Hewison and Tizard (1980) reported significant gains from encouraging children to read regularly to their parents from books sent home by the class teacher (see also Tizard *et al.* 1982). A rather more structured technique of parental involvement known as 'paired reading' has also proved attractive to a number of parents and teachers, and has had some success (Morgan and Lyon 1979; Topping and McKnight 1984; Topping and Whiteley 1990). This approach involves the parent and child reading together simultaneously in the early stages, and then the child moves on to independent reading, stopping when meeting a word he/she cannot tackle. Schemes of this kind have shown sufficiently promising results to justify further experiment, particularly as they encourage co-operation in learning tasks between teachers, parents and children. Nevertheless, it has to be recognized that there may be parents who are unable to adopt a relaxed attitude in any kind of teaching situation where their own child is concerned, and others who are so overwhelmed by their personal problems that they cannot give time or attention to a teaching role.

Communication between home and school over curriculum, school policies and records of progress

School curriculum and policies

Under the 1980 and 1988 Education Acts, schools are now required to provide parents with information about their teaching arrangements, the curriculum, and other matters such as the pastoral care system and provision of sex education. Many schools have for some time sent home a regular newsletter, but they now have to issue an annual prospectus to parents (see Docking 1990).

It is important that much thought should be given to the way in which material such as prospectuses or newsletters is presented to parents. An attractive format is important, even if due attention is given to the content, language and tone. It is helpful to involve parents in the preparation of material aimed at providing information, and some parents will have relevant skills to contribute.

Communication between home and school over the curriculum and other policy matters need not, of course, rely predominantly on written material. Dye (1989) gives an account of a project involving the reception classes in four infant schools in outer London, in which parents from a wide variety of ethnic and social backgrounds met each week to talk with the teachers. Practical suggestions were made about simple activities which children and parents enjoy at home. Evaluation of this programme showed that it produced gains on a variety of tests and assessments of the children's progress and development, and that excellent relationships were fostered between parents, pupils and teachers. Dye stresses that the nature of the programme and the timing of its implementation are both of importance. In particular, a programme of this kind should begin by focusing on the parents and family before branching out to cover wider concerns and interests.

Records of progress

Recent legislation ensures that the school keeps records for each pupil, and that the child's performance in mastering the National Curriculum should be communicated to parents.

The 1988 Education Reform Act provided that parents should be told the results of their child's assessments at the end of four 'key stages' (7, 11, 14 and 16 years) of the National Curriculum. Parents also have to be informed of the aggregated test results for each school for pupils of 11 years and over, in order to help them make informed choices of school. Under Section 22 of the Act, Education (Individual Pupils' Achievement) (Information) Regulations have been issued, and are explained in the DES Circular 8/90 (see also DES 1989b). Circular 8/90 has the following objectives: fuller reporting to parents on pupils' achievements; documenting achievement for the pupils' own purposes; and related formative processes, such as target-setting, review and forward planning.

In brief, the Regulations require a written report on each pupil's achievements to reach his parents by a specified date each year, from the summer of 1991. Such reports must cover the pupil's performance in all National Curriculum subjects and include the results of any public examinations taken, apart from giving concise particulars of the pupil's achievements in other subjects and activities undertaken during the year.

The Circular stresses that the Regulations comprise minimum reporting requirements and commends the practice of fuller and broader reporting on achievement. It lays down a firm basis for ensuring that parents receive adequate information on their children's progress at school; but, additionally, schools need to give parents ample opportunities for reacting to the information they are given, and for making their views known to the school.

Role of the support services in enhancing home–school relationships

The school should be, and often is, the focal point where teachers, parents and the various agencies which support both home and school meet to co-operate in the best interests of the pupils. This applies to all pupils, but most particularly in cases of children with special educational needs or problem backgrounds. The main support agencies involved will be discussed briefly under three headings – educational, health and social services (see Fitzherbert 1977; 1980; Sainsbury 1977; Baugh 1987).

Educational services

All sectors of LEAs should be prepared to help and advise parents. The main educational services supporting the school include the School Psychological Service and the Educational Welfare Service. Among its various functions, the School Psychological Service contributes to the assessment of pupils, especially those with special needs, the planning of individual programmes, and the in-service training of teachers. Educational psychologists, who now work mainly in the school context rather than from a clinical base, seek to involve parents from the earliest stage, in assessment as well as in programme planning. Many educational psychologists, too, play a leading part in fostering home–school links through schemes such as Portage and paired reading, mentioned above.

The Educational Welfare Service has an important role in setting up a dialogue between parents and teachers. Its responsibilities include not only dealing with non-attendance at school but, additionally, other aspects of family welfare, such as negotiating material assistance and advising parents on educational matters. As educational welfare officers visit the homes of a number of pupils, they are often well informed about relevant aspects of children's family background.

Health services

The school doctor and health visitor/school nurse advise parents on health problems; the health visitor knows many of the families in the school catchment area very well as a result of regular contact. Any child with a disability can be seen by the school health service from the age of 2 years onwards, if not before. Other professionals, such as speech therapists, paediatricians and psychiatrists work with children, teachers and parents, often on school premises.

Social services

Social Services Departments work with families faced with considerable stress, and cases of child abuse and neglect. They have certain statutory responsibilities in regard to the welfare of children. Co-operation between school, social workers and parents is highly desirable, but not always as effective as it should be. There is certainly a need for schools to have a greater knowledge of the functions of the Social Services, and for social workers to have a better understanding of schools.

EFFECTING CHANGE IN FAMILIES

Families may fail children for many reasons, including financial pressures, faulty child-rearing practices, marital disharmony, neglect and abuse. Attempts to effect change in families may focus on providing material aid, help in the home or advice or therapy to individual families; or they may be on a larger scale, aiming at bringing about improved home conditions in a number of families, for example those in socially disadvantaged areas.

Family therapy

In addition to the many agencies, statutory and voluntary, providing advice and/or material help to families in need (Sainsbury 1977; Baugh 1987; Herbert 1988), family therapy has been developed with the main aim of improving relationships within the family. Family therapy is especially called for when there is a malfunctioning family group affecting a child's development. As faulty intra-family relationships are often a factor in emotional and behavioural difficulties in children, and contribute to problems with academic work, the school needs to be brought into the picture. Family therapists work with the family as a whole and tend to focus on the establishment of rapport with the members of the family; the fostering of a trusting relationship within the family; making the problems explicit; and planning and executing a programme of action. Campion (1985) and Dawson and McHugh (1986) discuss the application of a family systems approach in educational settings, stressing the value of co-operation between educational psychologists, teachers, psychiatrists and family therapists in ensuring that family therapy is not divorced from the concerns of the school.

Therapy is not always the most suitable form of help required by families, some of which may be overwhelmed by health problems, severe budgetary difficulties or an inability to cope with daily life. However, family therapy can enable many malfunctioning families to come to terms with reality, and to cope with their problems more successfully.

Programmes of intervention

Large-scale programmes aiming at effecting change in families have focused mainly on those living in conditions of social disadvantage. The American Head Start programme, for example, launched in 1965 with government support, aimed at helping disadvantaged under-fives and their families; it was complemented about two years later by the Follow Through programme, directed at older children. These programmes attempted to improve children's performance in the school system as well as the standard of living within the family (Rutter and Madge 1976). To this end, the programmes have included measures to alleviate poverty and poor housing conditions, as well as efforts to change teaching approaches and conditions in school. Parents have been included in many such compensatory projects as the main agents of intervention: approaches to parental involvement have endeavoured to improve contacts between home and school, and to help parents to understand and enhance their children's cognitive and emotional development.

In the United Kingdom there have been government-sponsored

urban aid programmes for some time, but intervention programmes to help disadvantaged children have been on a smaller scale than those in the USA, and not as well sustained (Marland 1980). The Educational Priority Areas (EPA) Project was, for example, a national action-research programme with the broad objectives of raising the educational performance of children, improving the morale of teachers, and increasing the involvement of parents and the community; but it lasted only three years, finishing in 1971, even if some of the initiatives continued after the end of the project (Halsey 1972).

Two major home visiting projects in the UK have been described by Raven (1980; 1983) and Barker and Anderson (1988). Raven gives an account of a project set up in Scotland, in which home visitors (all trained teachers) were appointed to the staffs of nursery schools in six 'deprived' areas. The home visitors worked with 2 to 3-year-old children in their parents' presence for about one hour a week, with the main aim of encouraging the parents to take a more active role in promoting the educational development of their children. The project had a major impact on the understanding of the problem it sought to address and the mothers became better able to interact with their children and grew more aware of their own potential influence on schools. However, Raven concluded that, in their expert role as promoters of child development, the home visitors may have led the parents visited to feel less confident and competent than before. While they undoubtedly influenced the parents' attitudes and beliefs, they did not necessarily succeed in ensuring that parents took up the activities which they modelled.

Barker reports on the outcomes of a large-scale child development programme in the UK and Dublin, involving families with pre-school children and carried out mainly in areas of social and economic disadvantage. The support work in the UK was done by health visitors specially trained for the task of helping parents to find their own solutions to their child-rearing problems. Evaluation of the first phase of the programme, lasting from 1980 to 1983, indicated that it had been a considerable success, bringing about major changes in the home environments involved, even if only moderate gains were achieved in the developmental levels of the target children when compared with controls. Parents, health visitors and managers of health authorities participating in the programme were widely supportive of the initiative. However,

Barker acknowledges that a short-term support programme cannot bring a disadvantaged sample up to the level of a considerably less disadvantaged sample of children; rather, it can reduce the gap between them, and help to prevent conditions leading to failure in the home environments of the disadvantaged.

Programmes of intervention such as Head Start and Follow Through have been extensively evaluated in the USA (see, for example, Zigler and Valentine 1979; Lazar and Darlington 1982; Lazar 1985). As Osborn and Milbank (1987) observe, the findings have been far from clear-cut. However, in general the evidence suggests that early intervention programmes can increase children's potential and have lasting effects, provided that the programmes are carefully planned and executed, with specific and well-defined objectives and with the full involvement of parents. In his review of the pre-school intervention programmes in the USA, Bronfenbrenner (1974) found that children who were involved in an intensive programme of parent intervention during, and especially prior to, their enrolment in pre-school or school, achieved greater and more lasting gains in the group programme. Osborn and Milbank, too, underline the importance of parental involvement and interest in ensuring that the benefits of pre-school experience are not lost.

Shipman (1980), reviewing the British and North American experience of active intervention in inner city education, stresses that these interventions have employed only marginal resources. He concludes that specific objectives can be attained by specially designed programmes, but that there are no simple solutions to complicated educational and social problems; one-shot small-scale projects are unlikely to have lasting effects; if programmes are not sustained the final impact may be negative; and that no great outcome can be expected from any programme as long as it is isolated from mainstream education.

On a more optimistic note, Rutter and Madge (1976) assert that, while continuities in regional and ethnic disadvantage are marked, familial continuities are fairly slight for many aspects of family life: at least half the children born into a disadvantaged home do not repeat the pattern of disadvantage in the next generation. Topping (1986) expresses a positive view of parent training programmes, especially those based on behavioural principles. He concludes that there is no longer any doubt about the durability of gains accruing from parent training programmes, though generalization of improved behaviour from home to school does not seem to happen.

Family life education in schools

Preparation for parenthood and family life at school can make a valuable contribution to giving parents relevant skills and a knowledge of child development as well as of the educational system. Admittedly, courses in parenthood for adolescents at school may not have the same impact and relevance as they have for those who are actually, or about to become, parents. However, schools and further education establishments are increasingly providing courses which help in the acquisition of parentcraft and home management skills. Surveys by Grafton *et al.* (1983) and Pugh and De'Ath (1984) found that examined child care and development courses have proved popular, though they tend to be optional, of low status and rarely taken by male pupils. Projects in personal and social education, health education, and pastoral work reach a much wider range of pupils, often permeating many subjects in the curriculum.

Pugh (1984) concluded that, while there had been a growing number of courses in family life education in schools in recent years, the extent of provision was still patchy, and a policy on family life education at local and national level had yet to be formulated. There is no doubt that family life education in schools and colleges can help young people to make better informed decisions about the personal choices that crucially affect them. It is to be hoped that family life education is not crowded out by the demands of the National Curriculum.

CONCLUSION

This chapter has shown that material, cultural and psychological factors relating to the home exercise a powerful influence on children's development and progress at school. However, factors at school, including its organization, policy, curriculum and general climate, interact with home factors, and may compensate to some extent for adverse features in the family environment. Further, children react differently to conditions at home and are often very resilient, succeeding in school despite social disadvantages.

A wide range of attitudes to parental participation in the educational process exists among both parents and teachers. While many examples can be cited to demonstrate home and school sharing mutual understanding, teachers sometimes have misperceptions of parents' views about involvement in school, and parents do not always have full insight into teachers' aims and functions. It is desirable that this gap in understanding should be bridged, and that pupils should experience as much continuity between home and school as possible.

In recent years parents have been given more choice, for example in decisions about which school their child should attend; but frequently this choice is more apparent than real. Parents have also achieved more rights and powers, but they do not always use these to the full. Activities aimed at fostering home–school links have greatly increased in volume and variety; but not all schools do as much as they might to welcome parental involvement. Thus there remains ample scope for further developments in enhancing home and school relationships.

REFERENCES

Alcock, P. (1987) *Poverty and State Support*, London: Longman.
Anderson, E. M. (1973) *The Disabled Schoolchild: A Study of Integration in Primary Schools*, London: Methuen.
Bailey, G., Bull, T., Feeley, G. and Wilson, I. (1982) *Parents in the Classroom*, Coventry: Community Education Development Centre.
Barker, W. and Anderson, R. (1988) *The Child Development Programe: An Evaluation of Process and Outcomes*, Bristol: University of Bristol, Early Childhood Development Unit.
Bastiani, J. (ed.) (1987) *Parents and Teachers, 1: Perspectives on Home-School Relations*, Windsor: NFER-Nelson.
—— (1988) *Parents and Teachers, 2: From Policy to Practice*, Windsor: NFER-Nelson.
Baugh, W. E. (1987) *Introduction to the Social Services* (5th edn), London: Macmillan.
Becher, T., Erault, M. and Knight, J. (1981) *Policies for Educational Accountability*, London: Heinemann.
Bernstein, B. (1977) 'Class and pedagogies: visible and invisible' and 'Social class, language and socialization', in J. Karabel and A. H. Halsey (eds) *Power and Ideology in Education*, New York: Oxford University Press.
Bluma, S., Shearer, M., Frohman, A. and Hilliard, J. (1976) *Portage Guide to Early Education*, Windsor: NFER.
Branston, P. and Provis, M. (1986) *Children and Parents Enjoying Reading: A Handbook for Teachers*, London: Hodder & Stoughton.
Brind, R. J. (1984) 'Home/School Liaison Project', *Links* 10: 17–18.
Bronfenbrenner, U. (1974) *A Report on Longitudinal Evaluation of Pre-School Programmes*, vol. 2: *Is Early Education Effective?*, Washington, DC: US Children's Bureau.
Campion, J. (1985) *The Child in Context: Family-systems Theory in Educational Psychology*, London: Methuen.

CACE, Central Advisory Council for Education, England (1963) *Half Our Future (The Newsom Report)*, London: HMSO.

—— (1967a) *Children and Their Primary Schools (The Plowden Report)*, vol. 1: *Report*, London, HMSO.

—— (1967b) *Children and Their Primary Schools (The Plowden Report)*, vol. 2: *Research and Surveys*, London: HMSO.

Chapman, E. K. (1978) *Visually Handicapped Children and Young People*, London: Routledge & Kegan Paul.

Chazan, M., Laing, A. F., Cox, T., Jackson, S., and Lloyd, G. (1976) *Studies of Infant School Children I: Deprivation and School Progress*, Oxford: Basil Blackwell/Schools Council.

Coleman, J. S., Campbell, E., Hobson, C., McPartland, J., Mood, A., Weinfeld, F. and York, R. (1966) *Equality of Educational Opportunity*, Washington, DC: National Center for Educational Statistics.

Cyster, R., Clift, P. S. and Battle, S. (1980) *Parental Involvement in Primary Schools*, Windsor: NFER-Nelson.

Davie, R., Butler, N. and Goldstein, H. (1972) *From Birth to Seven*, London: Longman/National Children's Bureau.

Dawson, N. and McHugh, B. (1986) 'Application of a family-systems approach in an education unit', *Maladjustment and Therapeutic Education* 4: 48–54.

DES (Department of Education and Science) (1975) *A Language for Life (The Bullock Report)*, London: HMSO.

—— (1977) *A New Partnership for Our Schools (The Taylor Report)*, London: HMSO.

—— (1978) *Special Educational Needs (The Warnock Report)*, London: HMSO.

—— (1982) *Mathematics Counts (The Cockcroft Report)*, London: HMSO.

—— (1985) *Education for All (The Swann Report)*, London: HMSO.

—— (1989a) *Discipline in Schools (The Elton Report)*, London: HMSO.

—— (1989b) *The Education (School Records) Regulations 1989 (accompanied by Circular 17/89)*, London: DES.

Docking, J. (1990) *Primary Schools and Parents: Rights, Responsibilities and Relationships*, London: Hodder & Stoughton.

Dye, S. (1989) 'Parental involvement in curriculum matters', *Educational Research* 31: 20–35.

Edwards, V. and Redfern, A. (1988) *At Home in School: Parent Participation in Primary Education*, London: Routledge.

Essen, J. (1979) 'Living in one-parent families: attainment at school', *Child: Care, Health and Development* 5: 189–200.

Fitzherbert, K. (1977) *Child Care Services and the Teacher*, London: Temple Smith.

—— (1980) 'Strategies for prevention', in M. Craft, J. Raynor and L. Cohen (eds) *Linking and School*, London: Longman.

Fogelman, K. (1975) 'Development correlates of family size', *British Journal of Social Work* 5: 43–57.

Fogelman, K. (ed.) (1983) *Growing Up in Great Britain* (papers from the

National Child Development Study), London: Macmillan (for National Children's Bureau).

Gingras, G., Mongeau, M., Moreault, P., Dupois, M., Herbert, B. and Corriveau, C. (1964) 'Congenital abnormalities of the limbs, II: psychological and educational aspects', *Canadian Medical Association Journal* 91: 115-19.

Goldstein, H. (1980) 'Fifteen Thousand Hours: a review of the statistical procedures', *Journal of Child Psychology and Psychiatry* 21: 363-6.

Grafton, T., Smith, L., Vegoda, M. and Whitfield, R. (1983) *Preparation for Parenthood in the Secondary School Curriculum*, University of Aston: Department of Educational Enquiry.

Gregory, R. P., Meredith, P. and Woodward, A. (1982) 'Parental involvement in secondary schools', *Journal of Association of Educational Psychologists* 5: 54-60.

Grieve, R. (1990) 'Development in home and school environments', in N. Entwistle (ed.) *Handbook of Educational Ideas and Practices*, London: Routledge.

Halsey, A. H. (ed.) (1972) *Educational Priority*, vol. 1: *Problems and Policies*, London: HMSO.

Halsey, A. H. (1973) 'Reading standards in educational priority areas', *Remedial Education* 8: 16-23.

Hannon, P. and Jackson, A. (1987) 'Educational home visiting and the teaching of reading', *Educational Research*, 29: 182-91.

Heath, A. and Clifford, P. (1980) 'The seventy thousand hours that Rutter left out', *Oxford Review of Education* 6: 3-119.

Herbert, M. (1988) *Working with Children and their Families*, Leicester: British Psychological Society/Routledge.

Hewison, J. and Tizard, J. (1980) 'Parental involvement and reading attainment', *British Journal of Educational Psychology*, 58: 209-15.

Hirst, K. and Hannon, P. (1990) 'An evaluation of a pre-school home-teaching project', *Educational Research*, 32: 33-9.

Humphrey, M. and Humphrey, H. (1988) *Families with a Difference: Varieties of Surrogate Parenthood*, London: Routledge.

Johnson, D. and Ransom, E. (1980) 'Parents' perceptions of secondary schools', in M. Craft, J. Raynor and L. Cohen (eds) *Linking Home and School: A New Review*, London: Harper & Row.

—— (1983) *Family and School*, London: Croom Helm.

Jowett, S. and Baginsky, M. (1988) 'Parents and education: a survey of their involvement and a discussion of some issues', *Educational Research*, 30: 36-45.

Kogan, M., Johnson, D., Packwood, T. and Whitaker, T. (1988) *School Governing Bodies*, London: Heinemann.

Laing, A. F. (ed.) (1979) *Young Children with Special Needs*, University College of Swansea: Department of Education.

Lazar, I. (1985) 'On bending twigs and planting acorns: some implications of recent research', *Association for Child Psychiatry and Psychology Newsletter* 7: 28-32.

Lazar, I. and Darlington, R. B. (1982) *Lasting Effects of Early Education:*

A Report from the Consortium for Longitudinal Studies, Monographs of the Society for Research in Child Development, serial no. 195.

Leonard, M. (1989) *The School Governors' Handbook*, Oxford: Basil Blackwell.

Mackintosh, N. J., Mascie-Taylor, C. G. N. and West, A. M. (1988) 'West Indian and Asian children's educational attainment', in G. Verma and P. Pumfrey (eds) *Educational Attainments: Issues and Outcomes in Multiracial Education*, London: Falmer Press.

Marland, M. (ed) (1980) *Education for the Inner City*, London: Heinemann.

Meighan, R. (1986) *A Sociology of Educating* (2nd edn), London: Holt, Rinehart & Winston.

Mitchell, A. (1990) *Divorce and children*, London: National Children's Bureau, Highlight no. 93.

Morgan, R. T. T. and Lyon, E. (1979) 'Paired reading – a preliminary report on a technique for parental tuition of reading-retarded children', *Journal of Child Psychiatry and Psychology* 20: 151–60.

Mortimore, J. and Blackstone, T. (1982) *Disadvantage and Education*, London: Heinemann.

Mortimore, P., Sammons, P., Stoll, L., Lewis, D., and Ecob, R. (1988) *School Matters: The Junior Years*, Wells: Open Books.

Osborn, A. F. and Milbank, J. E. (1987) *The Effects of Early Education: A Report from the Child Health and Education Study*, Oxford: Clarendon Press.

Pugh, G. (1984) *Family Life Education in Secondary Schools: A Review of Practice*, London: National Children's Bureau, Highlight No. 62.

Pugh, G. and De'Ath, E. (1984) *The Needs of Parents: Practice and Policy in Parent Education*, London: Macmillan.

Raven, J. (1980) *Parents, Teachers and Children: A Study of an Educational Home Visiting Scheme*, London: Hodder & Stoughton.

—— (1983) 'Language in its social context and the role of educational home visitors', in A. Davies (ed.) *Language and Learning in Home and School*, London: Heinemann.

Registrar General (1966) *Classification of Occupations*, London: HMSO.

Reynolds, D. (1982) 'The search for effective schools', *School Organization* 2: 215–37.

Reynolds, D. (ed.) (1985) *Studying School Effectiveness*, Lewes: Falmer Press.

Rutter, M. and Madge, N. (1976) *Cycles of Disadvantage: A Review of Research*, London: Heinemann.

Rutter, M., Maughan, B., Mortimore, P. and Ouston, J. (1979) *Fifteen Thousand Hours: Secondary Schools and Their Effects on Children*. London: Open Books.

Sainsbury, E. (1977) *The Personal Social Services*, London: Pitman.

Sallis, J. (1988) *Schools, Parents and Governors: A New Approach to Accountability*, London: Routledge & Kegan Paul.

Sharpe, L. (1987) 'The management of home–school relations in the secondary school', in J. Bastiani (ed.) *Parents and Teachers, 1: Perspec-*

tives on Home–School Relations, Windsor: NFER-Nelson.

Shepperdson, B. (1988) *Growing up with Down's Syndrome*, London: Cassell.

Shipman, M. (1980) 'The limits of positive discrimination', in M. Marland (ed.) *Education for the Inner City*, London: Heinemann.

Smith, T. (1990) 'Parents and pre-school education', in N. Entwistle (ed.) *Handbook of Educational Ideas and Practices*, London: Routledge.

Stierer, B. (1985) 'School reading volunteers: results of a postal survey of primary school head teachers in England', *Journal of Research in Reading* 8: 21–31.

—— (1988) 'A symbolic challenge: reading helpers in school', in M. Mills and C. Mills (eds) *Language and Literacy in the Primary School*, Lewes: Falmer Press.

Sturmey, P. and Crisp, A. G. (1986) 'Portage guide to early education: a review of research', *Educational Psychology* 6: 139–57.

Templeton, J. (1989) 'Creation of a Home–School Council in a secondary school', in S. Wolfendale (ed.) *Parental Involvement: Developing Networks between Home, School and Community*, London: Cassell.

Thomas, G. (1987) 'Extra people in the classroom', *Educational Research* 29: 173–81.

Tizard, B. (1977) *Adoption: A Second Chance*, London: Open Books.

Tizard, B. and Hughes, M. (1984) *Young Children's Learning*, London: Fontana.

Tizard, B., Mortimore, J. and Burchell, B. (1981) *Involving Parents in Nursery and Infant Schools*, London: Grant McIntyre.

Tizard, J., Schofield, W. N. and Hewison, J. (1982) 'Collaboration between teachers and parents in assisting children's reading', *British Journal of Educational Psychology* 52: 1–15.

Tizard, B., Blatchford, P., Burke, J., Farquhar, C. and Plewis, I. (1988) *Young Children and School in the Inner City*, Hove: Lawrence Erlbaum.

Tomlinson, S. (1984) *Home and School in Multicultural Britain*, London: Batsford.

Topping, K. J. (1986) *Parents as Educators: Training Parents to Teach their Children*, London: Croom Helm.

Topping, K. J. and McKnight, G. (1984) 'Paired reading and parent power', *Special Education Forward Trends* 11: 12–14.

Topping, K. J. and Whiteley, M. (1990) 'Participant evaluation of parent-tutored and peer-tutored projects in reading', *Educational Research* 32: 14–32.

Topping, K. J. and Wolfendale, S. (eds) (1985) *Parental Involvement in Children's Reading*, Beckenham: Croom Helm.

Wedge, P. and Prosser, H. (1973) *Born to Fail?*, London: Arrow Books.

White, M. and Cameron, R. J. (1988) *Portage: Progress, Problems and Possibilities*, Windsor: NFER-Nelson.

Wiseman, S. (1967) 'The Manchester Survey', appendix 9, CACE (1967b) *Children and Their Primary Schools (The Plowden Report)*, vol. 2, *Research and Surveys*, London: HMSO.

Wolfendale, S. (1983) *Parental Participation in Children's Development* and Education, New York: Gordon & Breach.

Wolfendale, S. (ed.) (1989) *Parental Involvement: Developing Networks between Home, School and Community*, London: Cassell.

Woods, P. (1988) 'A strategic view of parent participation', *Journal of Education Policy* 3: 323–34.

Zigler, E. and Valentine, J. (eds) (1979) *Project Head Start*, London: Collier Macmillan.

Name index

Subject index